DERBY DAY
AND OTHER ADVENTURES

Books by

A. Edward Newton

———

THE AMENITIES OF BOOK-COLLECTING
(1918)

A MAGNIFICENT FARCE
(1921)

DOCTOR JOHNSON
(1923)

THE GREATEST BOOK IN THE WORLD
(1925)

THIS BOOK-COLLECTING GAME
(1928)

A TOURIST IN SPITE OF HIMSELF
(1930)

END PAPERS
(1933)

DERBY DAY
(1934)

ROUNDING TATTENHAM CORNER

From original painting owned by A. E. N.

DERBY DAY
And Other Adventures

By

A. EDWARD NEWTON

WITH ILLUSTRATIONS

BOSTON

LITTLE, BROWN, AND COMPANY

1934

Copyright, 1932, 1933, 1934,
By A. Edward Newton

Published September, 1934

THE ATLANTIC MONTHLY PRESS BOOKS
ARE PUBLISHED BY
LITTLE, BROWN, AND COMPANY
IN ASSOCIATION WITH
THE ATLANTIC MONTHLY COMPANY

PRINTED IN THE UNITED STATES OF AMERICA

Sixty years ago, in Rahway, New Jersey, my playmate was

WILLIAM C. VAN ANTWERP

now a distinguished citizen of
San Francisco

To him I dedicate this book

A. E. N.

"To adjourn Parliament over Derby Day is a part of the unwritten law of England." — LORD PALMERSTON

"Authors, like running horses, should be fed but not fattened."
— OLIVER GOLDSMITH

Publishers generally endorse this statement. — A. E. N.

"Be fair or foul, or rain or shine,
The joys I have possess'd, in spite of fate, are mine;
Not heaven itself upon the past has power;
But what has been, has been, and I have had my hour."
— JOHN DRYDEN

CONTENTS

ILLUSTRATIONS

xii   ILLUSTRATIONS

DERBY DAY
AND OTHER ADVENTURES

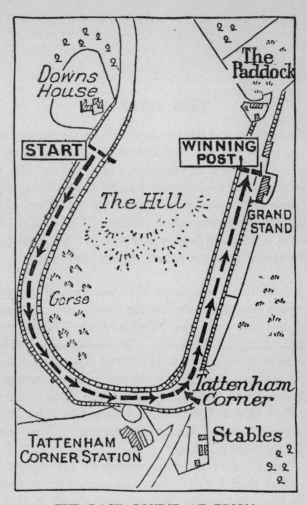

THE RACE COURSE AT EPSOM

I

THE DERBY

"Our English spring has opened with its customary severity"; so wrote Horace Walpole to Sir Horace Mann, his famous correspondent in Florence, a hundred and fifty years ago, just about the time that an Earl of Derby was establishing a horse race which has eclipsed all the other achievements of a very distinguished family. The trouble, however, is not with the spring — it is with us: we expect more from the spring than the spring is prepared to supply.

On a cold raw evening in May an English gentleman and I were sitting in the dining room of a mansion in London not far from the Marble Arch. A comforting fire was burning in the grate; the ladies had withdrawn and we were alone. We were indeed not quite alone, for between us was a decanter of old port, almost empty, and if there is a more delightful companion than a decanter of port after an excellent dinner, I should be glad to know what it is. "Cigars," you might suggest. "Yes, but not until the decanter is empty."

"Sir James," said I, "I am going to the Derby next week. How shall I go?" My host paused for a moment, lifted his glass and let the light shine through it, then put it down and replied, weighing every word. "Edward," he said, "the first thing to do is to go to Lincoln, Bennett's in the Burlington Gardens and get a white topper," meaning thereby that I was to go to the most expensive hat shop in

the course to the finish post; and while there may be joy in heaven over the repentant sinner, I declare here and now that it is nothing to the joy when "the favorite" wins the Derby — which he very seldom does. It is the difference of opinion that makes horse racing and stock markets. We play the market, the English the horses; both sports are full of excitement and chicanery. I am told that men go to the Derby and do not bet. It may be so, but it is certain that millions bet who are unable to go.

It is not my purpose to moralize on the subject of betting, but it is quite clear to me that it is as impossible to legislate effectively against gambling in England as it was to enforce what we called "prohibition" in America. An Englishman will profess horror at the prevalence, in this country, of knowledge as to what is going on in the stock market. He will tell you that the barkeep who shakes up your cocktail has a hundred shares of General Motors, that the barber who cuts your hair is interested in Steel, that the elevator boy knows what "they" are doing in Radio, and that the bootblack has inside information about G. E. This is true and perhaps to be regretted, but on the other hand we as a people know very little about horse racing, and nothing whatever of greyhound racing, which in England is the latest sport. It is, I think, fair to say that betting on the horse races, which are daily events all over England during a large part of the year, is much more general than was "speculation" in this country even during the great bull market which came to such an untimely end in the autumn of 1929. In ethics I can see no difference between betting on Pierpont Morgan's Steel and the Duke of Grafton's Whalebone. Most of the people who bet know very little about either the one or the other, but betting on them affords a subject for conversation. In taverns and public houses in England one sees signs to the effect

that betting on the races and the passing of betting slips
are forbidden by law. This law is a dead letter: everyone
bets; everyone always has, everyone always will. Let me
quote from an editorial in one of the best-known London
evening papers that rare day in June, the year 1932, when
I saw my first Derby: —

To-day there assembled on Epsom Downs the largest crowd
that gathers for any sporting event in any part of the world. No
one has succeeded in estimating the numbers of the Derby crowd,
but they cannot have averaged less than a quarter of a million
since the War, and they seem to be increasing from year to year.

Among the crowd there are every year a good many
Americans witnessing this amazing spectacle for the first
time. It would be an odd American who, finding himself
on his first visit to London in June, did not somehow by
hook or crook get to Epsom.

Let us suppose that one of them is escorted by an English
host, who on the way down has been chatting amiably,
but a little patronizingly, as Englishmen sometimes will
to Americans, of their general disregard for law. "Queer
that the United States makes so many and such ridiculous
laws and then fails so notoriously in their enforcement."
At this point they reach the Downs, and, observing the
immense concourse, the American is impressed. He also
observes the bookmakers, and hazards the remark that he
had always thought that gambling was illegal in England.

His English friend then explains to him that under certain conditions gambling is permitted by the law. Naturally the American wants to know what the conditions are
and the Englishman begins to tell him as much as he can
remember. "You may back a horse," he says, "so long
as you do not in person resort to a place in order to do so;
you must send your bet by post, by telegram, or by telephone. You must not, of course, send money with it."

"But," the American objects, "I can with my own eyes see numbers of people resorting to a place — namely, that stand over there occupied by a gentleman who describes himself as 'Honest Old Joe from Birmingham,' and to whom people are openly giving their money."

"A bookmaker's stand on a race course," the Englishman hastily explains, "is not a *place* within the meaning of the law unless it is *fixed*. If it is fixed it is illegal — unless," he adds, somewhat thoughtfully, "it is a 'tote.' "

"But I read the other day," the American continues to object, "of a prosecution for street betting. Now surely the street bookmaker has no fixed stand . . ."

The Englishman continues his explanation, finally becoming very much involved, until at last the American observes, "Well, your gambling laws seem quite fantastic and much more complicated than our prohibition laws were, and as little observed."

A few days after my arrival in London, the Irish Sweepstakes — the greatest and straightest racing gamble ever conducted in the world — were drawn. This race took place in Dublin, and after all expenses were deducted and a million dollars donated to Irish hospitals the balance was paid to successful ticket holders all over the world. The proceedings are known to be illegal, but what difference does that make? When twenty-eight units win £30,000 or £15,000 or £10,000 or £5000 each, and a thousand other lucky holders win lesser amounts, there is bound to be great excitement in the land. Newsboys dash frantically through the streets selling their papers containing alphabetical lists of winners. Their supply is immediately exhausted as men, women, and children leave their jobs, whatever they may be, buy papers, and eagerly scan the lists to see if by chance they are holders of winning

numbers.   One sees a cluster of girls on a street corner all
talking at once; one of them "knows a girl who has a friend
who won £1750."   A dignified gentleman wearing a silk
hat stops in front of a brilliantly lighted shop window, that
by its light he may look at a paper for a moment — and
then throws it away in disgust.   In imagination I can see
a noble earl telling his servant to fetch him an evening
paper immediately it comes, and a bishop, who in the
House of Lords is eloquently opposed to betting, retiring to
his closet to go over the lists in secret; for about half the
stakeholders conceal their identity under such pseudonyms
as "Goldfish" or "Misery" or "Hard Up" or "My Last
Hope" — and these are not such fanciful names, either.
Any day in London, as in many other cities in England,
early in the afternoon the newsboys are almost constantly
seen rushing about uttering weird sounds as though in
agony.   After a time one learns that they are crying, "All
the winners!"   In this rarefied atmosphere, who does not
think of the races?

There were horse races in Smithfield, in London, in the
time of Henry II — say two hundred and fifty years before
America was discovered.   They ceased in Tudor times,
jousting taking their place; they were revived by Charles
II, who became a patron of the turf, were neglected by the
early Georges, and were almost the ruin of the Prince Regent, afterwards George IV, whose racing debts were paid
by Parliament in order that he might not be deprived of the
sport in which all his subjects delighted.

I should like to make it clear at the outset that I am not
really a horsy man. I never was. There is a legend in
my family that a hundred years ago I, being then five years
old, interrupted the conversation of a presumably maiden

aunt who was declaiming the wonders of Niagara Falls, from which she had just returned, by asking, "And where do you think I have been?" And before my question could be answered I replied to myself proudly, "On Bob's back." Bob was an old plough horse and the ride I took was from a watering trough to the stable door, a distance of perhaps forty feet. Of actual equestrian experience this is my total, but in theory I yield to no man. I can, for example, tell one end of a horse from the other at a glance, and it requires only a casual examination to enable me to tell a lady horse from a perfect gentleman — unless someone has been tampering with him. My collection of sporting books is, however, another matter; modesty forbids that it be discussed here.

Prior to going to the Derby, the last race course I visited, which was also my first, was in Chicago in the World's Fair year, 1893. How it came that I, forty years ago, went to the races with James J. Corbett the prize fighter, John W. Gates of American Steel and Wire fame, who unsuccessfully attempted to "hold up" the late J. P. Morgan when he was putting together the United States Steel Corporation, Lillian Russell and two other actresses whose names I have forgotten, — a party of six altogether, — I do not now remember, but I do know that I felt like a fish out of water, and no doubt looked like one. But I remember well the peerless Lillian, and how happy I was when John Gates and "Gentleman Jim" left the box in the grandstand to place bets for the ladies, leaving me to entertain them, and how I hated the men when they came back, Gates for his wealth and Corbett for his good looks; and I remember, too, that when the horse won, it was Miss Russell's bet, and when it lost, it was John Gates's, and how content both were that it should be so. That's a long time ago — forty years. I have made many bets since; indeed, just before I left home I received a tip from a New England bookmaker, who had the effrontery to call himself an investment banker, to put ten thousand dollars on a sure thing called Ivar Kreuger. With confidence I backed this scoundrel, as did thousands of others, only to see my money turn to ashes in a week's time. So I went to the Derby in the frame of mind of John Gilpin his wife: "although I was on pleasure bent I had a frugal mind" — and I may say that this is an excellent mood in which to go to the races.

It was on an especially fine morning that I sallied forth from my little flat in Jermyn Street to go to the Derby. I could have "jobbed" a big motor car, stocked it with eatables and drinkables, and I might have done this had I not been afraid that, after going to a lot of trouble and expense, my car would have been parked in some position from which I could see practically nothing. I once had such an experience at a boat race on the Hudson. After getting up at dawn, — always a silly thing to do, — I went aboard a private yacht which steamed up the river and ultimately secured an excellent position. There we lay all day in the heat and glare until, just before the race, a great excursion steamer came in front of us and completely blanketed our view. We saw nothing whatever of the race and did not learn what crew had won until in the evening we got back to New York. I did not care to repeat this experience.

Or I could, for a matter of ten dollars, have secured a seat on the top of a motor bus and have been sure of an excellent lunch and "tea," — there is no escaping tea in England, — but then I should have been tied more or less to the spot allotted the bus, and in the event of rain, no unlikely occurrence, I should have been privileged to give up my place reserved inside to a lady and spend hours on end in a wet and miserable condition. "After much debate internal," with money in pocket for contingencies, I decided to go by train from Victoria.

As our taxi reached the station, I saw signs calling attention to "Special trains to Epsom and return, first class five shillings, third class three, class not guaranteed." This meant that, having bought a first-class ticket, I might have to be content with third-class accommodation; so, as I usually travel third anyway, I took third-class tickets, got excellent seats in a train that was just pulling out, and in a little over half an hour reached the Downs. It was not yet eleven o'clock, but already there was an immense crowd, people coming from all points of the compass and by thousands — quiet, orderly, well-behaved, plain people, intent, like myself, on having a good time. Some had been on the Downs for several days, living in motors, tents, in and under wagons, in the neighborhood — living any old way; for be it understood that, although there is but one Derby Day and the "Derby" is only one of several races run on that day, the Derby races are run for the best part of the week, and are followed by the "Oaks" and other races. Englishmen live for sport, for life in the open, to a degree quite unknown to us; therein, as in most other things, they are wiser than we. The racing season begins the last of March and continues until the last of November, by which time the fox-hunting season is in full swing and continues until the racing season begins again. Fox hunting is indeed a sort of steeplechasing, with the fox serving as the steeple, and Jack Jorrocks's dictum on this sport is well known: "Fox-hunting is the sport of Kings, the himage of war without its guilt, and only five and twenty per cent of its danger."

On the Sunday before the Derby, the Downs are themselves a great attraction. Uncountable thousands walk over the course, inspect the condition of the turf, watch the

gypsies take over their annual tenancies, and the bookmakers — their name is legion — locate their stalls. The
merry-go-rounds get agoing and the showmen erect their
tents, the hurdy-gurdies begin to grind out the most la-
mentable music, and refreshment booths are established
and do a thriving business. Derby Day is getting ready to
begin, and, in the midst of the noise and confusion, what
does one hear? Is it possible that some band of evangeli-
cals is trying to hold a religious service? Yes; and, while
it can hardly be a Church of England group, it is not the
Salvation Army, either, for the men wear white surplices,
stoles, and other ecclesiastical gear. A small and miserable
organ is being pushed along on a handbarrow. Farther
on one comes upon another group; ah, that 's the Salvation
Army! One hears singing, with a big drum carrying the
air. An anæmic-looking man is struggling with a large
banner on which one reads: CHRIST DIED FOR YOU.

I had intended to say that the horses are much too well
bred to attend these services — but let that pass. And
remember that at our national political conventions the
"deliberations" of both gangs of ruffians are always opened
by prayer; we are, I think, the most hypocritical people
in the world — as the French are the least.

The Downs station is about a mile from the grandstand,
which is, more or less, the objective of everyone who goes
to the Derby. Five minutes after leaving the station we
came upon a group of Welsh singers — singing very well,
too. On a sheet on the ground in front of them were a
number of small coins, for the most part copper, but with
a few sixpences and shillings, the latter doubtless intended
to suggest the singers' own appraisement of the value of
their concert. We had only listened for a moment when
an old hag, a gypsy, came up and wanted to tell my fortune.

She told me I should come into money, and for half a crown would tell me when and how. Meantime a man offered to guess my wife's age and weight. These matters being a profound secret, he was received with withering scorn; I really pitied him. Sellers of tips on the races were on every hand. Old 'Arry — "everybody knows Old 'Arry," a middle-aged man in threadbare clothes which had once been elegant, and were not now being worn by their original owner — Old 'Arry has been backing the winners for years, had taken his own advice yesterday and made a pot of money, offered much better advice to-day, and, to show how little he cared for money, lit a cigar with a ten-shilling note (stage money). Another man, an accomplice, rushing up, seemingly paid him a pound for some secret information contained in a sealed envelope, and disappeared. 'Arry had only one more left; this he would dispose of for ten shillings to effect a quick sale; he had important business elsewhere and was in an 'urry. A man with a small collapsible table before him was doing card tricks; the time-honored shell game was going on under one's very eyes, and a very primitive sort of roulette everywhere. "Violets, lovely violets, sixpence; well, then, tuppence; take 'em and God bless you." The crowd increases. Hawkers abound, seeking to sell toys, souvenirs, trash of all kinds; one wonders who would buy the stuff and burden themselves all day with it. Multiply the side shows of a country circus by a thousand, and you will have some idea of the Downs on Derby Day.

I have said that the race course is shaped somewhat like a crooked hairpin; to get into the space practically surrounded by the track takes time and effort. The course, which is perhaps eighty feet wide, is of turf, bordered on each side with a white fence, and is constantly patrolled to see that nothing, not a bottle or a box or a piece of paper, lies thereon to distract the attention of the racing horses. It was with some difficulty that we crossed the track and found ourselves in the centre of bedlam. The crowd and the shows and the sights of the circumference were as nothing compared to those in the centre. If the picturesque scenes and coloring of Frith's "Derby Day" were somewhat lacking, owing to the always leveling influence of democracy, the character of the crowd has not changed. Crowds out for a good time must eat and drink, and far off in large tents, erected by London *restaurateurs*, excellent food, with liquors of all kinds, was being served; but my object in subjecting myself to the hubbub and confusion of an English holiday crowd was not for the pleasure of eating at a fashionable restaurant, but to observe the crowd and watch individual members of it amuse themselves. Not to eat or drink with it; I did not care to regale myself with "fried fish and chips for ninepence," or, having bought a bottle of beer, make my way through the crowd drinking it from the bottle. Nor did I wish to indulge myself in a penny glass of lemonade. I never saw anything greener, not even Irish grass, than the liquid which called itself "lemon squash"; to add to the verisimilitude, two or three squeezed lemons were to be seen floating on the top of a large tankful of tartaric acid and water. Still less would I yield to the temptation of a scarlet drink as red as sin, which color was intended, no doubt, to suggest strawberries. My own fancy was for "stone ginger," although I knew it had been basking in the sun for hours, and I was careful to see that the glass I drank it from had just been washed in clean water, while to stay one's stomach one could buy a bar of excellent chocolate from a thousand hawkers.

I find that I must return to the subject of betting. I have always maintained that government, however necessary it may be, is a gigantic game of make-believe, and that the law which flows therefrom is a ass, an idiot; for this statement there is high authority, no less than that of Mr. Bumble. Whoever made the racing laws of England did so in a merry mood. The pivot on which they turn is the word "place." Gambling is a crime if carried on in a *place* in which by law it is not permitted, but it is legal if it is carried on in another *place* where it is. W. S. Gilbert in his most topsy-turvy moment never conceived anything better. What is a place, and when? Ay, there 's the rub. And wise old gentlemen, looking ferocious or benign in horsehair wigs, sit and debate this question for years, pass away and worms do eat them, and another generation — lawyers were children once — come upon the scene and are paid large sums for guessing what the lawmakers meant when they passed the Betting Act of 1853.

> "The Law is the true embodiment
> Of everything that 's excellent;
> It has no kind of fault or flaw,
> And I, my Lords, embody the Law."

So sings the Lord Chancellor, in *Iolanthe*. But even he does not know what a place is and takes a chance when he gambles on a horse race, just as the King does, and maybe the Archbishop of Canterbury. Meantime expensive and royal commissions have been appointed from time to time, to examine into the gambling laws of England and report what changes, if any, are desirable and practicable. Such a commission is sitting now, and it will debate the question pleasantly for a few years and then make some suggestions which, if adopted, cannot be enforced. Betting is and always has been so prevalent among high and low in England that the laws on the subject would probably have remained undisturbed, and more or less of a dead letter, but that it has been discovered that in the last few years over thirteen million pounds have gone over to the sweepstakes in Ireland. This is a lot of money; England is poor, and the English want to stop its flow across the Irish Sea. From the testimony already taken it was admitted, officially and publicly, that the laws relating to lotteries and sweepstakes cannot be enforced. The authorities have neither the ability nor the desire to carry out the letter of the law. As *Punch* said in a recent issue: "Street bookmakers are said to be taking penny bets on the races. Ruin is thus brought within the means of the poorest of us."

There were several thousand bookmakers on the Downs, hundreds of them in their little stands with their names and permanent addresses over them, and in addition there were representatives of old-established firms of gamblers who were as jealous of their reputations for square dealing as most of our investment bankers could be — and with better reason. Further, all during the racing season advertisements may be read in many of the London papers telling with whom and how and when and where to bet.

But we are living in a machine age, and it was inevitable that anything as general and as generally crooked as betting on a horse race should be "purified" by a machine which should be as incorruptible as mechanics and magnets could make it. With this end in view, an automatic betting machine called a totalizator — invariably referred to as a "tote" — has been installed at Epsom, Ascot, and other important race courses. It may be as stationary as the Bank of England or it may be in one place to-day and another place to-morrow, but it is not "a place" within the meaning of the Act; its existence is a legal triumph. The tote is not an individual machine, but rather a bank of machines, for on several of the courses there are as many as one hundred and fifty windows, each window equipped with ticket-issuing devices. In front of each window just before each race a long line of gentlemen and ladies may be seen, faultlessly dressed, waiting to record their bets. On one day last year over two hundred and thirty thousand pounds passed through one of these totes, which is as difficult to describe as it is easy to operate. This automatic bet-recording device is absolutely on the level; it is as accurate, indifferent, and impersonal as an electrically operated board in a broker's office. The idea comes from Australia; Joe Widener, one of our premier sportsmen, suggests that these devices be introduced in this country, giving a percentage of the takings to the state.

Here I should like to make a prophecy: namely, that within the next few years, the rich having been "soaked" to a standstill, totes or similar betting devices will be in operation all over the country. With the notably increased interest in racing, some means must be devised for the protection of those who wish to back a horse. Such a scheme will almost certainly be opposed by the same group which has deprived the nation of thousands of millions of dollars from the legitimate sale of liquor and, to the corruption of everybody, given it to the bootleggers. It is gambling pure and simple; it will lead to defalcations, petty stealing, and distress; but it ought not to shake the nation, it ought not to close our banks. I do not wish to labor the point unduly, but is it not sheer folly to permit the crookedest gambling game the world has ever known to function under the patronage of the New York Stock Exchange, with betting agencies in every city in the country, and at the same time to decry betting elsewhere? One frequently reads in the papers of the arrest of some poor devil for putting a five-dollar bill on a horse race, the while a pool of silk-hatted "bankers" send a selected stock up or down five or ten points in a single day to their own enrichment and to the destruction of a flock of innocents, well called "lambs."

I have no doubt that Charles James Fox would have looked upon a tote as a tradesman with whom no gentleman would wish to associate; but other times, other methods and manners. I never enter the club which he and others of his kind made famous, Brooks's, — and on several occasions I have had a card for it, — without thinking of the remark which Lord George Bentinck once made there on the eve of Derby Day.

"Does anyone present wish to lay three to one against my horse?" he inquired.

Whereupon Lord Glasgow replied, "I will lay it to you."

"Very good," said Lord George, "but I don't want small bets."

"Nor I," said Glasgow; "if ninety thousand to thirty will suit you, I will lay it." Whereupon Lord George confessed that he could not afford a bet of such a sum.

"I thought you were only talking big," continued Glasgow, who is reported later to have lost a hundred thousand pounds as the result of a single wager. Derby figures are indeed fantastic. It is said that three years ago the Stock Exchange Derby Sweep brought in so much money that the two prizes had to be duplicated. The first prize was worth one hundred and twenty-five and the second sixty-five thousand pounds — pounds, mind you. And once upon a time the Duke of Westminster, one of the richest men in the world, paid a thousand pounds for Flying Fox, won the Derby with it and forty thousand pounds, and then sold the animal for another forty thousand — a good day's work even for a duke. On the other hand, in 1919 it cost Lord Glanely, with Grand Parade, something like one hundred thousand pounds to win the "Blue Ribbon of the Turf," as Disraeli called it. The biggest win of all is attributed to a Mr. Merry, who in 1860, with Thormanby, won the race and half a million pounds to boot. Are the laws against betting a dead letter? I 'll say they are; but, more important, so does Lord Hewart, the Chief Justice of England.

A few days before the Derby, talking to a sporty friend at my club, — who could talk of nothing else, — I told him I wanted to bet against Orwell, the favorite, and asked him how to go about it. My friend told me I was mad. He was "betting both ways" on Firdaussi. This sounded to me like going long and short on the same stock (or horse), and subsequently I discovered, whenever I asked a question, that I became involved in a lot of racing terms which were to me pure Greek. Everyone told me that the favorite, Orwell, could not possibly be beaten, but for some reason I took a dislike to the horse and wanted to bet against him. However, the matter seemed too complicated; also, and most important, I wanted to place my bet with someone whom I could find, if I won, after the race was over. No one could have read as much about racing and betting as I without suspecting that, even if I were right in my "hunch" against Orwell, the chance of my being able to collect any substantial sum of money was about one to ten. It did not seem good enough, and in the event I did nothing.

But to return to the heath. We were, by this time, threading our way through a crowd so dense that our progress was measured by inches. Our objective was the starting post for the first race of the day. It was timed for one-thirty, and a few moments before that hour a group of nervous horses with their riders crouched well up on their shoulders were seen coming into the course. Who shall describe a magnificent horse — its head, its shoulders, its make and shape? Its coat as sleek as satin, its legs as beautiful and more highly regarded than any girl's; its

disappeared; they were at lunch. The restaurants were crowded; hampers were opened on the tops of motor buses, and cold chicken and salad were washed down with champagne. In the crowd in which we were, people sat down on the ground and ate the English equivalent of hot dogs and drank beer from bottles. I ate a block of chocolate and would have given something substantial for a glass of cold water, for which a warm stone ginger is a poor substitute. Then the side shows had their innings. Everything short of downright theft goes on Derby Day. One is expected to look after one's self, especially one's pocketbook. Suddenly quite close to us a man's frantic voice shouted, "Give 'im hair! Give 'im hair!" — and a circular space was made in the dense crowd by two men running round in circles and digging their elbows into the nearest persons, while on the ground we gazed with horror at a seedy individual in the throes of what appeared to be a fit. Then one of them, who had been most energetic in shoving the crowd back, produced a pair of greasy boxing gloves from under his coat which he threw to the man on the ground, who promptly scrambled to his feet and adjusted the gloves to his hands; the energetic one put on another pair and they began sparring, while the third man went round with a hat collecting the coppers which the good-natured and laughing crowd dropped into it.

Humor is characteristic of a crowd of cockneys. Let no one think he can, with advantage to himself, bandy words with one of them. It can't be done — they are upon their native heath. And I have learned by years of experience never to attempt to match wits with a cockney. In unexpected retort they are especially disconcerting. An English temperance lecturer once said in a public speech, "I have lived in this town all my life. There are fifty pubs in it, and I have never been in one of them."

From the back of the room a heckler inquired, "Which one have you missed?" They talk and argue and persuade: "I 'm Wopsy Willie. Everyone knows me. If anyone attempts to use my name, stop 'im. I 'm 'ere to tell you the result of the next race. Is n't it worth an 'arf a crown to win ten poun'? I 've rode Lord Rosebery's Cicero when 'e won the Derby, and I 've a friend who knows just what is goin' on. Don't pay no attention to what nobody says; specially don't mind what that bloke over there says. 'E 's discredited in his hown 'ome, where 'e 's known."

We move on. At two-thirty there was another race. This we determined to see from Tattenham Corner, but a hundred thousand other people were like-minded and we saw only the flash of color of the jockeys urging their horses to the utmost. The first bend in the hairpin course is a broad turn which occasions no trouble; the second turn is difficult and dangerous. By the time this is passed the winner will almost invariably be picked from the first half-dozen horses. Tattenham Corner safely turned, there is the home stretch, a straightaway of perhaps half a mile. Horses without staying power begin to fall behind. There is a brief pause, and almost unnatural quiet, until far off, on high standards, the result of the race is announced from the winning post, followed by a rush for the bookies to secure the winnings — and another pause.

Then comes the DERBY — the race to see which this enormous crowd congregates year after year, in fair weather or foul, and which perhaps one person in ten actually sees. There are paddocks and enclosures for the elect or the very rich, relatively tiny spots crowded with jockeys and owners and race-course habitués, men and women from whom a nod is as good, almost, as an invitation to dine with a duke. Do you remember the story, years ago, when the great

Mrs. Astor bowed to Mrs. Gould as she entered her box
at the opera, how from a hundred lips there came partly
suppressed murmurs, "She 's in"?   Such occurrences are
always taking place in Society with a capital S.   Or maybe
they are not taking place — in which event the hope is for
better luck next time.   Had I had the least hope of being
seen by anyone I knew, had I understood the language
spoken, had I known the pedigree of a single horse, had I
known a jockey, or even had I been able to call a stableboy
by name, I might have bought myself the white topper and
the rest of the sartorial adornment;   I might even have
indulged myself in an expensive field glass, overlooked by
my friend in his specifications.   But being, so to speak,
alone in London, — and one is never so much alone as in
a crowd, — I used my imagination and saved my money.
What I saw — and I saw enough — cost me exactly a
shilling for an empty fruit box on which to stand.

I saw the horses canter obliquely to the starting tapes.
I felt rather than saw the nervousness of the jockeys; for
the owners the agony would be over in ten minutes, in five,
in two.   "Orwell is sure to win," says one; "I fancy Miracle," says another; "Keep your eye on 'Esperus," says
a cockney to me confidingly.   No one gave a thought to
April the Fifth, except perhaps his owner and his rider.
"They 're off!"   A low meaningless rumble is heard from
the throats of thousands on the other side of the course as
the horses stream along; they disappear, they appear
again, they round the corner; the rumble becomes something very like a cheer — they are rounding the Tattenham
Corner.   "Here they come!"   Miracle leads!   Where is
the mighty Orwell?   April the Fifth is winning; the betting was 100 to 6.   It is a bad moment for the bookmakers;
they stand to lose a fortune.   Everyone holds his breath.
Had Orwell been in the lead, the crowd would have torn

the heavens with their cheers. As it is, the race is run in something like silence, everyone having a bet on Orwell. In ten seconds it will all be over: "Miracle, Miracle!" "Dustur!" "April the Fifth!" "My God! April the Fifth has won!" "Well, I'll be damned," murmurs a man as though in prayer. Tom Walls, an actor, with an unknown horse that he has trained himself, has won the Derby — and a fortune. "Believe it or not."

And what of Orwell? The hottest favorite in many years, with odds 11 to 8, and just before the race 5 to 4, he comes in *ninth*, if you please — walking. Did n't have the legs for the distance. I wanted to say, "I told you so," but to whom should I say it? By this time the result of the race was known in Dublin, in New York, in Bombay, in Shanghai, and millions of money were changing hands. Oh, Orwell, Orwell — the pity of it!

Tom Walls and his horse and its rider are being congratulated and weighed, photographed and what not. To-night the owner will dine the guest of Majesty in Buckingham Palace, with other members of the Jockey Club, the most exclusive club in the world. Immortality. Immortality in just two minutes and forty-five seconds. The King sends for Walls and shakes him warmly by the hand. "One touch of nature makes the whole world kin." Mrs. Walls is in a flood of tears; would she change places with any lady in the land? Not she — her husband has won the Derby!

Only those intimately concerned with horse racing can have any idea of the care, expense, and anxiety which go to make a Derby racer. The moment a horse becomes prominent in betting circles he must be watched night and day to prevent unscrupulous touts from getting at him. The food that he eats and the water that he drinks must be constantly tasted. No opera singer is more carefully guarded from drafts, and no royal baby is more carefully groomed. This is not surprising when one considers what is expected of him. He must be able to travel at about fifty feet a second, and when he has won his race he has a precarious value up to fifty thousand pounds, and possibly more. He may, with luck, win that amount for his fortunate owner, and after his racing career is over he may, for breeding purposes, for some years be the equal of an annuity of ten thousand pounds a year. About a guinea an ounce is reckoned the value of a Derby winner.

It was for us the end of a perfect day; there would be another race and then another, and then, *hic et ubique*, TEA. Seemingly every motor bus and taxi and private motor in England was on the Downs by this time. We had enjoyed what used to be called, when I was a boy, "Queen's weather." We had been walking and standing about for seven hours without food. I was tired, and, to quote once more that excellent horseman Jack Jorrocks, "my stomach thought my throat was cut." Let us stroll over to the Downs station and catch an early train back to town.

A special train was leaving just as we reached the station; in forty minutes we were at Victoria and found it crowded with men and women and motors and taxis and buses, as though there were no such thing as Derby Day. You may take half a million people out of London and not make a dent.

London! We who are about to dine salute you.

II

ASCOT

Ascot is a horse of another color; it was royal to start with and has remained so. Queen Anne began it in 1711. She raced horses under her own name if not under her own colors, and the last important change in the course, or rather in the grandstand, was made by Edward VII. Ascot is only six miles or so from Windsor Castle, and there are paintings showing George IV, plump and well corseted, driving himself to the course in what appears to be a sort of glorified baby carriage drawn by horses as plump as their master. In those good old days there was a redoubtable racing stallion, Eclipse, a horse that was never beaten. This gave rise to the saying, "Eclipse is first and the rest nowhere." This famous sporting phrase has been given currency by Lord Macaulay in speaking of James Boswell as the first of biographers. "Boswell," he says, "has distanced all his competitors so decidedly that it is not worth while to place them. Eclipse is first and the rest nowhere." This is one of the few downright statements of Macaulay that have never been disputed. Eclipse himself did not win a Derby, — Derby Day was after his time, — but a father would rather see a son win honors than win them himself, and three of Eclipse's sons achieved this distinction. The horse was very much at home on the Ascot course, as he was foaled in Windsor Great Park and bred by the Duke of Cumberland, the brother of George III.

Like Epsom, the Ascot is a free course, but it is very fashionable. Of course common people go, — I have gone myself, — but there were only seventy or eighty thousand of us and we were almost submerged by the swells. It was on a glorious day in June that my wife, and Tinker, dear old "Tink" of Yale, and I took our seats on soap boxes just by the rail and opposite the Royal Pavilion, there to see Royalty and the races in the order named. It was at just the proper hour that we heard, "Here they come," and presently, in an open landau drawn by four greys, appeared the King and Queen, the Prince of Wales, and the Duke of Gloucester, followed by other members of the Royal Family, and certainly no family ever received a more hearty welcome. The course is in every respect much finer than Epsom. The stands, the buildings, — and there were many of them, — had been freshly painted and gayly decorated with flags and flowers, the white of the rails contrasting strongly with the green of the turf and lawns. Beauty, elegance, and fashion, dressed as they are only at Ascot, unrolled themselves under an Italian-blue sky. Surely there never was a lovelier sight. As one paper said, next day: "The elements conspired with humankind yesterday to stage the finest, most glorious, and rarest day that has graced the King's Meeting for many a year. And to greet it there were present the King, the Lords, and the Commons in their happiest mood."

The members of the crowd in which we were seemed to know everyone by name. "There 's the Princess Royal" — a name recently conferred by the King upon the young woman whom we used to call Princess Mary; and soon, as someone in the crowd said, "The Royal Box will 'ardly 'old hany more, Hi 'm thinkin'," which is exactly the conclusion I had reached myself.

How the English people love to talk about the weather!

ASCOT

"Here they come"

It means so much to them, the greatest out-of-door folk in the world, given to sport for the pleasure of playing the game quite as much as for the pleasure of winning. A bright, pleasant day calls forth comment from everyone. They pet it along and write love letters about it to the newspapers, and when some famous race, or some wonderful cricket match at Lord's, or strongly contested tennis match at Wimbledon, is blessed by especially glorious weather, even leader writers drop their carping and forget that gold is leaving the country and that the budget is unbalanced, and let themselves go in this fashion: —

The weather promises to be all that can be desired for the Ascot races, and we hope the promise may be kept, for to-day begins the gayest festival in all our calendar, a festival supreme in its pageantry of color and in its appeal to men and women of all classes, from palace to cottage. Its setting and its traditions are characteristically English. There is nothing else just like Ascot anywhere in the world. This year it might have been thought that other anxieties and the general impoverishment would have detracted somewhat from its customary glory; yet, if the preparations are any guide, it promises to be brighter and more carefree and to assemble greater throngs than ever, and if its fleeting brilliance can drown sorrows we shall all be the better for it. The world would not be less awry if we were to sit down in sackcloth and ashes and leave Ascot Heath deserted this mid-June.

Ascot is what it is to the English race because of its intimate associations between people and Court. It is a semi-state occasion, when the King joins freely with his people in the common enjoyment of our premier sport. Bereft of the Royal patronage and presence, it would be undistinguished from the race meeting of every day. It is in effect an open-air Court, a circumstance which makes the dresses of its ladies as important as the form of its horses. People go to Epsom to see the whole world; to Ascot to see Society: the one is the greatest of all fairs, and the other the finest of all family parties. And it would be a sad day for

England were she to be ever so absorbed in her sorrows as to forget the form of the one and the pride of the other.

To which I say, "Amen."

We hardly needed this stimulation to go to Ascot, our pleasant Derby Day experiences being such a cordial memory. And we went in our oldest clothes, I wearing a cap — think of me in a topper when I could, and not unsuccessfully, pass myself for a cockney. But generally women — and men too — dress for the Ascot with as much care as though they were going to the opera; indeed the opera is an exotic in England, while horse racing is indigenous. An Englishman is a peacock and he preens himself with extreme care. In imagination I can hear a woman say to herself, "I 'll make that old flowered silk of mine do for the Derby and see if I can't, somehow, wangle a new crêpe de Chine for Ascot." Not so her lord and master! Does fashion dictate a long black coat with one button? He would die rather than be seen in a coat with two. His trousers must be creased and his spats freshly laundered. His topper must be irreproachable, and have we not all heard of Ascot ties? An Englishman will be careful not to commit a sartorial anachronism. Shakespeare may give Bohemia a seacoast and make clocks strike in Ephesus if he will, — Shakespeare was a law unto himself, — but a properly turned out Englishman will wear the right thing for a given hour or go into hiding.

Of the extreme refinements of "what and when" the average American knows nothing. A few years ago the British Bar Association entertained the American Bar, and the British lawyers, who had, many of them, enjoyed the splendid hospitality of the Americans, said, "We must make this thing a success." And they did. Houses, palaces, and galleries were thrown open, dinners and luncheons given. And then there was a garden party;

and when the English stage such an event, it *is* a party! Everyone was invited and everyone attended, and the question arose, "What shall I wear?" "A black morning coat, striped trousers, and spats by all means" — and many men wore spats for the first time. That same evening the King gave the more important delegates a dinner at Buckingham Palace, and many men, still rejoicing in their spats, thought it would be a nice thing to wear them. Mercifully someone discovered what was being done and word was passed, "Get rid of your spats." It was almost too late. A line of taxis was forming along Constitution Hill, leading to the Palace, filled with apoplectic old gentlemen trying, hurriedly, to remove the damn things, which is not so easy in a taxi. Then arose the question what to do with them. Along Constitution Hill is a high brick wall enclosing the Palace Gardens. "Throw them over the wall," someone said. This was done, and the next morning the shrubbery was seen, white with spats. They say the King will not have to buy a pair of spats for years. It's an ill wind . . .

The difference between a group of English men and a group of American men is the difference between day and night. The American, at a party, usually looks as though he were short of a rising market and his shoes were one size too small for him. In a word, we do not know how to enjoy life; we work like the devil and save our money, only to be robbed of it by our politicians and the bookmakers who call themselves bankers. In racing parlance, we do not even get a run for our money.

The Ascot course is an oval exactly two miles in circumference and almost level. Since that eleventh of August in 1711 when Queen Anne, in an interval of giving pledges of her affection for her husband, Prince George of Denmark (she gave seventeen of them), attended in person the first race, Ascot has been a regal affair. Farmer George, the third of that ilk, gave it a royal push, and Edward VII made a number of desirable improvements. He enlarged and rebuilt the stands, which were parallel with the course, — the worst possible position for seeing a race, — and placed them at an angle with it. He also enlarged the Royal Enclosure, but he did not let down the bars — not he. The Royal Enclosure was made more isolated than it was, as, in place of the road behind it, which was formerly used by occupiers of the grandstand to get to the paddock, a subway was constructed so that these should not contaminate the air breathed by the frequenters of the holy of holies! And although the Royal Enclosure had been enlarged, the numbers were limited to 1200, and so strict were the rules that any lady with unfortunate matrimonial experience who might have received a ticket for the Jockey Club stand from a member of that club was unable to use it, by reason of the fact that she would have had to pass through the Royal Enclosure, from which she was debarred, to get to the stand.

Knowing all this, as we did, upon our arrival at the course we sought the subway and, buying our soap boxes for a shilling each, took our places as nearly in front of and as close to the Royal Box as we could get, which I may say was not very close. But what came we out for to see? The crowd of course, a pageant with real Kings and Queens and things like that for the leading actors. I confess that we were more than a little pleased when Majesty observed us standing on our soap boxes — at least, he raised his hand and pointed towards us, and the Queen too appeared interested as she looked in our direction through her glass. Tinker is accustomed to be pointed at, but for me it was a new experience.

ASCOT

The Royal Enclosure

The weather was superb, as promised, and as one event after another was run off, — Ascot differs from other race meetings in that every event is one of major importance, — the crowd increased in numbers. First came the Prince of Wales's Cup, then the Queen Alexandra Plate, then the Gold Vase for the two-mile, and above all the Ascot Gold Cup for the two-and-a-half-mile run. These trophies stood glistening in the sun quite unattended except by a hundred thousand people. The enjoyment of the mob increased. And not of the mob only, but of the crowd in the grand-stands and in the Royal Box. Handsomely dressed women curtsied low to His Majesty and were raised in glory when he lent them his glass and pointed out some sight which interested him. The Queen graciously waved her hand to one, shook hands with another, and kissed a third. It was, as has been said, an open-air court, and when Limelight, the King's horse, won a race, and when His Majesty and the Queen and the members of the Royal Family made their way to the unsaddling enclosure, and congratulated the jockey and received the congratulations of their intimates, — if any such there be, — then joy was unconfined. Is this snobbery? Certainly not. Does any thinking man or woman really believe in democracy; does any member of the animal or vegetable kingdom believe in it? Why do Rotarians and Odd Fellows and such like wear their silly decorations and badges? Is it not an effort on their part to raise themselves above the crowd? Who wants to be one of a mob? Even an undertaker takes precedence of a garbage collector.

The betting everywhere was enormous; everyone seemed to have plenty of money. Five-pound notes fluttered gayly, and those stiff green paper pounds which have displaced, for the time at least, the golden sovereign seemed as plentiful as half crowns. "Four to one bar one," cries a bookie, which means I will lay you odds of four to one against any horse except the favorite. "Do yourself a bit of good for tuppence," says another, hawking an ice of doubtful quality, to be followed by another who seeks to sell "Ices that you *can* eat, Lyons' ices, sixpence," while a poor woman thrusts into your hand a bunch of "Violets, lovely violets." "Yes, my dear, the horses will begin to run around the circle in a few minutes, and then you will be able to pick out the one you like best," explains a father to an anxious child who wants to know when the fun will commence. You make your way slowly through the crowd until you see a bookmaker you think you can trust to be found after the race, or you can go to the "tote." In a word, you can back your fancy to any extent, for, as Lord Hewart, Chief Justice of England, has said, "The law can enforce successfully only that which the community has agreed in thinking right." In which respect he differs from that exploded Methodist Bishop who, when he appeared at the last Democratic Convention in Chicago, was greeted with boos and cries of, "Your broker wants you." If we in this country could only learn to take our laws from lawyers and not from meddling ministers, how much happier and wiser we should be. But why should we be wise? No nation has ever been wise, except the French — and who wants to be French?

On our happy Ascot excursion Herr Professor Doctor Tinker (as the Germans would say), of Yale, added much to our pleasure. He had some idea of blowing himself to a white topper and the rest of Ascot gear, thinking it *infra dig* for a Sterling Professor of Yale and Keeper of the Rare Books in its wonderful new library not to be also the glass of fashion, the mould of form, and the observed of all observers, but I would not permit it. "Save your money, Professor; I shall need it," I said, "when I come to pay for that replica by Reynolds of the portrait of Boswell in the

National Gallery that Gabriel Wells is this very minute buying for me, and then if there is any left over you may consider taking that *Lyrical Ballads* with the Bristol imprint, which is well worth all that Lionel Robinson is asking for it." So in great good humor we went to Ascot and in the same good humor we returned, and we had hardly seated ourselves in our little drawing-room of our flat in Jermyn Street, and poured out our whiskey and sodas, when Gabriel came in fresh from the sale at Christie's. "Well, I 've bought the Boswell," he said. "Which of you gets it?"

"Don't be silly, Gabriel. You know perfectly which of us gets it. It 's mine by right of discovery, but if you paid a high price it is Tink's, and mine only if you got it cheap. You very well know why — Tink is backed by Yale and I 'm out of a job."

"Very well. The Boswell is yours, and you shall have a year in which to pay for it, and if your wife don't want you to pay for it, I 'll give it to you. And right here and now" — for when Gabriel gets in expansive mood he is hard to check — "I 'll give you a hundred pounds profit on your bargain."

"And what do I get?" said Tink.

"Professor, you get an excellent dinner," said Gabriel. "We 'll all go to the Hungarian Restaurant and have paprika chicken and a bottle of . . ."

"We 'll do nothing of the kind," said I. "I can't talk against that band. And that overfed violinist will come up to my wife and play a Hungarian Rhapsody and it 'll cost me a pound. We 'll go to the 'quiet room' at Monico's. The dinner is on me. Do you remember, my dear, the day that we lunched there with E. V. Lucas and drank three quarts of champagne?"

And so it was settled. Why is it not possible to have these pleasant meetings elsewhere? When E. V. called London my spiritual home, he knew why.

III

OFF TO THE GRAND NATIONAL

WHEN Uncle Sam pitched upon the fifteenth day of March for the filing of one's income-tax return and the first payment of one quarter of the total amount, he gave no consideration to the fact that his date might conflict with that upon which the Grand National is run. And, even if he had, he would no doubt have kept right on in his arbitrary course; that is the way governments have. And that is why I am against 'em. There is no denying, however, that they have the last word, and in spite of the best efforts of a secretary, a chartered accountant, an income-tax expert, and a lawyer, to the end that the word might be soft, — the kind of word that turneth away wrath, — I say that, in spite of all these, the word when it was spoken caused a feeling of violent pain.

I can look back upon the time when one never came in contact with the United States authorities except upon returning from Europe, when one slipped a five-dollar bill to a customs inspector with the same regularity that one did to one's steward, and when one went to the Federal office only to decide upon the color and portraiture of a postage stamp. In those days the surplus of income over expenses was a cause of worry. And economists told us that what we needed was a big national debt — an economist will tell you anything. Now what a change! The asking of personal questions is no longer the prerogative of one's physician. Anyone, everyone, feels privileged. Why did

you buy B. & O. at 136, and New York Central at 200?
Why did you not buy your Steel Common at the bottom
rather than at the top? Did you take advantage of the
"split-up" in G. E. at the time "you disposed" of your
rights in Radio? Above all, why did you allow the emis-
saries of those sterling financiers, Al Wiggin and Charlie
Mitchell, to wangle you into the purchase of bank stocks at
a price which makes it impossible for you to look into a
mirror without loss of self-respect? Is the bushel of grass
seed you bought in your wife's name to be charged to
capital outlay or expense? These and a hundred similar
problems arise to vex you. And, finally, why did you take
au pied de la lettre the saying of a famous banker, the slogan,
"Never sell America short"?

We were to sail for Liverpool in the *Adriatic*, but it did
not seem wise to do so, and one evening after dinner, lighting a cigar, I observed to myself that if this was a specimen
of the last of life for which the first is made, I wanted more
of the first. "Never sell America short!" America has
provided the best short sale in all history. No doubt we
shall work out of our problems, but when, and where shall
I be? John Brown's is not the only body which will be
a-mouldering in the grave. Then the words of that sum of
all philosophers, Christopher Sly, occurred to me. "Let
the world slip. We shall ne'er be younger." And so, a
few days later, we took passage on the *Bremen*, the fastest
boat afloat, and, leaving her at Southampton, — with our
teeth intact, but badly shaken, — made our way quickly
to Liverpool.

Need I say that the Grand National is the sportiest horse
race that has ever been run in the world, that it is a steeplechase which has been a fixture for almost a hundred years,
and that it is distinctly not a race to watch from the grand-

stand unless one has placed big money on the result —
which is more foolish at the National than at other races, for,
as someone has said, "at the National the only thing certain
is the unexpected." To see the race properly one should
walk over the course the day before, study the obstacles
which the racers must overcome, and make up one's mind
what particular incident in the race one wants to see at close
range.

One can, of course, leave London early in the morning
on the day of the race in the magnificently appointed
special Pullman trains which run directly to the race
course and bring you back the same day. In this way
you are sure of a luncheon, a reasonably good dinner, and
an excellent cup of tea, but it makes a long and fatiguing
day, so I had made up my mind to spend several days in
Liverpool.

It is admitted that one of the best hotels in England is the
Adelphi. It does not capitalize dirt and antiquity as so
many hotels in Britain do, and was built just before the
Great War, which had the effect, among many, of diverting
the American traffic from Liverpool to the Channel Ports.
I felt quite sure, however, that having made no reservation
at the Adelphi I should be unable to secure accommodation,
and in this I was not mistaken. But we had no difficulty
at the Exchange Station Hotel, and this was a bit of good
luck, as special trains run from the Exchange Station every
few minutes to and from the race course at Aintree on race
days, and almost as frequently at all times — the distance
is only five miles. And so to Aintree we went as per
schedule on the day before the race, walked over the course,
examined the jumps, and decided upon what we thought
would be a good point from which to view the amazing
spectacle. Aintree is, except for the race course, not much,
although it is almost equally famous for its marmalade.

The race is run over a course two and a quarter miles, which is traversed twice, making a run of four and a half miles, but the second time round, two famous obstacles, the Open Ditch and the Water Jump, are omitted, so that the race finishes on the straightaway directly in front of the grandstand. Having traveled more than three thousand miles to see this race, weather or no, we prepared for whatever weather might come: a pestilent breeding fog, a heavy rain, and a strong wind, even a snowstorm, for the race has frequently been run under any of these conditions. The grandstand affords a certain amount of protection, but we chose to stand about near the course in the open. And we dressed for the occasion! Wraps and rugs and galoshes. And besides plenty of whiskey my medicine kit contained liniments, lozenges and lotions, pills and other pneumonia preventives. In brief, we were prepared to cope promptly with such intimations of mortality as might result from deadly exposure, and, to dismiss this subject well in advance of the race, let me now say that when race day came the weather was on its best behavior and we wished our impedimenta to the very devil. People took us for Eskimos.

A shout of ribald laughter went up from my friends in London when I told them that I had come over to *ride* in the Grand National, for, as all the world knows, the riders must be meagre little men, skilled not only in riding powerful brutes of horses but also in tumbling off them, not portly old gentlemen who should be doing their Now-I-lay-me's, thus preparing themselves for a better world. Better? I wonder! And in my wonderment I am not alone. I observe with interest that people, orthodox people, who affect to believe in the impossible seem in no more haste than I to leave this vale of tears. I am quite content with this wicked world as I know it, and shall see my number go up with the utmost reluctance.

Having chosen to see the race from the course, we were in some doubt as to whether it would be from Becher's Brook or the Canal Turn; finally deciding on the latter, we returned to Liverpool and, after a substantial lunch, went upon a voyage of discovery. It is difficult to become enthusiastic over Liverpool. It is a cold, hard, dirty city possessed of some magnificent buildings built of granite, black and grimy with smoke and age. The only feature of interest to the tourist is the new cathedral now building, work upon which has been going on for years; it will, when completed, be one of the largest in the kingdom and would seem to be entirely unnecessary. Is not the day of cathedral builders done? I think so. Abject poverty is the rule in Liverpool, as it is in Glasgow, and for the same reason — the decay of shipping and shipbuilding; and one might wish that the good people of Liverpool had been moved by greater consideration for the poor and less by ostentatious vanity. And now the Roman Catholics are passing the hat into which coin must be dropped, that they too may build a monster cathedral and thus not be outdone by their Anglican brethren.

Upon the occasion of a visit to Liverpool several years ago, on a Gilbert and Sullivan pilgrimage, we had neglected to see the new cathedral, and this time determined that we would attend a service, if one was going on. But there was only one woman kneeling in prayer in the vast "fabrick," — as Dr. Johnson would call it, — and one or two sight-seers like ourselves. Presently and seemingly afar off we heard the strains of a powerful organ and then a magnificent choral service. In imagination we could see a band of ecclesiastics in colorful array and a white-robed choir of men and boys with superb soprano voices. But where did the sounds come from? The crypt, probably. We descended — nothing, no one. Presently the music suddenly stopped

THE GRAND NATIONAL.
The field taking Becher's Brook

and out of the silence came a clear, well-trained voice:
"Hello, everybody.   This is the British Broadcasting . . ."
I was horrified; perhaps I should not have been.   But a
cathedral suggests, to me, mediæval religion and not the
latest development in radio.   Just then a poor, dirty, un-
dernourished ecclesiastic of low degree passed by, and I
asked him where the service was being held which had been
"broadcasted" so magnificently.   He did not know —
"from Lambeth," he thought.   This I knew to be nonsense,
and I passed on more than ever convinced that a new cathedral is an anachronism for which there is no excuse.

The Derby is a country fair the great feature of which is
a horse race for three-year-olds.   Ascot is a very swell
garden party patronized by Royalty which anyone with a
few shillings can attend through the wrong end of a field
glass.   The Grand National is a steeplechase, a horse race
in excelsis, interspersed with jumps many of which would
seem to be impossible.

I am indebted to Father Sheedy, of Altoona, Pennsylvania, for the origin of the steeplechase; the good Father's
cathedral deserves a fine steeple.   He tells me that "in the
County Cork, there are two small towns about three and a
half or four miles apart — Buttevant and Doneraile.   One
evening two officers stationed at the garrison in Buttevant
were dining in Doneraile.   Each had a well-bred horse, this
part of Ireland being noted for its fine horses.   The officers
were very proud of their mounts, and a challenge to race
was given and accepted.   'How shall we race?'   'Across
country,' was the answer.   'Where shall we start, and where
finish?'   On the main street of each town was a church
with a steeple.   'Let us start at a steeple and end at a
steeple.'   It was agreed; the race was run across country,
over hedges and ditches.   And a fine exciting race it was;

a steeplechase indeed. Now the name remains, although steeples no longer function."

At Aintree the race is run over a predetermined course on which the obstacles or jumps are artificial and planned to test to the full the endurance of the horse and the skill of its rider. Four and a half miles is a stiff run for any horse, even for such magnificent brutes as are entered in the National, but the length of the course is the least of it. It is the thirty "jumps," at which horses and riders frequently part company, which make it difficult and dangerous. These fences — say hurdles, rather — are of varying heights, widths, and composition, including ditches full of water, one of which, the famous Open Ditch, is a thorn hedge five feet two inches high, three feet nine inches wide, guarded by a rail eighteen inches high, beyond which is a ditch six feet wide and two feet six inches deep, full of water. There is also the Water Jump, of a total width of fifteen feet, twelve feet six inches being water two and a half feet deep, with a preparatory hedge thirty inches high. There remain two more difficulties to be successfully overcome, Becher's Brook, which is no longer the brook it once was, and the Canal Turn, where, after an especially high hedge, there is immediately a sharp turn in the course. This was the point from which we chose to see the race — and for excitement it is to be recommended.

In "flat" races, as they are called, such as the Derby and Ascot, speed only is considered, but the development of the Grand National, as it came to be called, at Aintree, was due entirely to hunting men, centuries after flat racing had become popular. Hunting men who "ride straight" have to negotiate whatever comes in their way, and to simulate the difficulties of the hunting field the obstacles at Aintree have been dug or erected. At one time a stone wall was included in the jumps, but this was thought to be too dan-

gerous and was removed. Becher's Brook became celebrated from the fact that when the first race was run, almost
a hundred years ago, a certain Captain Becher, going
strong, approached the brook, when suddenly his horse
stopped dead, throwing its rider head over heels into the
water. Luckily he had the presence of mind — which is
the next best thing to absence of body — to remain in the
brook under the protection of the bank until the remainder
of the riders had jumped over him. From that day to this
his name is associated with a jump at which many a gallant
horse and rider have come to grief. But Becher's Brook
is now no longer a brook; it is merely a relatively narrow
drain on the far side of a high hedge, but I observed with
interest that several stretchers were concealed near by and
an ambulance was not far off, in case of accident. Both
were requisitioned in the course of the race, but the accidents were not serious. There have, of course, been many
accidents during the century of racing at Aintree, but I think
in all that time only one was fatal to the rider. On the
other hand, the horses have suffered severely, and for this
reason the race is sometimes criticized. Both men and
horses are taught by experience how to fall, and the effort
which a horse will make not to step on a man when he is
down is almost unbelievable.

Wellington, the great Duke, once remarked that he had
"spent a great part of his life wondering what was going on
on the other side of the hill." This must be very much the
state of mind of the rider approaching a jump in the National. Have the horse and rider who have preceded him
fallen, and, if so, are they down to stay, and where? He
can only guess and hope for the best. To make the jumps
more difficult, the ground is usually lower on the landing
side, in one case as much as nineteen inches lower, than
the take-off side. But the true huntsman is never tired of

quoting the lines of that prince of sporting poets, Adam
Lindsay Gordon: —

> No game was ever yet worth a rap
> For a rational man to play,
> Into which no accident, no mishap,
> Could possibly find its way.

The course as originally laid out consisted of "turf and
plough" — that is to say, of grass interspersed with rough
or furrowed fields; in 1885 an all-turf course was decided
upon and the character of the jumps changed. There
could be — doubtless there has been — assembled a whole
anthology of almost unbelievable happenings at Aintree
since the first race was run. On one occasion a horse
named Lottery made a jump of thirty-five feet! Horses
have been known to jump a hedge, turn a complete somer-
set, get up, and, riderless, win the race, if so it might be
called but that, to win, horse and rider must stick together. Once twenty-four horses in all came to grief at
the Canal Turn, and in 1929 sixty-six horses started — it
constituted a "bumping match": the falls of horses were
thirteen in number, as were the jockeys unseated, their
horses not down; ten horses finished, and the remaining
"died," refused, were pulled up or interfered with. The
value of this race to the winner was just under thirteen
thousand pounds. A horse has been known to throw his
rider at the first fence but keep right on in the lead for
over four miles! And I may say that nothing is feared
more than a riderless, that is to say a guideless, horse, for
he may suddenly stop or as suddenly cut across an on-
coming horse, to the certain grief of all concerned. In
brief, the course may be strewn for its entire length with
men and with horses in the most fantastic attitudes, or
they may be bunched together in an almost inextricable
mass.

It is a great race to watch, is the National.   The jumps which constitute records are almost unbelievable and are always being talked about.   For a long time the greatest distance jump was thirty-nine feet, made in 1847, but this is now said to have several times been exceeded, while some time ago at the Concours Hippique in Paris, a high jump of seven feet ten inches was made — the record is said to be eight feet and a fraction of an inch.

Like the Derby, there are a number of minor races run on the day of the Grand National, but *the race*, over the whole course, is set for a quarter past three in the afternoon.   In the race we saw on that fine day in March 1933, thirty-four horses started and eighteen finished; the others fell by the wayside.   The start we did not see, but a loud murmur through the crowd told us, "They 're off."   And presently in the distance over Becher's Brook came the horses, first one, instantly two more, and soon what was left of the entire field; in another moment they were at the Canal Turn, over which they came streaming like water. In another moment they had disappeared, and for some minutes we stood around quite nonchalantly as though indifferent to the fact that a great race was being run. Presently a loud murmur advised us that the horses would soon be clearly in sight again.   "Here they come!" There is a little suppressed cheering and once more the horses pass out of our sight, and for us the race — the race we had come so great a distance to see — is history.   It seems rather curious that a world-rocking sporting event can be decided in a couple of minutes — but so it is with horse racing.   There are so many preliminaries; months, perhaps years, are occupied with them.   Horses have to be chosen and trained; likewise men, and then fitted together.   "They 're off!" — "Here they come!" — a cheer — a groan — and it is all over.   But it is put down in the books and in men's minds and talked over for years to come.

Our race will long be spoken of somewhat in this fashion: "I remember back in 1933 when two horses with similar names, Kellsboro' Jack and Pelorus Jack, were neck and neck at the last fence. Pelorus Jack seemed to be going a trifle easier than the other Jack, though neither was too comfortable, when Stott, who was on Pelorus, a bit too eager, landed his horse right on the last fence and turned him over. I was standing right there and saw the tears streaming down Stott's face. Poor fellow, it was his race up to that minute. Williams was on the other Jack. He was owned by a lady — an American, I think she was."

And then there will be a dispute and more reminiscences: "I remember my father telling me of how a parson rode in the National in his day and came damn near winning the race, too. His name was Drake, but he rode as Mr. Ekard, which is Drake spelled backward. Someone went to his bishop and told him that one of his clergymen was bringing a scandal upon the church by riding in a steeplechase. 'Did he win?' inquired the bishop. 'No,' was the answer. 'I'm glad I did not know he was riding,' said the bishop; 'I certainly would have put some money on him.' It was worth a man's while to be a bishop in those days." Even bishops are not what they were.

And another will then tell of the wild enthusiasm when the Prince of Wales, afterwards Edward VII, in 1900 won the National with his horse Ambush, and how much he paid for him, what his winnings were, and what became of him. "I remember," replies a listener, "he dropped dead after a gallop at the Curragh" (a famous racing park near Dublin).

It is not until the race is over and the Captains and the Kings have departed that one knows all that actually happened, and I fancy that the best place to see a horse race, after having seen a good many, is in a moving-picture theatre; at any rate, I saw the pictures of my National and heard its story told with a great deal of pleasure. But to enjoy the pictures thoroughly and understand them properly one must have seen the race itself. And there is also the radio. One can wait very patiently to read what King, President, or politician has to say about this, that, or tother issue, but it is a very different thing, seated comfortably at home, to hear a voice at one's elbow saying: "Seven horses are now entering the home stretch; in another ten seconds the race will be decided. . . . Alpine Hut is improving his position and Remus is going well. . . . The riderless horse is leading, but Kellsboro' Jack wins . . . with Really True second . . . and Slater third. The race is over, in the fastest time ever recorded, nine minutes twenty-seven and two-fifths seconds, almost five seconds cut off the record time." Think of a whole nation, of many nations, listening in for twenty minutes to three or four men's description of what is taking place at that moment under their very eyes. No one person, however well or highly placed, can see all of a race; most persons can see little or nothing: a murmur, a dash, a flash, and it is all over.

The National, as shown in the picture theatres, was interesting as parades and crowds in movement are apt to be. One gets an excellent idea of the speed and excitement of the race, and the camera accurately records happenings which escape the human eye. The sections in slow motion were especially curious in that they seemed to show the riders gliding gracefully or clumsily leaving their mounts for no reason whatever, while the horses seemed to choose the most inopportune moments and places in which to lie down. This, of course, is far from being the

case: in reality horses and riders fall with a crash while
going at their utmost speed, and their falls are due to some
accident or interference not shown in the picture.

The winner of the race was Mrs. Ambrose Clark, an
American lady about whom and her husband the papers
had much to say the next day.   And it was all to the lady's
credit, for if there is one thing that the B. P. (British Public)
admires more than a good sportsman it is a good sports-
woman.   So, along with the gossip as to why Golden Miller
had done this and Remus had done that, came the story of
how Mrs. Clark came to be the owner of the winner, Kellsboro' Jack — which goes this way.   It seems that one day
Mr. Ambrose Clark's trainer came to him and said, "You
are the unluckiest man that I have ever trained for.   If
you will give Kellsboro' Jack to your wife he has more than
a good chance to win the race."   Mr. Clark, who had
bought the horse in Ireland a year or two before, turned
the matter over in his mind for a moment, and then offered
to *sell* the horse to Mrs. Clark for one pound.   The lady
produced the money and, when he won the race, pocketed
the very substantial sum of seven thousand and some odd
hundred pounds, which in the drab days of the spring of
1933 was a shiny spot of money.   Mrs. Clark was not the
first woman, by several, to win the great race, but I make
no doubt she is the first winner with a horse that cost only
a pound.   She is said to have told a friend that she was
tempted to put some money on her horse, but that she had
made it a rule never to bet.

When we got back to London there was a good story
going the rounds of the clubs, to this effect: —

Living in Paris was a young sportsman, Freddy Procter
by name, of the far-famed Ivory Soap family.   It was
Procter's habit to forgather with a group of friends at the
cocktail hour at the Ritz Hotel, and even those who do not

know the Ritz know of Frank, the genial, canny head bar-
man of that institution; he has been and is the guide, philosopher, friend, and banker to a whole generation of
Americans.   Well, one day a group were clustered around
the bar waiting for Frank to shake them up a "Side Car"
or a "September Morn."   Meanwhile, Frank, never object-
ing to doing a little business on the side, was selling books
of tickets for the Irish Sweepstakes, ten tickets to a book.
Procter declined to buy, but one of his friends "fell" for a
book.   This was in the fall of 1932.   The purchaser, after
buying his book, examined the numbers and, finding one
that he did not like, tore it out and gave it to Procter, saying, "Freddy, here is a number that has always been unlucky for me; you take it, perhaps it will be lucky for you."
Procter took it and, wishing to conceal his identity and
ownership, adopted, as is usual, a disguised name suggested by the place he was in, signing himself "Barritzki,"
and giving the address of his apartment in the Rue Jean-
Goujon.   Several months later the Paris *Herald* announced
the names of successful ticket holders residing in Paris,
suggesting that one of the luckiest was the Russian butler
of an American residing in the Rue Jean-Goujon.   The
butler's name, the article went on to say, was Barritzki, but
when interviewed he seemed confused and not in the least
overwhelmed by his good fortune.   Naturally enough, the
butler was not Russian, his name was quite different, and
he knew nothing whatever of the matter.

Not so Freddy, however; he immediately flew to London: there he sold for one thousand pounds a half interest
in the ticket that had been given him, retaining the other
half, and when Kellsboro' Jack won, Pelorus Jack having
fallen at the last obstacle, Freddy's ticket was worth thirty
thousand pounds.   History does not record the emotions
of the man who gave the ticket away, nor Freddy's feelings

got the cheers but not the purse, which must have been a heartbreaking experience for its owner, trainer, and one-time mount. All of which will get into the books and be read and commented upon when this mortal shall have put on immortality — and after.

perhaps for this reason it is popular in Scotland.   Cricket,
which every Englishman plays until his whiskers are as long
as Rip Van Winkle's or W. G. Grace's, was once played a
good deal in Philadelphia, but its name only survives in
the Merion Cricket Club, which is now largely given over
to golf.

Perhaps our pleasures are so few and attenuated because
of our unlucky inheritance.   New England was Puritan,
and the Puritan put his foot down on all games; when in
playful mood he sang psalms through his nose.   Pennsylvania was Quaker, and the traditions linger.   New York
was Dutch, and the Dutch seem to have exhausted their
sporting proclivities in inventing golf.   The South saves
us — if we are saved; in Virginia men rode and shot, and
to some extent still do, but we business men are corrupting
them.   I am speaking generally: there are exceptions to
all rules.   The emigrants who have descended upon us
since Colonial days have brought with them no games.
It is indeed remarkable that aliens almost invariably leave
such good qualities as they possess at home and, coming
over here, promptly adopt our least admirable habits.   The
necessity of subduing a frontier country and working hard
long after there was, or should have been, need for so doing
has left its impress upon all of us.   In brief, we are not a
sport-minded people, but I think I see traces of our becoming so.   If we are to have a shorter working day and week,
as now seems likely, let us learn to spend our leisure in the
open.   We shall be healthier and happier.

Motor, as I have recently been doing, through the English countryside, and wherever you go you will see great
crowds of men and boys playing football and cricket, and
girls and boys playing tennis, from late in the afternoon
until dark.   And in the northern latitudes, in which good
fortune has placed the English, with a good climate and

with the help of daylight saving, darkness and bedtime come almost simultaneously.

A history of the amusements of the English people would include many sports which are no longer permitted, but which were very common a century ago. (I say nothing of prize fighting, which I know only from its literature, which is extensive and colorful, even in black on white, as in the pages of Hazlitt, where, in a famous essay, he describes the fight between the Gas-man and Bill Neate.) There were also bear baiting, cockfighting, and rat catching. A century ago, a celebrated dog, Billy, killed a hundred rats at one bout in a pit at Westminster, to the ecstatic delight of all who were able to witness the exhibition. But it remained for a group of sportsmen, or gamblers, quite recently to discover the immense possibilities which, for good or evil, lay concealed in greyhound racing. This, the latest English sport, is sweeping over the land like an epidemic, and there are signs of its coming to this country.

In spite of the seeming cruelty of such sports as I have referred to, the English people are animal-loving as no other people are. I once made this statement in the presence of a German, who very ineptly referred to something he had seen at Naples which led him to say that the Italians, also, were an animal-loving people. A shout of derision went up, whereupon my friend said that he had never seen a horse in Naples with a bit in its mouth. He was somewhat nonplused when my old friend, Billy Scott, remarked that it was unusual to see a horse in Naples with a bit in its stomach. But let that pass.

Greyhound racing provides the common people of England at one and the same time with outlets for two of their strongest emotions — their love of animals and their love of gambling. It has frequently been said that the English take much better care of animals than they do of themselves,

and I think this reproach will fairly lie against them.   More
than once I have seen a man in the City, in that square mile
of old London of which St. Paul's Cathedral is the centre, a
man in all the panoply of a frock coat and a silk hat, stoop
down and tenderly stroke a cat, which received his atten-
tions with supreme indifference.   This man would hardly
show the same interest in a child.   It is axiomatic that a
good sportsman will care for his horse before himself and
lavish affection upon his dog which might perhaps be
slightly annoying to his wife.   But any animal will excite
the interest of an Englishman.   Introduce a horse, a dog,
or a cat upon the stage in any theatre, and a curious murmur of kindly emotion will pass through the entire audience.

And the English have always been great gamblers.   Fantastic stories of gambling of all sorts pack the biographies of
many of the characters of the eighteenth century, when
money first became plentiful, and even to-day, when most
of us are bankrupt, the sums won and lost on horse races
are almost beyond belief.   These have been touched upon
in other essays and need not be repeated here.   But it remained, as I have said, for a new form of vice — if it be a
vice — to sweep the country; the whole nation is "going to
the dogs."   There is much to be said for and against it.   I
shall try and state the case fairly.

It will be admitted even by one who knows little about
the game — but who finds an afternoon at Lord's, the aristocratic home of the Marylebone Cricket Club, delightful
— that cricket is *par excellence* the outdoor sport of the Englishman.   Bets may be laid upon results, but it is not pri-
marily a betting game; probably the same thing may be
said of tennis.   Horse racing, however, means betting, and
betting with a capital B.   It is a business in which thousands make their living and have reputations for fair dealing
which many of our bankers might envy.   They have their

established places of business, they advertise their skill and integrity and call attention to the legality of the functioning of the tote. But there is objection in certain quarters to legalized betting and the law frowns upon it, but the more the law frowns the more the people laugh. Such laws are to the English what "prohibition" used to be with us. Thank heaven, one can now speak of it in the past tense. When some heavy swell begins to talk about the evil of betting upon dog races, he is met with the rejoinder: "Why should a poor man who wishes to make a small bet on a dog be deprived of the opportunity which is available to the rich man who wishes to make a large bet upon a horse? Have we two sets of laws in this country, one for the rich and another for the poor?" In England it is not considered good form to ask such questions. So as long as horse racing is permitted, and there is at present no possible way of stopping it, betting on the dogs will continue. Indeed, many of the laws of England are in fantastic shape just at present. One can buy a lollipop, a poisonous-looking piece of candy, until nine-thirty or ten in the evening, but not a box of matches. But who expects logic from a lawmaker? Logic is wasted in the House of Lords — it may indeed be wasted anywhere. The Bishop of Carlisle recently stated that it takes four days to publish the names of the winners of the Irish Sweepstakes and that it would take almost five years to publish the names of the losers, who have one chance in four thousand! "That's quite good enough for me," people say, and the betting continues.

It is undoubtedly the poor, decent, generally law-abiding, if somewhat unhealthy and underfed, man and boy who, one would say, cannot afford to bet that, for the most part, patronize the dogs. They study the newspapers — there are at least two which are entirely devoted to greyhound racing — and reports of past performances and prophecies for the future are as carefully studied as stock-market reports are with us.   More so, in fact, for I venture the statement that where, over here, one person gambles in stocks, in England a hundred gamble on horses or dogs, or both.

A man with twenty pounds may, with luck, come away from the dogs with five hundred in his pocket.   I went to the dogs several times, but I did not bet; I did not know how nor did I care to, but one day three friends told me their experiences.   Two had lost a few pounds.   One made five small bets, unsuccessfully; he then noticed on the official card, which costs sixpence, a dog with the amusing name Lady in Bed.   On this lady he placed ten pounds at odds of eighteen to one, and in five minutes he was the richer by one hundred and eighty pounds.   Someone will finally get this man's money — I rather think that it will be some crook who, in New York, calls himself a banker. It is admitted that gambling leads to shiftlessness and recklessness.   But consider that it gives the poor something to think about; that it takes their minds off their misery. Consider the "homes" from which these people come and to which they return.   We pampered mortals who do our courting under the most favorable conditions, why should we seek to reform some poor lad who perhaps denies himself, not luxuries, but almost the necessities of life, in order that he may take his best girl to the dogs?   It is a pleasant change from doing one's courting on a bench of a wet night under an umbrella, with a not too sympathetic policeman near by.

From my point of view, the life of "the lower orders" is more interesting than that of the class to which I suppose I may consider I belong.   I have spent many an evening with my wife in a pub in London chatting with men and women about the state of the nation and other states, and I am more at home in the Elephant and Castle than I am in the Ritz — indeed, for years it was my distinction that I had never entered the portals of that lordly establishment. It is in no way different from other Ritzes in which I feel fairly at home. The Elephant and Castle! That's my house of call. For several centuries the sign of an elephant with a pagoda (hence castle) on its back swung at the door of a tavern in the South of London where crossroads meet. It is now one of its busiest — circuses, it should be called. Shakespeare recommends it in *Twelfth Night*. "In the south suburbs, at the Elephant it is best to lodge," he says; but my wife balks at "lodging": she says that Shakespeare may have known all the anfractuosities of the human heart, but that he had no taste in plumbing.

To one who has not seen a greyhound race as at present run in England the spectacle is a little difficult to describe: let me make the attempt. In the first place, there have been erected in England, particularly in London, since the War, enormous stadiums in which football is constantly being played. Football is not, as with us, played in the autumn only, but practically all the year round. One day in May of last year there was an attendance of one hundred and twenty-five thousand at Wembley to see a football match, and it is estimated — I don't know how — that an equal number were unable to secure admittance. Greyhound races are usually run at night, so these races provide an important, if secondary, use for a large and expensive structure which, without them, might be deserted for a great part of the time.

You are to imagine a great bowl, exactly such bowls as we have in our college towns, with seats or benches for spectators rising to a great height all around. These may or may not be open to the weather. The arena is of turf, but it is surrounded by a wire fence, perhaps five feet high. About fifty feet outside this fence — we are looking at it from the outer side — is a wooden housing or shed which, several feet high at its outer circumference, slopes down to almost nothing at its inner. This housing conceals a track, to all intents and purposes a railway track, upon which runs a truck set upon four wheels. The mechanism is operated electrically, just as are our trolleys, but all this mechanism is concealed from the spectators. The only thing which one sees protruding, and one scarcely sees that, is a short iron rod upon the end of which is mounted an immense stuffed hare. Under the hare is a small wheel which supports it and which rides upon its own track level with the ground. The stage is now set. A bugle is blown and the dogs, each with its trainer, enter. A certain style is observed — the English do everything in style: the trainers wear what we should call long white linen dusters, and each hound is led around the whole circuit. How tiny they seem, these little animals, in the immense arena! Each dog has its number upon its little colored coat, and they give every sign of nervousness. After completing the circuit the hounds are placed in their individual kennels, from which they can see the great stuffed hare, which they are to chase, in its turn make the circuit of the arena, slowly at first, but with increasing celerity, until it is back to the starting point. The hounds almost go crazy. Here is, seemingly, a large hare which their instinct tells them is made to be chased and nothing chasing it, and here they are "cabin'd, cribb'd, confin'd." What is the meaning of it? Suddenly, a bugle is blown, a flag drops, the doors of the kennels open, and the animals are released and are after the hare like a flash. There is a burst of speed, of intense excitement on the part of the spectators, and in thirty seconds or so the race ends. The hare has made its circuit and disappears into a hole which, providentially, saves it from the hounds, and all is over — but the shouting.

GREYHOUNDS AT WEMBLEY

There are seven greyhound racing tracks in London. I visited two, Wembley and the White City. Wembley is the largest; the White City is, I believe, the best adapted to its purpose. The electric lighting of the track is as clumsy as is British plumbing, but equally efficient. Mechanical music, much amplified, relieves the monotony of a quarter of an hour or so between the races, time which may, profitably or otherwise, be spent in arranging one's bets. This is not usually a matter of luck or chance. Men and boys make a profession of following the dogs with all the knowledge and intelligence that God or Devil has blessed them with. The pedigrees of the dogs are known for generations back and are as carefully studied as those of horses. Knowledge of their performances on this track and that is a necessary part of one's betting equipment, and thousands, perhaps hundreds of thousands, live entirely upon their winnings. I dare say it is all wrong, but who are we that tolerate stock exchanges to criticize?

There are flat races and hurdle races, as in the more famous horse races, and indeed it is a beautiful sight to see these tiny, graceful animals cascading over the little fences of bush in their mad and always unavailing chase for something that looks like a hare. How fast do they go, you ask. Well, at Wembley the official records, with distances, are as follows: —

525 yards, flat	29.68 seconds
525 yards, hurdle	30.65 seconds
700 yards, flat	40.72 seconds
700 yards, hurdle	42.10 seconds
900 yards, flat	61.20 seconds

This, it will be admitted, is speed. And usually seven races constitute an evening's entertainment. The races are run under rules which have been laid down by the

National Greyhound Club and are as strictly followed, if
not as time-honored, as the rules of the Jockey Club.

Greyhound racing is merely an elaboration or glorifica-
tion of whippet racing, which has for some years been a
sport in Ireland and the North of England. A whippet is
a greyhound in miniature, a cross between a hound and a
terrier, which is enticed to make for a towel, or some such
object, shaken violently at the end of a straight course,
usually a hundred yards or so from the start. Nothing is
required for the indulgence in this sport except a few dogs
and a straight path. It affords a cheap amusement; bets
may be made in sixpences or even pennies, and there you
are — sport for the working man. I hope the New Deal
will give it him.

Have I too long deferred a few words upon the greyhound itself? It will, I think, be admitted that nature
made many animals in a sportive mood. The old farmer,
it will be remembered, when told of the giraffe, denied the
existence of such an animal, and anyone regarding the
fishes in a first-class aquarium will be tempted to doubt his
eyes. Most dogs seem to have been especially intended for
the purpose for which they have come to be used. Their
names suggest their activities: a bulldog will throw a bull,
a pointer points, setters set; lap dogs lap more than
other dogs, and terriers scratch or dig the earth (*terra*).
But greyhounds! Animals which have unmistakably greyhound characteristics are represented on prehistoric tombs
in Egypt, and the first syllable of their name is lost in antiquity. They need not even be grey. A good greyhound,
like a good horse, may be of what color it will. Hunting
is the oldest sport in the world; it was indeed, also, the
first business of our ancestors. In this business or sport the
greyhound had its part. It became through centuries of
breeding and training immensely fast. It is probable that

they are now faster than they have ever been, but less strong than formerly, for we can hardly imagine these relatively small dogs — they seldom weigh over sixty-five or seventy pounds — bringing down animals much larger than themselves. The greyhound is deficient in its sense of smell; on the other hand, its sight is remarkable. In these characteristics greyhounds and foxhounds oppose each other. Both are speedy animals, but the greyhound is the speedier, being, seemingly, all legs, lungs, and heart. They are, too, of a snappy disposition — one frequently sees a greyhound muzzled. The chief end of its existence is to course and catch something. I wonder if it has ever occurred to the greyhound that one sees at Wembley and elsewhere that, notwithstanding the immense amount of coursing it does, it never catches its hare, — Mrs. Glasse's first rule, — an electric hare being something quite beyond its philosophy.

But at the races one overhears the most intricate conversation, to the uninitiated, about the points which must or should be taken into consideration when one makes one's bets. That the dog's pedigree must be known and satisfactory, and its trainer's reliability unquestioned, goes without saying. But, much more than that, its chest must not be too small for wind or too wide for speed. Are its front legs straight enough, and its hind legs sufficiently spread to permit them to pass the forelegs when galloping? Dr. Johnson, who prided himself upon knowing something of everything, once got into a dispute with a clergyman — a sporting parson who claimed to have the finest bull in England — about a dog which he said was "perfectly shaped." Johnson regarded the animal attentively and then took issue with its owner. "No, sir," said he, "your dog is not well shaped. There is not the quick transition from the thickness of the forepart to the tenuity, the thin part, which the dog ought to have." Tenuity in a racing dog is very important — its belly must not get in its way, and its tail must be long and flexible, for it serves somewhat as a rudder.

I had always thought when I saw pictures of animals — including elephants — galloping, and noticed that their hind legs seemed to outrun their front legs — I had always thought, I say, that I was looking at caricatures, but it seems not.   There are almost as many points to be considered in judging a racing horse or dog as a first folio of Shakespeare, and a hundred thousand to one is about the proportion of people interested in the animal rather than in the book.   I had the feeling of being a very lonely and ignorant old man when I went to the dogs.

V

ADVENTURES IN LONDON
MORNING

It has frequently been said that a Sunday in London is to be avoided at all costs. Certainly, if one has the artificial pleasures of a Continental Sunday in mind, a London Sunday is likely to be accounted dull, but if a rational human being of mature years, with a teaspoonful of imagination, will put himself in my hands for twelve or sixteen hours, I think I can show him how they may be spent pleasantly and not without profit. I once met a fellow countryman in London who said to me, "You know this town; tell me something to do, will you?"

"Cheerfully," said I. "Go to a ticket office and buy a ticket back to the place you came from." But already I grow didactic.

I admit that it is by no means the proper thing to be found in London on a Sunday; if one wants to observe the social conventions, one should leave town on Friday afternoon and not be seen until lunch time on Monday — for, be it observed, as Dr. Johnson has said, "a London morning does not go with the sun." And the fact is, the English countryside is so inexpressively lovely that one can hardly be blamed for seeking it on every occasion. There is another thing — the English love of sport. It has always seemed curious to me that a nation which has for a thousand years been producing an uninterrupted succession of literary men — I say it is curious how loath an English

man or woman is to stay indoors, where literature is certainly produced, if not consumed.   It was, if I remember
rightly, Charles II who said that England had more days
in the year when one wanted to be out of doors than any
other country.   And this wish to be in the open, knocking
about some kind of ball, probably accounts for the desire
of the Londoner to get out of town.   But I have no such
wish; I have a distaste for all games, — except kissing
games, for which I am now too old, — and it pleases me
frequently to spend a Sunday in the great metropolis.

One usually sleeps late in London.   When one first
arrives one is apt to regard an eight-o'clock breakfast as
about the proper thing, but after a few days one finds that
it is nearly ten o'clock before one is through with one's
bacon and eggs and tea and toast.   By which time at home
— but never mind, we are not as clever as we think we are.
A New York banker once told me that he had his mail read
to him by his secretary as he ate his breakfast, *at the bank;*
by ten, he had dictated his mail and was ready for the business of the day.   But that banker is now a financial wreck
and he has spread disaster near and far; it would be much
better for the world if that industrious man had never been
born.   Occasionally the Stars and Stripes float over his
bank, but we know now that the skull and crossbones of the
pirate would be the correct emblem.   The name of the
bank is not important; there are several of them.

Instead of sleeping a little later than usual, as one does
at home on Sunday, it is sometimes my pleasure to get up
very early and, after a crust and cup of tea, "take a walk
on an empty stomach" — as Sydney Smith's physician
prescribed, to be met by the query, "Whose stomach would
you have me walk on?"   Now, were I prescribing a walk,
I should suggest a walk on an empty street.   I know no
sensation more curious than to walk through a street and

not see a human being, not even a cat — in a street which, a few hours before, has been thronged with humanity. "How London doth pour out her citizens!" says Shakespeare. It is no less true to-day. Early on a Sunday morning not a soul is to be seen and not a sound heard. "Dear God! the very houses seem asleep" — why should I not quote the whole of Wordsworth's famous sonnet? More especially because it so perfectly describes the feeling I have in mind.

Composed upon Westminster Bridge

Earth has not anything to show more fair:
Dull would he be of soul who could pass by
A sight so touching in its majesty:
This City now doth, like a garment, wear
The beauty of the morning; silent, bare,
Ships, towers, domes, theatres, and temples lie
Open unto the fields, and to the sky;
All bright and glittering in the smokeless air.
Never did sun more beautifully steep
In his first splendor, valley, rock, or hill;
Ne'er saw I, never felt, a calm so deep!
The river glideth at his own sweet will:
Dear God! the very houses seem asleep;
And all that mighty heart is lying still!

It will be remembered that Wordsworth did not have the present Westminster Bridge in mind, but an earlier and finer structure, built of stone, of less than half the width of the present bridge, which is built of iron. But the view must have been then, as it is now, magnificent. The bend in the river seems to relocate, curiously, some of London's great "towers, domes and temples," notably St. Paul's. All of the views in Paris are man-made; nothing, seemingly, has been left to chance. In London, with the exception of one or two vistas from and toward Buckingham Palace, they are almost as accidental as the bends in the river.

No London-lover, and I here proclaim myself to be one,
but has, I suppose, his favorite walk. At home, walking is
a lost art.   Our cities are, for the most part, hideous, and
our countryside has disappeared — has become, in fact,
merely a raceway for the automobile.   In London I can
walk for hours without fatigue, and, my usual habitat
being in Jermyn Street, my favorite walk, on which I shall
ask my obliging reader to accompany me, is through St.
James's Park, by Whitehall to the north end of Westminster
Bridge, then keeping company with the river for two or
three hours until we are lost in the purlieus of Wapping.
"Sir," said Dr. Johnson, "if you would know London, explore Wapping."   But we must not hurry through one of
the most wonderful walks in the world; let us retrace our
steps and begin over again.

We are walking down St. James's Street — not St. James
Street, mark you (just why this street is always referred to
in the possessive I think I know, but never mind).   We
are on the left-hand side and are passing a famous hat shop,
Lock's.   On week days, hats of a rare and curious vintage
chock the windows, but on Sundays equally antique black
shutters have been erected, suggestive of a protracted siege.
Next door but one, No. 3, is Berry Brothers, the wine merchants.   The Berrys look down upon the hatters as mere
upstarts in trade, for the Berrys have been purveyors to
Majesty — St. James's Palace is just across the street — for
two hundred years and more.   Some week day we will go
in, purchase a bottle of brandy of the same age as the hats
next door, and get ourselves weighed and have our weights
recorded in a great book which contains the number of
stone and pounds at which every important man in England has tipped the scale for the last century or two.

Pall Mall comes to an abrupt end just where we cross it
to pass the high brick wall which gives privacy to the gar-

dens of Marlborough House, for many years the home of
Edward VII when Prince of Wales, and more recently the
residence of the beloved Alexandra after the death of Edward.   The present Prince of Wales should be living here,
but he prefers his bachelor apartments just opposite the
Palace in Stable Yard, as being less ostentatious and less
expensive to keep up.   Ostentation will, of necessity, come
upon the death of his father.   A memorial to the late Queen
Alexandra has recently been let into the brick wall, with a
stream of water running therefrom; just what it means its
creator has not made abundantly clear, if one may judge
from the remarks one overhears as one passes it.

As we approach St. James's Park we shall bear round to
the right, for we are going to Buckingham Palace, only a
short distance away, to make a proper start for the East End
of London.   That great long row of mansions is Carlton
House Terrace; it is the abode of many of the great swells
of the nation, foreign diplomats, and the like.   The Mall, as
it is called, is certainly the finest residential street in London.
At the top of the Mall is the Queen Victoria Memorial, a
really magnificent affair, in or on which sits the Queen, in
marble, looking towards London, with her back to the
Palace.   When the King is in residence the Royal Standard
is flown, but he is at Windsor at present and we shall just
peep at the Palace through the bars of the tall iron fence.
Remember, if you please, that this is the last stronghold of
Royalty in the world.   Democracy has invaded all the
others.   I hope it may be long before this one falls, for if
and when it does the shock will be severe.   Democracy is
not yet safe for the world, and I doubt it ever will be.   I
never see the Palace without thinking of those lovely little
verses of A. A. Milne's, "They're changing the guard at
Buckingham Palace."   You remember it; it's too well
known to quote.   Now we shall turn our backs on the

Palace and, skirting the Park, walk briskly along until we
come to the Parade Ground behind the famous Horse
Guards.   Here greetings and farewells are exchanged between Majesty and his crack regiments, and here he takes
the salute upon his birthday.   We must not loiter here,
however, but move on into Whitehall, which I once heard
a cockney call the " 'eart of the Hempire."   The Horse
Guards, through the central arch of which we pass, is my
favorite building in this part of London.

Whitehall is not only the name of a street, it is the name
of a district.   Like Knightsbridge, it is a locality with a
roadway.   It has been a palace, also the place of execution
of a king.   Now, from ten to four every day, two sentinels,
in full fig, mounted on fine black horses, keep guard in two
small pavilions on either side of the main entrance.   Keep
guard of what?   I do not know, but the function of changing the guard is a colorful proceeding which a good Londoner would not have abridged for anything.

Now we shall pass the Cenotaph, and presently the
Abbey, St. Margaret's, Westminster Hall, and the Houses
of Parliament will come into view.   I remember well the
"Silence," at the stroke of twelve on the first anniversary
of the Armistice (November 11, 1919), when the Tomb of
the Unknown Warrior in the Abbey was dedicated as a
national shrine by the King, assisted by a million people,
myself among them, trying to enter Parliament Square,
and how I got no nearer the Abbey than the National
Gallery — half a mile away.   But there is nothing, not
even a sound, to impede our progress this morning.

What shall be said about the Abbey?   There it stands,
unique in all the world, a monument to the magnificent
continuity of the English people, their sovereigns, their
heroes, and, noblest of all, their unapproachable literature.   And I never pass Westminster Hall without mur-

muring to myself that purple patch of Macaulay's in his essay on Warren Hastings — " The Hall was worthy of the trial, it had resounded with acclamations at the coronations of thirty kings," and the rest of it.

As we approach the Houses of Parliament, Big Ben strikes six. You see we made an early start. I am not a slavish admirer of the great Gothic palace — let us push on. What I want is a glimpse of the river. I followed it once from the Cotswolds, where it rises, to the Nore, where it loses itself in the ocean; it is only a matter of two hundred miles or so, but distance, like time, should be measured by events: this would give Father Thames greater length than the Amazon and Mississippi placed end to end. And, as we come down the river from its source, its interest increases as London is approached, until at last the river, in a sense, is London. The story goes that once, when James the First was King, he wanted a large amount of money which the Commons would not vote him. He then applied to the Lord Mayor of London, who also declined; thereupon the King threatened to move his Court and Commons to Winchester and make Westminster a desert. "What, then, will become of you?" he said.

"That depends, Sire, upon what you decide to do with the river," was the reply.

My wife, who can be very annoying at times, always makes fun of my interest in the Thames, and we never cross it or see it without her asking, provokingly, "What did you say was the name of this river?" To get even, I always tell her that well-known story of John Burns's. It is, and deserves to be, quite as famous as Dr. Johnson's remark that "the noblest prospect a Scotchman ever sees is the highroad that leads him to England." John Burns was once entertaining upon the Terrace of the House of Commons two men, one from Canada, the other from the United

States, and he was singing the praises of the River Thames.
Said the Canadian, "Mr. Burns, have you ever seen the St.
Lawrence?"   And the American chimed in, "Or the Mississippi?"   In a voice of thunder, the Honorable John replied, "Gentlemen, I have seen those rivers: the St.
Lawrence is water, the Mississippi is muddy water; that
river, gentlemen, is liquid history!"   And so it is.

It is as difficult for us to visualize the Thames as it was
once painted by the poets — a placid, silvery stream, flowing between green banks, choked with all sorts of fish, with
swans floating upon it — as it is for us to think of it when
historic pageants incident to weddings, to coronations and
to beheadings, were being performed on its bosom.   How
many and how royal were the prisoners conveyed on it to
the Tower and thence to the block!   It was once London's
greatest highway, with three or four times as many boats for
hire thereon as there were hackney coaches — which term,
with time, has, with us, degenerated into "hacks."   For all
its narrow width the Thames may be very rough, and it has
a tide which has frequently carried the careless boatman to
destruction.   London Bridge was accepted — it was almost
prehistoric;   but generally the erection of bridges was
attended by scenes of riot on the part of the watermen,
who felt that they were going to be deprived of an existence.
In those days, one set out from "stairs" on one side for stairs
on the other, by no means certain at what stairs one would
land.   As was once said of a reverend gentleman, looking
for preferment, when he embarked: —

> With the tide he must swim,
> To St. Paul's or to Lambeth,
> 'T is all one to him.

As we approach the north end of Westminster Bridge we
notice a great allegorical figure of Queen Boadicea on the

left-hand side, and this gives us our turning point, for our way is along the Embankment as far as Blackfriars. It is a broad and noble avenue, a short cut to the City, with gardens of exquisite loveliness on one side and "liquid history" upon the other. On the other or the "Surrey Side" of the river are the fine new buildings of the London County Council, and some day, when the whole of the hideous river bank has been made to conform architecturally with the Embankment side, and the unspeakable Charing Cross Railway Bridge has disappeared and a noble structure has taken its place, to connect Trafalgar Square with the Waterloo Station, John Burns's dream will come true. I was in hopes that I should live to see this great development when I heard that the roof of the Charing Cross Station had fallen of its own weight and ugliness, — there was much talk of it, — but the great shed was in part reërected, and this much-needed improvement is reserved for another generation.

I am thinking of Scotland Yard, which is just over there. Once the home of the Kings of Scotland, it has been for over a century the headquarters of what is by common consent the most efficient police force in the world. It is not "in politics," or in league with the criminal class, as our police are, but in theory and in practice opposes it. Although Mr. Sherlock Holmes made it perfectly clear to his friend and colleague, Dr. Watson, that he did not hold its detectives in high esteem, the thought of Scotland Yard strikes terror to the criminal. For most of us it merely means the place we seek when we wish to retrieve the new umbrella which we very stupidly left in our taxi: we shall recover it without a doubt.

We are not sorry to turn our backs on the Charing Cross Bridge and enter the Embankment Gardens. There is the old Water Gate of York House, now high and dry, built by

Inigo Jones, and reminiscent of the haughty and profligate noble, Buckingham, who must frequently have stepped from it into his almost royal barge. That fine office building occupies the site of the Hotel Cecil, but the great hotels are disappearing from this part of London and are moving westward, although the famous Savoy remains. If we do not think of the Adelphi, with its mysterious brick arches below and its historic mansions above, or the Chapel that once belonged to the Savoy Palace, which has long since disappeared, it is because we are thinking of the Savoy Theatre when it used to be the home of such good fun and melody as no nation has ever had before. There is the bust of Sir Arthur Sullivan, whose music has been ringing in our ears for over half a century. There is the tablet to his amusing colleague, Gilbert, "whose foe was folly and whose weapon wit." Almost am I content to be old when I think of the delightful performances I have seen and heard during the palmy days of the Savoy. "Age cannot wither, nor custom stale . . ." Do you see that obelisk over there? Cleopatra's Needle, they call it. I never gave it very much thought (it is only about half the size of the one in Rome, in front of the Lateran Church) until, a few years ago, I was shown in Heliopolis the place where it was originally erected in 500 B.C. or thereabouts.

Never heard of Heliopolis? It was once a great city in Egypt, a few miles from Cairo; now a total ruin, nothing of it remains except, in a field surrounded by a ditch and a dilapidated wooden fence, a red granite obelisk, the mate to this one — they were always erected in pairs. Even then I was not much impressed, until later, at Assuan, five hundred miles or so up the Nile, near the first cataract, I visited granite quarries and saw where that bit of stone came from. I take off my hat to the transportation facilities of those early Egyptians. The English had a hell of a time (if you 'll ex-

cuse my language) in getting it here.   It came from Alex-
andria by a steamer which was wrecked in the Bay of Biscay;
as a result the obelisk was abandoned.   Later it was recovered and taken to Spain; finally they got it safely on to
the Embankment.   It had been the intention, originally,
to erect it in front of Westminster Abbey, but it was suggested by authority that moving it through the streets of
London would be quite a chore, and it was decided to erect
it where you see it.   They tell me it has suffered more from
its exposure of fifty years in London than from its twenty-
five hundred years on the banks of the Nile.   Fog eats right
into granite, but it's good for the complexion of English-
women — like a certain soap which I am not paid to advertise.

How many and varied are the reminiscences that a walk
through the streets of London evokes!   Every few moments
one comes upon some statue, bust, tablet, or token which
lifts one above the dull, sordid, and monotonous life of to-
day into, if not another world, at least another period to
which distance has lent enchantment.   And these little
oases are the more delightful when they are stumbled upon
unexpectedly.

DR. JOHNSON LIVED HERE: instantly one thinks of his
"Sir, to seize the good that is within our reach is the great
art of life" — and a hundred other sayings so perfectly
minted that after a hundred and fifty years' circulation they
show no signs of wear.

DISRAELI LIVED HERE WHEN PRIME MINISTER: one
thinks of his definitions of "misfortune" and "calamity."
"If Mr. Gladstone fell into the Thames it would be a
misfortune; if anyone pulled him out, that would be a
calamity."

W. E. GLADSTONE LIVED HERE: of whom it has been
said that if he were caught in a card game with an extra ace

up his sleeve, he would insist that God had put it there for
some good purpose, and he would play it without scruple.

And it is interesting to take some sordid little street, Hanway Street, for instance, and try to think how it must have
looked when it was once a popular street for antiquity shops.
Not one Londoner in a thousand knows where Hanway
Street is. It is said to be named after Jonas Hanway, the
philanthropist, and the inventor of the umbrella. The
streets of London are, for me, never deserted; they are
always thronged with ghosts. Do you see that one? Do
you know who he is? That is Charles Lamb. And there
. goes Charles Dickens, and that tall, melancholy-looking
man is Henry Irving. You never saw him act with Ellen
Terry in *Olivia* or in *Charles the First?* Ah, well, age has its
compensations.

It is regrettable that we cannot easily enter the historic
Temple Gardens except from the Strand, which this morning is off our course. How I wish I could live in the
Temple! How lovely it is, how central, yet how secluded!
Packed with lawyers, though, for whom, as a class, I have
no love. "Lawyers, I suppose, were children once," and
lived in a state of innocency; grown to man's estate, they
wear wigs the better to mask their villainy.

We reach Waterloo Bridge. It is a pity that this noble
structure, the finest bridge in London, shows signs of sink-
ing; one end of it is and has been shored up for several
years. The fact is that such enormously heavy structures
— that is to say, heavy in themselves and carried on piers
erected on a scouring bottom — are not suited to the conditions of modern traffic. That, however, is not my
problem.

The Embankment ends at Blackfriars, and here we leave
the river for a bit. If it were seven in the evening instead of
seven in the morning I should pay a call at a certain public

house just over there, famous for its white port — and newspaper men, for the office of the London *Times*, alias "the
Thunderer," is not far off, just beyond where Upper
Thames Street plunges beneath the hideous railway via-
duct.   I have never quite understood why such immense
sums of money are spent on public works only to have them
utterly mutilated by "private enterprise," as it is called.
We are now in the City; presently we come to Queen
Street, which is the approach to the Southwark Bridge,
which would take us to Shakespeare's London but that
neither hair nor hide of it remains.   So let us keep right on
until we reach the Monument; then let history resume its
sway.   The Monument was designed by Wren to commem-
orate the Great Fire.   It stands two hundred feet high and
was intended to be surmounted with a colossal statue of
Charles II, in whose reign it was erected, but finally a huge
brass "flame" was decided upon.   On the base of the monument are four long inscriptions; the only one which need
detain us is the one which is *not* there.   It stated in many
words that "This pillar was set up in perpetual remembrance of the burning of this Protestant City by the treachery and malice of a Popish faction in order to effect its
horrid plot for the extirpating of the Protestant Religion
and Liberty and to introduce Popery and Slavery."   After
the death of Charles, who did not give a single damn what,
if any, inscription was placed upon the pedestal, his successor, James II, being a Catholic, had it obliterated; but
after he had dropped the great seal of England into the river
and run away, the lettering was recut, deeper than before.
Finally, in 1831, reason prevailed, and the silly inscription
was erased forever.   Verily, as Dr. Johnson says, "in lapidary work a man is not under oath."

Leaving the Monument, we must make a detour, for a
moment, and have a look at London Bridge.   There have

been several bridges just about here, all known as London
Bridge. For over a thousand years this has been the principal approach to London from the South of England and
from the Continent, for at this point the river is narrower
than it is either above or below. Until within comparatively recent times this bridge was built of wood and was the
most picturesque structure of its kind in the world. Almost
a thousand feet long, it was sixty feet above the water at
low tide; it seemed rather a street than a bridge. In
Queen Elizabeth's time it was thought to be magnificent
and no doubt was. It had a beautiful Gothic chapel
erected to the memory of Saint Thomas à Becket, the murdered Archbishop, whose shrine, at Canterbury, was the
most costly and popular in Europe. And "Nonsuch
House," which spanned the bridge on an arch in the centre,
near a drawbridge, was a small but magnificent palace
built, in Holland, entirely of wood, richly carved and gilded,
taken down, brought to England in sections, and reërected
without the use of nails, pegs of oak being used in their
stead. There were a number of shops with dwellings above,
and there was at least one mill, operated by the swiftly
flowing water below, for the many wide piers acted somewhat as a dam and to shoot the bridge at certain stages of
the tide was a dangerous operation. In those days there
was a saying, "Wise men go over the bridge and fools go
under it." At either end was a high gatehouse around
which riots, almost deserving the name of battles, occasionally took place, with the result that these gatehouses were
constantly adorned with the heads of the vanquished.
Several times all the structures on the bridge were destroyed
by fire, one fire resulting in large loss of life, but the bridge
itself was saved. Sections of it were constantly falling
down, hence the song which we used to sing as children,
"London Bridge is falling down." Finally, and just about

a hundred years ago, a new bridge of stone was erected
near the old bridge, which finally came down for good.

Except early on such a morning as we have chosen for
our walk, there is a constant stream of traffic, in four lines,
moving across London Bridge in opposite directions, and
the wide footpaths, considerably widened only a few years
ago, are always thronged with men and women hastening
to and from work.   Only on such a morning as this is the
bridge lacking in groups of idle men, with occasionally a
woman, staring, vacantly, over the parapet on the eastern
side — at what?   The sea, perhaps, for, in a sense, below
the bridge is the sea.   What are these loiterers thinking of?
Do they know that a million years ago

> . . . this water of mine,
> Was once a branch of the River Rhine?

Or, knowing, do they care?   Or are they wondering when
and where they shall next eat and sleep?   Or are they
thinking of taking a long journey, by water?   How many
poor and broken men, and women too, have taken a short
cut to eternity from London Bridge!

"I smell fish," you say?   Yes, and if it were not Sunday
morning you would smell them more abundantly.   Right
over there is Billingsgate, the greatest fish market in the
world.   At 5 A.M. on any week day is the properest time to
come.   It's a wonderful sight.   But it is not the size of
London's appetite that surprises one so much as the bounty
of the sea.   The trade is as old and highly specialized and
localized as any in England.   Billingsgate gave its name to
a language which gets but slowly into any dictionary.
Time was when a filthy word or a bloodcurdling oath was
the best that could be expected out of the mouth of a fish-
monger, but that is largely a thing of the past.   I once

heard a man, under great provocation, indulge in a line of vile language which, so far from inviting a return in kind, only led to the quieting retort, "Sh-sh, norty, norty!"

But one hears not a word this morning, and we must push on to our objective, Wapping Old Stairs. We are now in Lower Thames Street and have to skirt the Tower on the north side, the river front being "No thoroughfare." Here is Trinity Square, which is not and seemingly never has been a square. It is the home of the Trinity Brethren, which was once, and still is, a rich and powerful corporation with many privileges and some duties connected with lighthouses, buoys, and the like. Some day I shall know more about it. That great building over there, with its truncated pyramidal tower, is the head office of the Port of London Authority. We think, sometimes, that we are extravagant in the erection of our public buildings, in Washington, say, but London beats us all hollow. Our office buildings, however fine, are intensely practical — space and material are not used lavishly; London's great buildings are all monumental in character. This one took ten years a-building.

Here we are on Tower Hill; a slab of granite marks the spot where *public* executions took place, and there were plenty of them; only *privileged* persons were executed within the confines of the Tower walls. The site of the scaffold, near the Chapel of St. Peter ad Vincula, is enclosed in heavy iron chains within which a raven and his consort strut about croaking, "Never, never more." Up to a year or two ago, as time is reckoned in the Tower, there were three ravens, but during the Great War one of them committed suicide. It is said that it observed with horror a famous regiment dismissed by an ignorant officer, *with fixed bayonets*. Whereupon he croaked, "It's not done! It's not done!" But, no attention being paid to him, he walked right down to the river, plunged in, and, resisting all efforts to save him, sank to the bottom. "And quite right, too," said the King when he was told the story.

I am not now a hardened church-goer, but I once attended a most interesting service in the Church of St. Peter ad Vincula on the occasion of some special event which made it necessary for officers and men, Beefeaters and the rest, then on duty in the Tower, to turn out in all their historic magnificence. This church is not to be confused with the Chapel of St. John in the White Tower, which dates from the time of the Conqueror. The axe was in such constant use hereabout, in Henry the Eighth's day, that it must have seemed hardly worth while to remove the scaffold and "the appurtenances to it appertaining." Anne Bullen, Lady Jane Grey . . . but why call the roll? In the Tower, as in the Abbey, one is lost in close upon a thousand years of history; suffice it to say that this is one of the saddest spots in the world.

At last one reaches the Docks — that colossal terrain ruled by the Port of London Authority. It takes the tides as they come; everything else it rules with an iron hand, and its jurisdiction extends from above Hampton Court to the Nore. The Docks are not too easy to see; indeed, only from the air can one gain any idea of their enormous extent and magnificence. A fleet of steamers, large and small, comes up the river on every tide. Heavy gates swing open automatically, huge mouths with narrow throats leading to bellies insatiable. Into these the ships enter and disappear: London has been fed. As someone has said, "London swallows its ships, each one a morsel, as deftly and neatly as a warehouse swallows its chests of tea or its bales of tobacco." Such is the impression one gets from the river. From the land one sees even less. Great basins of flat, dirty water surrounded by huge warehouses — water and warehouses alternating for more miles than the eye can reach. Occasionally a steamer can be seen lying alongside its dock; sometimes a forest of masts or the funnels of great ships seem to be growing out of a row of mean houses. How did they get there? Will they ever return to their element again? At the proper time and in the proper manner, yes. The Port of London Authority will see to it.

"Where are you going?" my wife once said to me as she heard me dressing one morning in the dark. "Not Wapping again?"

"Yes, my dear, and when I get back I 'll tell you all about it."

"I know all about it. Have n't I been there time and again?"

Now, my wife hates Wapping as much, perhaps, as John Burns and I love it. And the fact is that one sees in Wapping only what one takes there in one's mind. One thinks of John Taylor, the "Water Poet," and of the watermen fighting on the stairs for their fares, as a generation ago our hackmen used to do at the railway stations and ferries. In reality, except warehouses, there is little to be seen, and of warehouses one soon tires. It is a dull, drab, reasonably clean, orderly area, as little picturesque as any part of London. The High Street, which parallels the river, resembles a tunnel from which the top has been removed; it is a narrow canyon of brick and stone which conceals everything except a narrow strip of dull sky immediately above one. During the week, towering overhead cranes lower into great trucks — lorries, the English call them — bales or boxes of merchandise by thousands of tons, or perhaps this process is reversed. But on a Sunday morning there is nothing to be seen, nor is a sound heard; it is highly ordered monotony.

WAPPING OLD STAIRS

From a rare colored print by Rowlandson

It is difficult in these surroundings to visualize this same riverside as it must have been when its low green banks sloped down to an untormented water. Tiny villages, each with its parish church, dotted the banks for miles on either side of the river. These villages have now lost their identity and only their names remain: they have been absorbed in that immensity which we call London, but from these villages came the men who, with the help of God and wind and weather, destroyed the Spanish Armada and sowed the British Empire throughout the world. And it was from these same villages that, two hundred years later, came the men who destroyed the sea power of France at Trafalgar.

When Queen Elizabeth came down the river to Deptford in her royal barge to greet and make a knight of Francis Drake, after he had circumnavigated the globe in his *Golden Hind,* Wapping was by no means as important as it subsequently became, but even then its people were seamen and were saying to one another, "There is no land uninhabitable, no sea innavigable to an Englishman." Rough brutes, pirates, if you please, they had begun to have a knowledge of the Bible and some little fear of God, if of nothing else. "Fear God, Honor the King" was their motto, and if the King was a woman, "she was one who had," as she said, "the heart and stomach of a man, and of an Englishman too" — and England had never a better.

> England.
> The narrow seas are found too straight
> For thy capacious heart.

And a rude sort of justice was awakening.

> So shall thy rule, and mine, have large extent:
> Yet not so large, as just and permanent.

Three hundred eventful years have passed since the
spacious days of Queen Elizabeth, and again Wapping
becomes important and as picturesque — if the horrible
can be picturesque — as it formerly was.   It is now known
in every land penetrable to an English sail; it has become
a part of London, and to many it is the best known part.
It is a place where one can get drunk for a penny and
dead drunk for tuppence.   Its once shady lanes have
become busy, noisy, filthy streets stinking to heaven.
Mean houses, hovels, dens of iniquity, have sprung up
everywhere.   It has become the most cosmopolitan spot
in all the world; every nation under heaven is represented, every language is spoken, and every crime known
to man is practised.   From out of the miserable hovels,
public houses, brothels, and the rest, drunken sailors come,
swearing, tumbling, quarreling, and fighting.   Wapping
has grown, its boundaries have disappeared, so that few
know whether they are in Wapping or Ratcliff or Lime-
house, on one side of the river, or in Bermondsey,
Rotherhithe, or Deptford on the other.   Wapping has
given its name to an area.   'T is all one; poor, dirty,
and vicious.   Sanitation is unheard of.   Godliness and
cleanliness are alike unknown.

During the Napoleonic Wars all England, especially the
south coast, was in a ferment.   The villages on the Thames
below London Bridge teemed with the raw — the very raw
— material out of which sailors were made.   They were
emptied by the press gangs of the navy of men and boys,
who were forced into the service of His Majesty.   And the
searchers were not too particular in their methods; they
drugged their victims with vile liquor, and when they grew
sober they were by way of becoming seamen, for the British
navy is built upon the broad base of her common seamen as
well as upon her admirals.   Look!   Here comes a slender

lad of fifteen years, say, staggering under the weight of a
sea chest which he is carrying on his shoulder. Take a good
look at him, as he inquires his way to Old Stairs. He is on
his way to join the *Seahorse*, which lies in the river, fitting
out for the West Indies. If you live long enough, you will
see him standing on top a tall shaft in Trafalgar Square.
His name is Horatio Nelson.

An early historian says of Wapping: "I remember when
there was never a house standing, only a gallows, where
pirates and others who had committed crimes at sea were
hung at low water, there to remain until at least three tides
had overflowed them." Presently this gallows is removed
further down the river almost to Ratcliff, on Execution
Dock; it was thought that a highly salutary influence was
exerted upon seamen coming up the river to see a man or
two hanging from the gallows, around which a flight of
crows were gathered. Well might Dr. Johnson, who could
in a phrase sum up every human situation, say, "No, sir,
no man will be a sailor who has the contrivance to get
himself into a jail, for being in a ship is being in a jail with
the added chance of being drowned," and "a man in jail
has more room, better food and commonly better company."

But the legend of the gayety of the sailor's "life on the
bounding blue" persists in song and story. Charles Dibdin,
with his sea songs, is the true laureate of the navy. His
songs were sung by English sailors all over the world; their
author declared, and with truth, that he had done more to
"man the navy" than all the press gangs in the hire of the
Admiralty.

Listen! It is Molly singing: —

> Your Molly has never been false, she declares,
> Since last time we parted at Wapping Old Stairs,

to be interrupted by Jack, who says: —

> I sails the seas from end to end
> And leads a joyous life;
> In ev'ry mess I finds a friend,
> In ev'ry port a wife.

While a drunken sot, not old, for men die young in His Majesty's service, insists upon breaking in with " 'Earts of Hoak."

Hearts of oak, indeed, they must have had; a voyage over, back come the men to Wapping, with a bit of money of which they are promptly relieved by the harpies who are awaiting them. Poor devils! Their money gone, sadder but no wiser, they go to sea again, swearing that they will be true to their wives and sweethearts, as they stagger to the Old Stairs, from which they are rowed to their ships lying in the river. And they keep their oaths, too — until they reach the next port, and their women keep theirs, until the anchor is weighed and the ship on a flood tide stands out to sea. It was a rough age and Wapping was a lawless quarter. To-day one should see Wapping with the mind's eye. I can see it as well, better perhaps, in the comfort of my library at home. There I can enjoy W. W. Jacobs's longshore watchmen and skippers with their wit, wisdom, and folly. Have we anyone to compare to Jacobs? Yes, I think we have; at least we had — Finley Peter Dunne. Mr. Dooley's friend, Mr. Hennessy, the philosopher saloon-keeper of Archey Road, Chicago, is badly needed these days to puncture the solemn folly that emanates from Washington. Let us thank God for Will Rogers.

Beyond Wapping is the Isle of Dogs, so named because centuries ago some king kept his kennels there. It was a peninsula then, formed by a bend in the river; it only became an island when the India Docks were made. On the other side of the river is Greenwich, one of the most interesting spots in London, too little known even to

Londoners.   We cannot go there this morning, although a tunnel would take us there in no time.   But our walk on an empty stomach — very empty by this time — is over.   We can take a tube train at Wapping Station and be back in the West End in a few minutes.   We have well deserved the excellent breakfast that awaits us.

VI

ADVENTURES IN LONDON
NOON AND NIGHT

NOON

I SHALL have to ask you to finish that cigar promptly . . .
I know, no one better, the joy of an after-breakfast cigar —
naturally it 's the one your physician would deprive you of.
But we are going to church.

To church!

Yes, to church — to chapel rather, and we must be on
time to the minute.   My first idea was to go to the service
at the Royal Military Hospital at Chelsea, but we should be
late.   The gates to the grounds are closed promptly at
eleven o'clock, as I very well know, for I walked all round
them on a bleak Sunday morning not long ago, and I
found every gate locked, and in the process I lost something — namely, my temper.   The next Sunday I was in
time, but I got into the chapel given over to the soldiers of
the present, whereas I wanted to attend the service, as I
have since done, in the chapel of Sir Christopher Wren's
historic building which faces the river.   It is a pretty legend,
that which gives Nell Gwyn the credit for suggesting to her
royal lover, Charles II, the establishment of this hospital or
place of refuge for old or disabled soldiers.   It is a lovely
place and they are a picturesque lot, these Chelsea pen-
sioners, as they are called.   One sees them walking about
— there are over five hundred of them — in their long

scarlet coats lined with blue, and they attend service in a body on Sunday mornings in a noble chapel, drifting thereto from an equally noble common room or lounge in which they enjoy all the comforts of an Englishman in his club. But it is too late for Chelsea, so we shall go to the Guards' Chapel, Wellington Barracks, which you will enjoy as much, perhaps more.

And five minutes later we are wedging our way through the crowd which is watching the evolutions of the guards alongside of St. James's Palace. On week days this colorful bit of pageantry takes place in Whitehall, but on Sunday, for some reason, when the King is not in Buckingham Palace, it is shifted to the short street which runs from Pall Mall to the Mall. We cross the Park, stop for a moment to look at the view, both east and west, from the little suspension bridge, watch the ducks being fed by men and children, some of them, seemingly, in need of food themselves, and almost immediately are in Birdcage Walk — so called because Charles II kept birds, of which he was fond, in cages, along what was, in his day, a walk through private grounds.

Charles II, what a king! He had a son by Nell Gwyn, his favorite mistress — who was no virgin when she went to him, for she called her royal lover her Charles the Third. In due course the King visited her to have a look at his offspring.

"Bring the little bastard in," she said.

"Nay, nay, Nellie, that won't do," said the King; "he 's got to have a name," and he thereupon was christened, with a sword, Charles Beauclerk, first Duke of St. Albans.

Religious feeling, or what passed for it, ran high in those days, and there is a story that one of his Catholic mistresses, whom he had made the Duchess of Portsmouth, had been attacked in the streets by Protestant rabble. "Are you not afraid to go out?" said one of Nell's women as her mistress was preparing to take the air.

"Not at all," said Nell, and, writing on the door of her chair, "I am the King's Protestant whore," she received quite an ovation as she was carried through the streets. The King thought this an excellent joke. "The task of composing a list of all Charles's mistresses would be too arduous," says some writer, but when the King's end was near his last thoughts were of Nell, and, apologizing for being "so unconscionably long a-dying," he urged that poor Nellie be not allowed to starve. We all have a sort of tenderness for Nell, the Sweet Nell of Old Drury of the play; she was so pretty and witty and generous. "Had no enemy but herself," as people say. But this gossip is no proper preparation for the sermon we shall presently hear in the Guards' Chapel. That is our objective and we must push right on.

I came to be a more or less regular attendant of the services at the Guards' in a rather curious way. A friend, to whom I was complaining of the difficulty of hearing a good sermon or good music in a London church, suggested that I write a note to the chaplain of the Guards' Chapel asking for two tickets for the service on the following Sunday, and enclosing a self-addressed stamped envelope. "And when your tickets arrive," said she, "go to the chapel a few minutes before eleven, for it is apt to be crowded." I did as I was told. Now it happens that I very well know a good sermon from a poor one, for my sponsors in baptism took very seriously their solemn vow, promise, and profession that I should be called upon to hear sermons. I have heard thousands — good, indifferent, and bad, chiefly the last. In the Church of England, in town or country, it makes small difference whether the sermon be preached in St. Mary's Billingsgate, in Westminster Abbey, or in Somerset-

shire where the lovely churches are; 't is all one — the
sermons are awful.   As Anthony Trollope says in one of his
novels, a poor actor will play to empty benches, a poor
lawyer will get no fees, a poor doctor will kill his patients,
but from a poor preacher there is no escape.   There is,
however, one difference between a sermon in the small
church and the large ones.   In the small church the
preacher always addresses *you;* in the abbeys and cathedrals
he addresses first those on his right, then those in front of
him, then those on his left.   This has a great advantage:
one hears only one third of the discourse — a discourse
which would do no credit to a lazy lad of sixteen.

Occasionally one may be deflected in one's walk of a
Sunday by seeing the door of a church open which perhaps
one has tried in vain to enter on a week day.   I do not advise this course.   There are some City churches that will
repay as many visits as one can make to them, but not when
a service is going on.   They have, very largely, served their
purpose and are now deserted by their congregations, having become little local museums into which occasionally one
is beguiled by a promise or threat of music.   The rector,
who may live as much as fifty miles from the church, enters
it rarely — only often enough to qualify for the stipend
which is attached to the job from which he can only be
detached by an act of Parliament.   And I have heard sermons read or preached by decrepit old men which were
merely a string of almost meaningless words.   In reply to
my criticism my English friends say, "We don't go to church
to hear sermons, but for the service."   To which I, logi-
cally, reply, "Then why have 'em?"

But we are approaching the Chapel.   It is a classical
temple of brick, not too large, painted a dark slate color.
The interior, however, has from time to time been magnificently decorated in mosaic, so that it reminds one, forcibly,

of the churches in Sicily. There is no organ, but the congregation, which takes part in the service with a will, is led by a full military band under the direction of a competent bandmaster. At the stroke of eleven, such guards as are in attendance enter. They come in with heavy tread, in their gorgeous uniforms, carrying their tall black bearskin headgear at rest, so to speak, upon their left arm, as though each man had been entrusted with a baby. The entrance march may be from *Aïda* or the "March of the Peers" from *Iolanthe*. There is a full choral service; the hymns are well known and are sung with a will; the sermon lasts twelve minutes, an address delivered by a he-man (how I hate that expression!) to men, at the end of which, after a hymn, there is a rattle of kettledrums and everyone in the church stands at attention, while "God Save the King" is sung. I indulged myself in a "His Master's Voice" record of this national air one day after hearing it sung in the Guards' Chapel, and I never spent three-and-six, or whatever it cost, to better purpose. The arrangement was Elgar's and the voices were selected from the Philharmonic Choir, and the London Symphony Orchestra did the rest. After the national anthem the guards march out and the congregation is dismissed.

It will be understood that I guarantee complete satisfaction, or money refunded, with this service in the Guards' Chapel. The penultimate time I was there I was so struck by the all-round excellence of the service that when I got back to my flat I wrote a letter to the chaplain and asked if he would instruct the bandmaster to play Blake's "Jerusalem" on the following Sunday, enclosing in my letter a one-pound note, which I said was to be spent in the best of all good works, namely, a bottle of whiskey and a little tobacco — and I hope it was. Anyhow, Blake's noble hymn was sung with a will.

"You score; that service was hundred per cent perfect," said my friend as we left the Chapel. "It's too early for lunch. Let's go back to our flat and rest a bit."

Good idea. But while we are here I want to show you some of Epstein's statuary which is embedded in the walls of the office building of the London Transport Company, ot far off. I think it is the very limit — there is no excu for it. If the sculpture which has received the approv of the world for two thousand years is right, then th work of Epstein is grotesque. I suspect a gigantic ho which has taken in the art experts of the world, tho superstitious men who, like the Athenians with w m Saint Paul reasoned, spend their time either in te ng or in hearing some new thing. Epstein first bec e notorious many years ago when he designed a tomb one for Oscar Wilde's grave in the Père-Lachaise, whic o shocked Paris that for years it was kept covered wit canvas. But Epstein kept on and his effrontery won a ast; now there are those who affect to regard him as a g t sculptor — only time will tell. To me, his work looks a ough it had been hacked out of a block of granite by a nsane man working with an axe — and the statuary o e new Bank of England is little better. There are a nur er of Epstein bits stuck into the walls of the buildings the Broadway, but the allegorical figures "Night" ar "Morning" are those which attract most attention

Som e sent a very clever limerick to the *Atlantic Mont y* a year or so ago. It went like this: —

> There 's a notable family named Stein;
> There 's Gert, and there 's Ep, and there 's Ein:
> Gert's poems are punk,
> Ep's statues are junk —
> Can't make head nor tail out of Ein.

I am in full accord with your idea of a complete rest for an hour or two, especially as we have a rather zigzag walk to Marble Arch before a better-than-usual tea.

It will be best, I think, for us to begin our walk at Leicester Square, thence to Hyde Park Corner and to Marble Arch.   And let me conjure up, as best I may, the streets as they were when I walked through them for the first time, fifty years ago.   Leicester Square had once been Leicester Fields, an open space surrounded by a paling fence, in the centre of which, where the statue of Shakespeare now is, there stood a large equestrian statue of George I.   It was once a rather famous place for duels, and Thackeray makes Henry Esmond kill my Lord Castlewood there.   Hogarth had his town house at the southeast corner.   Sir Isaac Newton and later Dr. Burney, Fanny's father, lived at the bottom; and Sir Joshua Reynolds, whose residence still stands and is now Puttick and Simpson's auction house, was on the west side.   Walking towards Piccadilly Circus through Coventry Street, we come to the Prince of Wales's Theatre, where, in June 1884, I first saw Marie Tempest — then an exquisite bit of Dresden china, with the loveliest voice imaginable — in the beautiful operetta, *Dorothy*.   It was my second night in London.   On my first night I went to the Gaiety to see Florence St. John in *Olivette*.   My third night took me to the Lyceum: Irving and Terry in *Much Ado*.   Hear me, ye gods!   Those were the days — and nights.   I had a tiny hall room in the back up two flights of stairs at 2, Rupert Street, for which I paid ten bob (a bob is a shilling) a week, with seven-and-six a week extra for breakfast.   No. 2 Rupert Street, one door from the corner of Coventry Street, still stands, and it is the only house in that immediate neighborhood that does — all the others have given way before the march of improvement.   When

I lived there the shop on the ground floor was occupied by a tobacconist; now it is a chemist shop. If the London County Council knew its business it would be marked: "A. Edward Newton lived here" — I shall take on this job myself when a suitable occasion offers.

In Piccadilly Circus there was, and is, a famous restaurant and theatre, the Criterion. The theatre is below the level of the street and was for many years the home of Charles, subsequently Sir Charles, Wyndham, who was one of the favorite actors of his day. He played *David Garrick* on and off for years, against his wife, known on the stage as Miss Mary Moore. His and her last appearance in this country was in a dainty and difficult play, *The Mollusc*. It failed upon its first production in New York, hearing of which Wyndham cabled over: "You don't know how to play it." Whereupon Wyndham was asked to come over with the entire English company, consisting of four persons only, and give the play, which he did, with great success.

Piccadilly Circus was then a circle much smaller than it is since it became a square, and as yet the famous statue of Eros was not. He disappeared and was greatly missed during the reconstruction of the Circus a few years ago, and his worshipers — they were many, and of both sexes — in this part of London would not be comforted until the graceful little archer was reërected and resumed his sport. Now just west of the Circus is Lyons' Popular Restaurant, where may be had the best and, all things considered, the cheapest food in London. I publish this advertisement without hope of reward, as did Arnold Bennett in his amusing book, *Buried Alive*, in which, in a chapter entitled "No Gratuities" (once the slogan of this establishment), there is a burlesque description of this famous restaurant. "As Alice Challice and her lover were conducted to their seats by a haughty gentleman in evening dress, a costume which seemed to be denied the diners, they noticed signs everywhere informing them that they need expect no gratuities, that gratuities were not to be had at any price. Everything else, but *no gratuities.*" Jack Lyons has passed on to his reward, but he has left a chain of the best hotels and restaurants in London, and the price of the shares in his company is as stable as those of the Bank of England. Of what shares dealt in on the New York Stock Exchange can this be said?

Just opposite "Lyons' Pop," as it is called, was and is Swan & Edgar's department store. It has extinguished, in this locality, the famous bookshop of Quaritch, which now occupies commodious premises in Grafton Street, just off Bond Street. I came to know Mr. Quaritch and his family intimately, and his daughter, now Mrs. Wrentmore, is one of my oldest and best friends in London. It was at the table of the Wrentmores that I ate my dinner last Christmas Day. With them I listened to the Empire chain of voices over the radio from London to Wales, to Scotland, to Ireland, Canada, British Columbia, Australia, India, back to London and Sandringham, from whence the King in a brief and moving message wished all his subjects around the world a Happy Christmas. Then we all stood, as probably millions of others did, and drank the King's health and said: "The King! The King!" As Kipling says, "What should they know of England who only England know?" The strength of the English King is that he is above politics. Not long ago, a stupid M. P. ventured to speak of this measure or that as being "opposed by Buckingham Palace." Instantly there was an outcry, and the M. P. found it necessary to spend much time in explaining that he did not mean what he said.

All the once-famous buildings which adorned the left-hand side of Piccadilly as far as the Green Park, except St. James's Church (which few of us realize that the great Sir

Christopher regarded as one of his best churches — I have passed it a thousand times, but I cannot remember ever to have entered it), have now disappeared, but on the right-hand side the Albany, Burlington House, and the Burlington Arcade still remain. Just beyond is Bond Street, the fashionable shopping street of London. To the eye of one accustomed to the magnificence of Fifth Avenue it does not seem to be much. It is quite narrow, in one place only wide enough for two traffic lanes, moving in opposite directions, but the shops are unsurpassed anywhere.

As I have said, it was once my proud distinction never to have entered the Ritz Hotel — if I had patronized fashionable and expensive hotels what sort of library should I have had? But a year or two ago, having to introduce four little children — my "cousins" — to such London society as I knew, I hired a drawing-room with its appurtenances and was pleased with the result and not shocked by the bill. In Albemarle Street to the left is a plain old seventeenth-century house whose plaque informs us that Sir Robert Walpole lived here; a little further on lived Charles James Fox, convenient to Brooks's, his favorite club; while just around the corner in a street which should be Jermyn Street, but is n't, is another house whose plaque says, "Lord Byron lived here." One thinks of his lordship living here, or perhaps a little further down, in St. James's Street, when on the morning of March 10, 1812, the poet, after the publication of *Childe Harold*, "awoke to find himself famous." The words ring in one's ears! Yet withal no poet was so modest as he: "I write verse because I can't manage prose," and, "The end of all scribblement is to amuse." How unlike Wordsworth! John Murray, Byron's publisher, then and thereafter had his town house and publishing business in Albemarle Street just off Piccadilly — how impressed I was with all that I saw there on the occasion of my first visit!

It is one of my favorite theories that experts, whether in theology, law, economics, medicine, politics, science, or what not, are almost invariably wrong. At the moment I have in mind the dire prophecies when gas was first introduced into the metropolis, something over a century ago, when even so great a man as Sir Humphry Davy proclaimed it as a wild and dangerous scheme. Our own Emerson declared that electricity was the toy of the laboratory and would do no work, and the suggestion that London be tied together with loops of railways running in tunnels was generally received with scorn. But gradually difficulties were overcome, and when I first visited London the Metropolitan Underground had been in successful operation for twenty years. A tunnel, of course, was no new thing, but running one through a labyrinth of gas, water, and sewer pipes, with here and there a submerged river, made the work difficult and expensive. The problem of ventilation was met by the designing of locomotives capable of "holding their breath," as the saying went. But the tunnels soon became indescribably foul, and people with sensitive lungs and throats had to abandon their use altogether. And when a heavy fog, of the famous pea-soup variety, descended upon the town and signal lights disappeared in the gloom, then London, unable to crowd itself into the horse-drawn buses, threw up its hands and walked. And, speaking of walking, I shall never forget my amazement upon my first day in London to see every man above the level of a day laborer going to business wearing a long frock coat and a high silk hat. Even schoolboys of ten or twelve sported their toppers, and to this very day it is *de rigueur* for every clerk in Coutts's Bank at all times to wear a long frock coat.

To-day London has one of the best transportation systems in the world. The railway stations, to be sure, are not magnificent like ours, but they are convenient and well suited to the traffic they are designed to serve. And we have few trains which compare favorably with the long-distance, high-speed, smooth-running "Flying Scotsman." I shall never know, personally, very much about the network of tubes in which the underground trains ply like shuttles. Access to them is for the most part by escalators, the very sight of which throws my wife into a panic. This is a pity, for like many other boys of my age I enjoy running up a descending staircase or running down an ascending one. I have tried to get my wife to join me in this inexpensive recreation, without success. But after all is said, the most agreeable means of locomotion remains the bus. Buses are quick, clean, convenient, and cheap, serving without prejudice Whitechapel and Mayfair. The beery old men of my youth, full of wise saws and modern instances, who drew the reins over horses almost as wise as themselves, have all been gathered to their fathers, and their places have been taken by quick and intelligent mechanics who tool their motors through traffic lanes which leave not an inch of space on either side. Considering the speed at which they travel and the immense number of passengers carried, accidents are very rare, and it is thought disgraceful for a man to bring in his bus with a fender dented or the paint scarred.

London in 1884 was still the London of Dickens. The great changes did not begin until about 1890, but since that time London has been practically rebuilt, and nowhere are the changes greater than in the West End. One change is not yet: the Albany remains. It is a fine old mansion fronting a small courtyard, entered from Piccadilly by a private passage. It was once the town residence of the Duke of York and Albany, but more than a century ago it was turned into residential flats. Its most interesting feature is in the rear, where a long, flower-bordered colonnade gives access to sixty sets of apartments, thirty on each side. This is typical eighteenth-century London. Quiet, unostentatious comfort, for men only, although I think a man and his wife with unimpeachable references might secure one of these apartments.

Almost opposite the Albany stood the Egyptian Hall. I remember it well: its façade, with its inclined pilasters and its walls covered with hieroglyphics, gave it a truly Egyptian appearance. In its early days it was a sort of human Madame Tussaud's, many of the exhibits being alive. The famous Siamese Twins, two young men, natives of Siam, with perfect bodies, uncomfortably united side by side by a short ligament, were first exhibited here, as were the Living Skeleton, the Obese Woman, General Tom Thumb, and hundreds of other freaks. The Hall was also used for concerts, lectures, and the like, and the famous Maskelynes, for a century or more masters of magic, and still functioning, gave thousands of performances there. Piccadilly, which has a pleasant dip and a slight curve in it, occasioned by a submerged creek or bourn, "Tybourn," before it becomes Knightsbridge, is the southern boundary of what is called Mayfair, a district which may be said to extend from the west side of Bond Street to Park Lane, and on the north to Oxford Street. It is the abode of wealth and fashion. Just behind the mansions on the north side there is a little slum now called Shepherd's Market, where for several centuries a fair was held in the month of May — hence the name, but it became noisy and disreputable and was finally suppressed. Almost opposite where the Ritz Hotel now stands, there stood, until a few years ago, Devonshire House, the London residence of the Dukes of Devonshire. Shops, offices, and flats now occupy the site. I was sorry to see the ugly old brick palace — for it was no less —

disappear, but no one should ever judge a London mansion by its exterior; its interior may be, and frequently, as in the case of Devonshire House, is, spacious and splendid. I entered it only once, for a few hours, when it was thrown open for some charitable purpose to "paying guests," many years ago, and was stunned by the magnificence of its state apartments; especially by the grand staircase of marble, alabaster, and crystal, at the top of which it was usual for Their Graces to receive their guests. It was once the home of the beautiful Duchess Georgiana, who kissed a butcher — in return for his vote, for she was a keen politician. Opportunities of being kissed by duchesses seldom come my way; I would have given a whole lifetime of votes for the privilege.

If any reader of these lines is a good Trollopean, as I hope for his own sake he is (I am going to start a Trollope Society very soon to "grub-stake" a much-needed complete and uniform set of his novels), he will remember that in *Phineas Finn* a certain Mr. Bonteen is murdered in a dark sunken passage which separates the gardens of Devonshire House from Berkeley Square. Phineas Finn is accused of the crime and is defended by that witness-harrowing lawyer, Mr. Chaffanbrass. He was, of course, acquitted. I walked through this passage, now brilliantly lit by electric light, one night some time ago, pleasantly meditating upon this matter.

Another mansion: just west of the site of Devonshire House there stands at the corner of Stratton Street a brick house built high above the street. It is much larger than it looks, and it challenges attention by reason of its enormous bow window which looks out over Green Park. The house is usually freshly painted a sort of buff color. Here romance enters, with a capital R. Almost two centuries ago there came to London two brothers, Scotsmen, Coutts by name, who entered the banking business. One brother died and the survivor, a bachelor, married his brother's servant and by her had several children — girls. In due course he became very rich; he always dressed, however, like a poor man, and standing by the door of his "shop" he was sometimes tipped a sovereign by a nobleman who had just obtained a loan from one of his partners. Being Scotch, he always took the money, thankfully. Finally, as a very old man, he became infatuated with a beautiful actress, Harriet Mellon, and, his wife providentially dying, then indeed the funeral baked meats did coldly furnish forth the marriage tables, for he immediately married the lady, and at his death, having previously given immense sums to his daughters, who had married well, he left his widow his entire interest in the bank, valued, it is said, at two million pounds. Mrs. Coutts thus became one of the richest women in England. She, becoming lonely in her old age, decided to buy herself a young and aristocratic husband, and pitched upon the Duke of St. Albans, the great-great-grandson of Nell Gwyn, of whom we have heard. She was able to make her husband rich beyond the dreams of avarice and yet retain an enormous fortune, which at her death she bequeathed to her first husband's favorite grand-daughter, Miss Angela Burdett. The Piccadilly house with the bow window which we have been admiring is the Burdett-Coutts town house, the lady having another beautiful home, Holly Lodge, in a park of its own, at Highgate. She gave away money right and left, and presently Queen Victoria ennobled her, made her a baroness in her own right. When I was a child one was constantly hearing of the good lady's philanthropies; not a subscription list but was headed by the Baroness Burdett-Coutts. Her romance was retarded, but it arrived nevertheless. She was plain, almost ugly in appearance, but in her seventieth year she decided to buy herself a lover, and her choice fell upon her secretary, a young man of twenty-five and, to make matters worse, an American. And she paid a pretty penny for him, too, for by marrying him she was to lose more than half of her fortune. But to the amazement of everyone and to the disgust of her friend, Queen Victoria, she persisted, and, living to be ninety, she was buried in Westminster Abbey. Her husband's name was Ashmead, a member of a well-known Philadelphia family, who upon his marriage renounced his name and nation, became a member of Parliament, and made a respectable if not a distinguished career for himself. When he died a few years ago, the library was sold, and some of the Baroness's books now adorn my shelves, and Joe Widener is now the possessor of the famous Coutts folios of Shakespeare.

The original Coutts lived over his shop, adding from time to time additional properties as they were required, and when I first saw Coutts's, in the Strand, it was difficult to believe that an assembly of unimportant brick houses was in fact the oldest and richest private bank in England. At the turn of the century the whole outfit was outgrown and it was decided to erect a proper bank building, and the Lowther Arcade was secured. I remember it well; it was on the opposite side of the Strand from the old bank and somewhat nearer Charing Cross — a long, wide, covered way with shops on each side for the sale of children's toys and trash. The new bank was several years a-building, for immense vaults for the safe-keeping of plate, papers, and the like, had to be constructed. Many of the parcels and chests of papers had not been opened for a hundred years. More than a century ago it became a sort of hall mark of wealth and gentility to have an account with Coutts's. Gilbert, Sullivan's partner, speaks of

> The aristocrat who rides and shoots,
> The aristocrat who banks with Coutts.

The bank was not only the privy purse for the English Royal Family, but for most of the rulers of Europe, who wanted an anchor to windward in the event of revolution; indeed, to-day, it is said that Coutts's largest single depositor is the former German Emperor.

In 1904, the new building was ready for occupancy, and there was much talk and to-do in the papers and on the streets as to how and when the transfer of all the bank's valuables would be made. The transfer was to be done between midnight and morning under a heavy guard of soldiers and police, it was said. The new bank was to be opened for the first time on Tuesday after the August bank holiday, and on that day the announcement was made that the transfer of everything had been made very quietly long before.

Sometimes it is easier to deposit papers with Coutts's than to get them again. A very distinguished family had this experience. In 1830 died King George IV, alias "the first gentleman of Europe," alias the "fat friend" of Beau Brummell. He was thought to be the third husband of Mrs. Fitzherbert, the most beautiful woman of her time and country, but she being a Catholic, and he the Prince of Wales, if he married her the marriage might not be legal: the King said it was not, the lawyers that it was. It was an ever-burning political-social-religious question, affirmed and denied as occasion demanded. Charles James Fox, who knew the facts, stated on his word of honor in Parliament that no marriage had taken place, but it was generally believed that he was lying. The lady, with a perfectly good wedding certificate in her pocket, suffered in silence, and presently the Prince was forced to marry Caroline of Brunswick, an ugly German woman whom he hated. After the death of the King, the Duke of Wellington, representing deceased Majesty, and Mrs. Fitzherbert burnt most of the papers, but certain important documents were preserved and deposited with Messrs. Coutts. Long after the high contracting parties had passed away an effort was made by the lady's family to secure the papers, but Queen Victoria would not permit it. She "never cheapened Royalty," but preferred that a lady's name should be besmirched rather than a rakish ancestor's crime should be revealed. But King Edward was a gentleman, and when he came to the throne he ordered the bankers to deliver the documents to his secretary, Lord Knollys, who turned them over to a historian for publication. Thereupon the most romantic and tragic love story of modern times was revealed: the King had been forced by Parliament to abandon his wife and marry the ugly and vulgar Caroline of Brunswick, whom he sought to divorce. The rest is history, but Mrs. Fitzherbert's honor had been vindicated and the papers in the case are now in the royal archives at Windsor.

But we are loitering, — that is the joy of a walk in London, — and at this rate we shall never get to Hyde Park Corner, much less to our objective, Marble Arch. Where were we? Walking on the north side of Piccadilly just east of Stratton Street. When Piccadilly was known as the "Road to Reading," great country houses with their out-buildings stood on the north side of it, but these gradually came down, giving way to smaller and finer houses, many of which ultimately became clubs, and some of them have now yielded to the demand of the times for modern hotels in the West End. One landmark I hope will remain. It is a small but noble house with a courtyard in front of it separated from the street by a high brick wall, in which are two gates; IN is lettered on one, OUT on the other. It is usually referred to as the "In and Out Club," but its proper title is the Naval and Military Club. It was built in the middle of the eighteenth century and was known as Cambridge House, after its owner, the Duke of Cambridge, son of George III; its last distinguished occupant was Lord Palmerston — who had no love for us, it will be remembered.

Every house in Piccadilly suggests something. If I were to become involved in the story of a house on the steps of which one winter's night a great nobleman found a little girl whom he befriended, I should find myself telling the story of the Wallace Collection, and I should have no time to speak of the Duke of Queensberry, "Old Q," the wickedest man of his age. Just think of a rich and vicious man of eighty spending his time at a bow window ogling every pretty woman that passed, and keeping a servant under it ready to carry a message to any passer-by who promised pleasure. He never married, he preferred to buy his love — one got more of it that way, he said. He was no fool, either, but kept a physician in his house at a big stipend which he was assured would cease with the Duke's illness; on these terms he lived until he was eighty-five.

What else did he do?

Well, he once bet a thousand pounds that he could cause a letter to be conveyed fifty miles within an hour. To accomplish this he enclosed a letter in a cricket ball and the ball was thrown from one man to another in a circle; at the end of an hour the letter had traveled many more than the required number of miles. "Old Q" was a great horseman and he spent a fortune trying to win the Derby, without success.

We approach Apsley House, passing first a short line of mansions setting back somewhat in their own forecourts, one of which is now the residence of the Duke and Duchess of York, with the young Princess who will in all probability become a second Queen Elizabeth. Another is the home of the present Lord Rothschild, whose nephew and heir is

a friend of mine and by way of becoming a great book-
collector. But Apsley House is No. 1, London. It got its
name from a certain Lord Apsley when it was built a
hundred and fifty years ago, and the Duke of Wellington
did not change it when, some years after Waterloo, he
acquired and very greatly improved the property. Shortly
after the Iron Duke took up his residence in the rather
gloomy-looking mansion, a mob, excited by the Duke's
opposition to the Reform Bill, attacked the house, breaking
the windows and doing other damage, after which iron
shutters were erected, on the west and north side, which,
it is said, have never since been opened.

Hyde Park Corner at last! It is difficult to visualize
this famous centre, now the busiest in all London, as it must
have been a century or two ago when it was one of the two
main approaches to London from the west. A toll gate,
which had originally stood near where the Ritz Hotel now
is, had been pushed westward to just about the site of Apsley
House. Both within and without the gate were taverns,
houses of good repute and ill, supplying refreshment for
man and beast. Of these the Hercules Pillars was the most
famous. Fielding makes Squire Western in *Tom Jones*
stop there. The original Pillars of Hercules were the
opposite sides of the Strait of Gibraltar — beyond which
was an unknown ocean. Beyond our Pillars was the country. Once the road narrowed to a gate; now it is the widest
traffic way in London, and according to recent count is used
by almost a hundred thousand vehicles a day. Some traffic!

Just opposite Hyde Park Corner, the main entrance to
London's greatest park, is a shabby old building, St.
George's Hospital; it is an old institution supported, as it
is never tired of telling the public, by voluntary contribu-
tions. It would seem that a more desirable site for a hospital could be secured, and certainly a more distinguished

building could be erected on what is undoubtedly the finest site in London. The difficulty is, I have been informed, that if it ceases to be used for hospital purposes, the land reverts to the descendants of the original donors.

But we must now make a sharp turn to the right and head for Park Lane, stopping only to give a glance — all it deserves — at a colossal statue of Achilles, a monument to the Duke of Wellington. It has been much criticized, which is the fate of most statues. It has been called a statue of Adonis draped only with a dirk, to the horror of Victorian ladies, who were expected to "eyes left" as they passed it when entering Rotten Row. As one walks through the Park, one notices a few benches and many chairs. The story of these chairs is unwritten history. About the middle of the last century, Queen Victoria, desirous of helping the widow of an old servant, presented her with five hundred chairs, with permission to place them in Hyde Park and charge for their hire. This became in due course a vested right, which was subsequently bought up by the Office of Works, which now realizes, annually, a very tidy sum from the monopoly.

Park Lane! Two hundred years ago it was a shady lane called Tyburn Lane, leading from Piccadilly to Tyburn Turnpike, a section of the road to Oxford. At the junction of the land and pike was Tyburn tree, a more or less permanent gallows. We shall come to this. At present we are walking north on Park Lane, where until recently there stood some of the finest mansions in London. Dorchester House, for example, the not frequently used palace of Sir George Holford, and Grosvenor House, the town residence of the Duke of Westminster. They, with many another mansion, have gone now and their sites are occupied by blocks of flats, architectural monstrosities, so ugly as to resemble great piles of blocks built by boys. They are universally condemned by Londoners, and an American, knowing how magnificent a skyscraper may be, is nettled somewhat to be told that they have been erected in the American manner. London is changing; I suspect that it has always been a changing city, but never more so than now, when it is rapidly becoming a city of flats or, as we would say, of apartment houses. The fact is, the day of the great landowner — "the Dukes," as Lloyd George called them — is done. There are men of immense wealth in England still, but they prefer to live in the country, and when they go up to London for the season they no longer care to occupy a palace which must be manned by a regiment of servants. How true the words of Tennyson: "The individual lessens and the world is more and more."

Just where Park Lane crosses Oxford Street and loses its distinction in the Edgware Road, there will be seen to-day a small triangular block of granite. It is not easy to find: a policeman can, and usually does, stand upon it. This spot for six centuries was the favorite place for public executions, not only for the executed but for the public, whose wishes and tastes in such matters were consulted. It was not in London, but it was not so far out as to be inaccessible, and the open country about it afforded room for the immense crowds that gathered to see a really fine hanging. "Sir," said Dr. Johnson, "executions are intended to draw spectators; if they do not, they don't answer their purpose. The old method was most satisfactory to all parties; the public was gratified by a procession, the criminal was supported by it." Boswell says care must be taken to distinguish between Johnson's talking for victory and talking to enlighten and inform. This is a good illustration, I take it, of his talking for victory, for it was the removal of the gallows which aroused his ire, he being against all innovation. On the site of the gallows was erected a toll gate,

and executions became semi-public functions behind the
walls of Newgate Prison.   It was Charles Dickens's vivid
description of a hanging which led to their suppression
altogether as a public show.   An authority says that a
moderate computation of the hangings at Tyburn would
place the number at fifty thousand, and of all this grim
procession nothing now remains but memory and a small
triangular stone set in the roadway.   From memory I shall
have to quote Dr. Johnson once more.   In his famous poem,
London, first published in 1738, he says: —

> Scarce can our fields, such crowds at Tyburn die,
> With hemp the gallows and the fleet supply.

Much the same sort of crowd which used to gather here
to see executions now assembles in that great open space
behind the Marble Arch to hear oratory of a Sunday afternoon.   Open stands, pulpits they might be called, from
which men talk till they are as exhausted as their hearers.
What do they talk about?
Subjects which are taboo in the drawing-room — chiefly.
Politics and religion; the wickedness and stupidity of the
party in power, whichever it may be, or the superiority of
Mohammedanism over Christianity.   Many of the talkers
are clever and take the heckling to which they may be subjected in good part.   The Salvation Army is always represented, and an address on the necessity for atheism is usually
drowned by the strains of "Onward Christian Soldiers."
Hundreds of policemen stand about maintaining order and
giving everyone a chance.   "Hi 've been a-'earing of this
for years," said one of them once to me.   "They blows off
their mouths till they are good and tired, then they goes
'ome and goes to sleep and feels better about it.   S'pose all
this horatory was bottled up and exploded — no man can
tell what would 'appen."

"Would you like to see what purports to be the grave of Laurence Sterne?" I asked my companion after we had moralized over Tyburn Stone.

"Yes, but why 'purports'?"

Well, it 's a long story, I 'll try to make it short. Sterne was living in lodgings in Bond Street when he died; he had expressed the hope that he would not die in his own house but rather in some decent inn, where the few cold offices his body would require might be purchased with a few guineas. And so it was, and he was buried "most private" in a graveyard in the Bayswater Road which had been enclosed and consecrated only a few years before. Now the story goes that a day or two after the interment the body was resurrected and sold to an eminent surgeon of Cambridge — the only way, at that time, that anatomical specimens could be obtained. After the corpse had been subjected to the indignities of the surgeons it was discovered with something of a shock that the body they had been dissecting was that of the celebrated author of *Tristram Shandy* and the *Sentimental Journey*. The story went the rounds and was affirmed and denied, but a sufficient number of people believed it to prevent the erection of a monument with an inscription which had been composed for it by Garrick. Then the scandal died, as scandal will, and some years later two freemasons who had enjoyed Sterne's writings took it upon themselves to erect a tall headstone with a long and silly inscription. They perhaps had never heard of the resurrection story. For some reason the graveyard never became a popular place of burial, although belonging to St. George's, Hanover Square, one of the most fashionable churches in London; in due course, however, it became crowded with graves of the poorer sort. A century passed, London overflowed its bounds, — as London has a habit of doing, — and the burying ground was closed to further interments and became overgrown with weeds and nettles, finally becoming little better than a dump for refuse. The neighborhood became fashionable and people forgot the graveyard, which was entirely surrounded by rows of tall houses. Then in 1893, a gentleman from the North of England, interested in Sterne, got busy and erected a *foot-stone* to the grave, on which a reasoned and coherent inscription was carved; he also recut the original inscription on the headstone, and there the story rests. Was Sterne's body exhumed or was the story of the disinterment started as a jest, as one authority suggests?   Nobody knows.

I set myself the task of finding the alleged grave some time ago, but first it was necessary to find the burying ground. I had frequently passed along the Bayswater Road on my way to the mansion of my friends, the Cecil Harmsworths, who live just off the road in Hyde Park Gardens, but in the course of my journeys I had never seen anything even remotely suggesting a graveyard, and it had not occurred to me at the proper time to inquire whether Mr. Harmsworth had any knowledge on the subject.   I interviewed, however, several policemen, who usually know everything, and had been assured by them that there was no burying ground near by.   Yet my good friend, Dr. Wilbur L. Cross, now Governor of Connecticut, the final authority, tells the whole story of the death, burial, and resurrection of Sterne in detail, and could not be mistaken. A grave may be lost, but not a burying ground whole and entire. . . .   I 'll find that burying ground or know the reason why, I said to myself, not once but several times.

About a quarter of a mile west of Marble Arch on the Bayswater Road, behind a fence, is a grass plot about fifty feet square, on which and facing the road is a small chapel, entered by a door in the centre with a smaller door on either side.   It is a sort of "Come ye aside and rest a while" struc-

ture, of which there are many in London. I never saw any
evidence of a religious service being held in it, although I
once saw therein an old woman kneeling in prayer. Somehow I became convinced that this chapel was in some way
connected with the burying ground I sought. The structure fitted snugly between two tall buildings, and it did not
seem possible to effect an entrance to a possible graveyard
from the Bayswater front. So I walked all around the
entire block — which was a very large one — of buildings
and courts and stable yards, eventually coming back to just
where I started, having discovered nothing. I inquired of
whomever I met, "Is there a burying ground in this neighborhood?" No one had ever heard of one. Then I walked
round the block again, this time carefully peering into every
court and alley. Presently I noticed that my progress was
everywhere blocked by a brick wall over which I could not
look; behind that wall was the burying ground I sought —
I became certain of it. At last, climbing a ladder which
was leaning against a house, I got a look over the wall, and
spread out before me was the promised land, as foretold by
Governor Cross. The wall which surrounded the burying
ground on all four sides served to prop up thousands of
old moss-covered tombstones, which left a large open space
except for here and there a single tomb more elaborate than
the rest, in the centre. The open ground afforded room for
several tennis courts; a number of allotments for vegetable
gardens, much neglected; chicken coops, sheds, and the
like; and an archery butts on which some women were
shooting at targets, bending their bows with strength and
skill. Where else but in London could such a sight be seen?

But how was I to explore the place? I am a little old for
scaling a high brick wall. So I continued my walk, taking
every turning which might by any chance lead to a gate.
Presently, on the west side, I entered a court, where I met

a woman who directed me to a gate which I pushed open, and there I was at last in the long-sought graveyard, and in two minutes I stood by the tombstones, if not by the grave, of Sterne.   Alas, poor Yorick!   That his grave should be in such a poor and neglected place!

I watched the archery practice for a time; whereupon a young woman, coming up, asked me if I was interested in the sport.   "No," I replied, "but I now understand how un-pleasant the English archers, under the Black Prince, made themselves to the French at the Battle of Crécy."   I don't think she knew what I was talking about, and to change the subject I said, "Tell me, how does one get into and out of this curious place?   I certainly have come in by the back way."

"Do you see that door to the right of the chapel?"   I said I did.   "Open that door and you will be in Bayswater."

I had looked at the Bayswater side of that door a dozen times and never thought of opening it.   Fool!

I think that some of these fine days, when my friend the erstwhile Professor Cross gets tired of governing the people of Connecticut, I shall suggest that it would be interesting to provide ourselves with spades — and permission from the proper authorities — and discover whether poor Yorick's corpse was violated by vandals, as the story goes, or whether it was allowed to rest undisturbed.   It is curious that no English student of Sterne has interested himself in settling the question beyond peradventure.

My friend had had enough, that was quite evident, but to please me he said, "I am willing to look at Sterne's grave, or the tombstones, or whatever it is, on one condition: that we can get there in five minutes, that you won't keep me there more than two, and that we then taxi to a good restau-rant and consume food.   Your idea of walking on an empty stomach is being carried to excess."

NIGHT

I have often thought that I should like to write a paper on the night clubs of London, but knowing nothing whatever about them, never having been in one, it would be necessary for me to put myself in the hands of competent teachers, lady specialists in fact, but to this I discerned objections, deep-seated objections, on the part of my wife. I suggested that I might meet — that is, see — Royalty, but even this argument failed to move her. We discussed the matter, not without heat on both sides, but with the usual result. If I know nothing whatever about the night clubs of London, blame my wife, not me.

But there are many other places of amusement not counting movie houses, of which there are several thousand. For example, there is the Gate. It is — that is to say, it *was* — a club; it has just gone "busted" now for about the fourth time, but it will be revived: the producer's, Peter Godfrey's, motto is NEVER SAY DIE. Admission is limited to members only, and their friends, but I feel quite sure it is much easier to pass the Gate than it is to become a member of the Carlton Club or even the Athenæum. The Gate is a tiny theatre situated at the bottom of Villiers Street, on the right-hand side, almost under the Charing Cross Railway Station. I have seen my old friend Wilfrid Walter act there in short and admirable little plays, and once, as the guest of Greville Worthington, I saw one Sunday evening a burlesque of *Uncle Tom's Cabin* which was excruciatingly funny. English burlesque is the best in the world: it always has been. They take a serious play, Victor Hugo's *Ruy Blas* for instance, "rag" it almost out of recognition, pack it with puns and rollicking music, and present the result, *Ruy Blas or the Blasé Roué*, to the most sophisticated audience in the world. Only a few weeks before we had seen in New York

VII

ADVENTURES IN GOUGH SQUARE

GOUGH SQUARE is not too easy to find. Going towards St. Paul's from the West End of London, the best way is to go directly to the Cheshire Cheese: motorbuses pass within a few feet of the "Cheese" and taxi drivers know it to a man. There are other ways that are not so good: the Strand becomes Fleet Street at Temple Bar — that rather ugly monument which marks the place where the historic gateway once stood — and there are several courts hard by, with interesting names, through which you can pass into Gough Square, but you will almost certainly get lost; so it is best to go directly to the Cheese, walk along Wine Office Court, which passes the door, as far as you can, then turn to the left, and in a few seconds you are in the tiny square and Dr. Johnson's House, the magnet which draws so many thousands to Gough Square, is looking at you — and you at it. One can enter the Square in a taxi from the north by way of New Street — but that way madness lies.

London is a delightful city to loiter in: in this it differs from our American cities, which are uninteresting, noisy, and dirty. In London, one turns a sharp corner or passes under an arch, and in an instant one is in the country. Fine old trees are growing on well-kept lawns, birds are twittering, the noise of the city is distant and forgotten: one has passed from the turmoil of the twentieth century into the calm of the eighteenth — the last century in which people really lived; for with all of our time- and labor-saving devices we have less time to live than ever before, and we work harder: something is wrong with our age, but I was not born to set it right — and, after all, as Voltaire said, *"C'est un monde tolérable."*

London is a city of ghosts: the people one sees are not important; they merely serve to clutter up the streets — they have no existence for us.   The actualities are the men and women one sees in one's mind's eye, with the help of a little imagination: it does not require much, the settings are so perfect.   Gough Square is in the heart of London; it was a very genteel neighborhood in Dr. Johnson's time, and the house was, for him, a most desirable residence.   He took it in a burst of enthusiasm after he had made his contract with the booksellers to supply a Dictionary of the English Language, for a sum total of fifteen hundred and seventy-five pounds, in which the words were to be not only "deduced from their originals" but "illustrated in their different significations by examples from the best writers": therein Dr. Johnson's Dictionary differs from the dictionaries that had gone before it, and therein lies a great part of its charm to-day — for charm this Dictionary certainly has.   We know how Dr. Johnson bedecked himself for the first production of his play, *Irene:* we read of his scarlet waistcoat with rich gold lace, and gold-laced hat; when he set up as a dictionary-maker to the English-speaking world, he may well have thought that a good address was desirable.   Practical considerations, too, no doubt, moved him: he desired to be close to William Strahan, the printer.   It was, however, Andrew Millar, the bookseller in the Strand, who had charge of most of the details of publication, and he it was who said to Johnson's messenger, who carried the last sheet of manuscript to him, "Thank God I have done with him" — upon hearing which Johnson remarked, with a smile, "I am glad that he thanks God for anything."

Many are the details which have been written and read with emotion and profit and amusement about this great work. Johnson's friends liked to question him about it, and he, great talker that he was, was by no means loath to gratify their curiosity. Of no other monumental work do we know so much. We know, as I have stated, just how much, or rather how little, he got for it, where he lived when he began it (in Holborn), when and why he moved to Gough Square, how many and who his amanuenses were, how he went about the job, in how short a time he expected to finish it, and how long he was about it. Boswell once suggested that he did not realize the immense scope of the work he had undertaken when he began, but Johnson set him right: "I knew very well what I was undertaking but I sadly underestimated the time."

"But, Sir, the French Academy, which consists of forty members, took forty years to compile their dictionary."

"Then, Sir, this is the proportion. Forty times forty is sixteen hundred: as eight is to sixteen hundred, so is the proportion of an Englishman to a Frenchman." In quoting Dr. Johnson, care should always be taken to remember that there were two Johnsons: one who "talked for victory," the other who "talked to enlighten and inform." Johnson permitted no one to poke fun at him, but he was not above making fun of himself, as when he refers to a dictionary-maker as "a harmless drudge." His first idea was to dedicate the work to the great Earl of Chesterfield, but when that nobleman neglected him until just before the appearance of the book, Johnson wrote him one of the most damaging letters in literary history. Speaking of it, his friend, Dr. Adams, accused him of pride. "Ay, Sir, but mine was defensive pride," was the significant reply.

Yet, withal, Johnson could, upon occasion, be as modest as a girl is supposed to be. From Gough Square he wrote to Dr. Burney, Fanny's father, one of his finest letters, in which, among other things, he says: "I remember with great pleasure your commendation of my Dictionary. Your praise was welcome not only because I believe it was sincere, but because praise has been very scarce. . . . Yours is the only letter of goodwill that I have yet received, though indeed I am promised something of that sort from Sweden." Think of our Lexicographer, the author of two great volumes in folio, pleased with the promise of a few words of goodwill from Sweden!

Scholars have long since been agreed that the Preface to his Dictionary is one of Johnson's finest bits of writing. It is at once manly, modest, and magnificent; above all, it is pathetic. He devoted, he says, to "this book the labor of years, to the honor of my country, that we may no longer yield the palm of philology without a contest to the nations of the continent. The chief glory of every people arises from its authors; whether I shall add anything by my own writings to the reputation of English literature must be left to time." He admitted that he had little hope of pleasing those who were not inclined to be pleased, and in illustrating the use of words his purpose was to omit the testimony of living authors, "save when some performance of uncommon excellence excited my veneration . . . or when my heart, in the tenderness of friendship, solicited admission for a favorite name." "The tenderness of friendship" — what a phrase! No man beneath a somewhat rugged exterior had a more tender heart. How true was Goldsmith's saying: "There is nothing of the bear about Johnson but his skin." And with that magnificent defensive pride of his he wished the world to know that his Dictionary was "written with little assistance of the learned and without any patronage of the great; not in the soft obscurities of retirement, nor under the shelter of academic bowers, but amidst inconvenience and distraction, in sickness and in sorrow." And he adds: "I have protracted my work till most of those whom I wished to please have sunk into the grave, and success and miscarriage are empty sounds; I therefore dismiss it with frigid tranquillity, having little to fear or hope from censure or from praise!"

Johnson must have been especially low in his mind when he wrote these words. Horne Tooke said he never could read this part of the Preface without tears, and Horne Tooke was not given to tears: he it was who, after his ordination, — for among other things he was a clergyman, — remarked that although "he had had the infectious hand of a bishop waved over him," the usual results had not followed, for the devil of hypocrisy had not entered his heart. In other words, he had taken Dr. Johnson's advice and "cleared his mind of cant."

After all this it is pleasant to turn to the words of praise of that arch-dyspeptic, Thomas Carlyle, from whom words of praise always come with difficulty. He says: "Had Johnson written nothing but his Dictionary one might have traced there a great intellect, a genuine man. Looking to its clearness of definition, its general solidity, honesty, insight and successful method, it may be called the best of all Dictionaries."

It is much to be regretted that until within recent years the general opinion of Johnson was derived not so much from his biographer, Boswell, as from Macaulay, who, to suit his own literary ends, greatly exaggerated Johnson's personal peculiarities, which, if the truth must be told, were in no need of exaggeration. If the gods who gave Macaulay so much could have given him a trace, only a trace of humor, it would have saved him from many blunders. Johnson was a Tory and hated a Whig; Macaulay was a Whig and hated a Tory, but there was always more than a

THE ATTIC ROOM IN JOHNSON'S HOUSE, GOUGH SQUARE

Where the Dictionary was compiled and the meetings of the Club took place

dash of humor in Johnson's hatred, while Macaulay's hatred for a Tory was his eleventh commandment cut in stone. In his usual cocksure manner he says Johnson was a "wretched etymologist." It may be so — how should I know? What of it? Judge the work as a whole. "Its undertaking was sublime and its fulfilment noble. Nothing like it, nothing within measurable distance of it had hitherto appeared in the English language. We should all bow down before such a monument of industry and talent."

And, having done so, let us rise and get what joy we can ("To seize the good that is within our reach is the great art of life") out of the Dictionary, remembering that it is the work not alone of a great scholar, but also of a great wit. In order that we may easily refer to his most famous definitions, we will take them, not in the order of their "risible absurdity," but "following the beaten track of the alphabet."

BLISTER — "A postule formed by raising the cuticle from the cutis and filled with serous blood."

BUXOM — "It originally signified obedient. Before the reformation the bride in the marriage service promised to be obedient and buxom in bed and at board."

CAMELOPARD — "An Abyssinian animal taller than an elephant but not so thick. He is so named because he has a neck and head like a camel; he is spotted like a pard" (a pard is a leopard) "but his spots are white upon a red ground. The Italians call him *giaraffa*."

CANT — "A whining pretension to goodness, in formal and affected terms."

CHICKEN — Among other things, "a term for a young girl."

COUGH — "A convulsion of the lungs vellicated by some sharp serosity."

ESSAY — "A loose sally of the mind; an irregular indigested piece; not a regular and orderly composition."

EXCISE — "A hateful tax levied upon commodities and adjudged not by the common judges of property, but by wretches hired by those to whom excise is paid."

FAVORITE — "A mean wretch whose whole business is by any means to please."

FLIRTATION — "A cant word among women."

GRUBSTREET — "Originally the name of a street in Moorfields in London, much inhabited by writers of small histories, *dictionaries* and temporary poems; whence any mean production is called grubstreet."

JOB — "A low word now much in use of which I cannot tell the etymology."

LEEWARD AND WINDWARD — Though of opposite meaning, are both described as "towards the wind."

LEXICOGRAPHER — "A harmless drudge that busies himself in tracing the original, and detailing the signification of words."

NETWORK — "Anything reticulated or decussated with interstices between the intersections." (This is a real glory: four big words to define one of three letters — NET.)

OATS — "A grain which in England is generally given to horses but in Scotland supports the people."

PASTERN — As everyone knows, was to Johnson "the knee of a horse." And equally familiar is his famous reply when taxed of his blunder, "Ignorance, madam, pure ignorance."

PENSION — "An allowance made to anyone without an equivalent. In England it is generally understood to mean pay given to a state hireling for treason to his country."

POETESS — "A she poet."

PRESBYTERIAN — "An abettor of Calvinistical discipline."

RUSE — "A French word neither elegant nor necessary."

SCAVENGER — "A petty magistrate whose province is to keep the streets clean."

STOCKJOBBER — "A low wretch who gets money by buying and selling shares in the funds."

TEA — "A Chinese plant of which the infusion has lately been much drunk in Europe."

TELESCOPE — "A long glass through which distant objects are viewed."

TORY — "A cant term derived I suppose from an Irish word signifying a savage." (And then follows one of his high-rolling sentences.) "One who adheres to the ancient constitution of the state and the apostolical hierarchy of the Church of England."

TRANSPIRE — "To escape from secrecy to notice."

WHIG — "The name of a faction."

Some of these definitions, as Boswell says, "cannot be fully defended and must be placed to the account of capricious and humorous indulgence."

After this noble work was completed its author was just as poor, if not poorer, than ever before. And into the Gough Square House came the bailiffs and arrested its author for a debt of five pounds, eighteen shillings; whereupon Johnson wrote to Richardson, who lived in Salisbury Court on the other side of Fleet Street, not far away, "entreating his assistance," which was instantly forthcoming. Even had Richardson not been the inventor of the modern English novel, he would nevertheless have a place in our hearts for his kindness to Johnson in his distress. My friend Mr. R. B. Adam, of Buffalo, owns this important holograph letter; I have frequently touched it, and never without emotion. In the lower left-hand corner is the endorsement in Richardson's hand: "Sent Six

Guineas." The late Lord Rosebery had another wonderful letter signed *"impransus* Sam. Johnson": signifying "not having dined" — perhaps starving. How prophetic were Johnson's lines!

> There mark what ills the scholar's life assail, —
> Toil, envy, want, the patron, and the jail.

It seems quite clear that Mrs. Johnson was living in the Gough Square House when she died. That Johnson felt her death keenly we know, for there is a letter from Johnson to Dr. Taylor, of Ashbourne, in which he says: "Let me have your company and instruction . . . my distress is great." Mrs. Johnson was buried in Bromley, in Kent. Dr. Johnson composed a funeral sermon, which for some reason was never preached, and it was not published until after his death; nor was Mrs. Johnson's grave marked until, a few months before Johnson passed away, he requested that a suitable stone be placed upon the grave and provided an inscription. When I was last in London I went out to Bromley, which is now a suburb of London, and with some difficulty found the grave, in the main aisle of the parish church, near the door, under a bit of carpet.

On my way back to town my train passed through and over one of those hideous districts composed of tens of thousands of ugly little houses, with tiny yards, in which clothes are always hanging, and a rhyme which I had once read came into my mind: —

> Daily she came from Bromley to the City,
> Pink underclothes of crêpe de Chine she wore,
> So that in each back yard she viewed with pity,
> The short and simple flannels of the poor.

What would Dr. Johnson's emotions have been could he have known that one hundred and eighty years after his wife's death, a man from the far-off Plantations — as

Dr. Johnson called this country — would journey to
Bromley to stand with bowed head at Tetty's grave?
Would he not have taken back his famous remark — "I
am willing to love all mankind except an American: they
are a race of convicts and ought to be thankful for anything we allow them short of hanging"? (This was
Johnson talking for victory, and shall not he who has given
us so much pleasure have his fun also?) Johnson always
loved nicknames: Goldsmith was "Goldy," Boswell was
"Bozzy," and "Tetty" was his favorite name for his wife.
Thirty years after her death we find him writing: "This
is the anniversary of dear Tetty's death . . . perhaps she
knows that I prayed for her; perhaps she is now praying
for me." Call this superstition if you like, I shall not
deny the word, but is it not exquisite devotion also? Had
Boswell been in London, we should have gone out to
Bromley together.

There seems to be good reason for believing that *Rasselas*,
or, as it was called in Dr. Johnson's day, *The Prince of
Abissinia*, was written in Gough Square, for on the twenty-
third of March, 1759, Johnson wrote to Mrs. Lucy Porter:
"I have this day moved my things and you are now to
direct to me at Staple Inn (Holborn). I am going to
publish a little story-book ('Rasselas') which I will send
you when it is out." But he soon moved again to chambers
in Inner Temple Lane, "where he lived," as has been
said, "in poverty, total idleness and the pride of literature."
The legend is that the book was composed in the evenings
of one week to defray the expenses incident to his mother's
funeral. When the work was completed, Baretti, Johnson's Italian friend, happened to call upon him and was
told by Johnson that he had just finished a romance, and
requested that he go to Dodsley, the bookseller, and say
that he wished to see him. Dodsley called, was shown

the manuscript, was asked what he would give, and replied one hundred pounds, which Johnson immediately accepted, but insisted that he receive seventy pounds at once. Any other person, says Malone, who tells this story, would have demanded four times as much, but Johnson never understood the art of making the most of his productions. Writing to his friend Strahan, who printed the book, Johnson said, "The story will make two volumes like little *Pompadour*" (a rather naughty French book which had appeared the year before), "that is about one middling volume." The success of *Rasselas* — to give the book its present title — was immediate: a second edition was printed within the year and it was translated into most European languages. Baretti made a translation into French: he never could, however, satisfy himself with the opening sentence, which in English is uncommonly lofty: —

Ye who listen with credulity to the whispers of fancy, and pursue with eagerness the phantoms of hope; who expect that age will perform the promises of youth and that the deficiencies of the present day will be supplied by the morrow; attend to the history of Rasselas, Prince of Abissinia.

One day, mentioning his difficulty to Johnson, the latter, after thinking for several minutes, said: "Well, take up the pen, and if you can understand my pronunciation I will see what I can do." He then turned the paragraph into what seems to me excellent French. (It will be found on page 154 of this volume.)

Enough coincidences coincide in life to hang a man. As I write these lines, a servant brings into my library a package: upon opening it I find a copy of *Rasselas*, in French, in a fine old morocco binding, done in Paris one hundred years ago for the Queen of Württemberg. It is a

present from an unknown lady who wants to secure a suitable home for a lovely book: she has done so and I am grate-
ful to her.   The English and French texts face each other.
The translator is unknown to me: it is by Madam ——
Who may she be?   Its opening sentence is quite different
from the translation Johnson made for Baretti.   The
curious thing about *Rasselas* is, however, that it antedated
Voltaire's *Candide*, with which it is so often contrasted, by
only a few weeks.   Each work is entirely in key with its
author, and both are famous and read a century and a
half after the death of their authors — fifty years more
than the period which, in the Preface of his edition of
Shakespeare, Johnson says is "the term commonly fixed
as the test of literary merit."

   After Johnson quitted Gough Square, the house fell
upon evil days, and apparently no one gave it a thought
until about 1831, when Thomas Carlyle discovered it,
"not without labor and risk," as he says, after two days'
search.   It had become a tenement, the tenant-in-chief
letting rooms to lodgers; subsequently it was freshened up
a bit and became a sort of family hotel, for a visitor from
Washington records that, about 1871, he stopped there
and the proprietor remarked as he assigned him a room:
"You 're a young lad and can climb, so I shall give you a
top room," adding, "but when you get older you will be
proud to say that you slept in the very room where Dr.
Samuel Johnson compiled his Dictionary."   "I believe,"
the visitor goes on to say, "that I remained in that room
for about a month, and, as I recall the circumstance, that
long room was divided into two, mine being the southern
end with the fireplace."   Finally the house was let to a firm
of printers, and it had reached the depth of its degradation
before Mr. Cecil Harmsworth bought it in April 1911.

The house purchased, the question immediately arose,
"What shall I do with it?" An accomplished architect
was consulted, a careful inspection of the premises made,
and a conclusion reached: to do nothing not absolutely
necessary and to restore the house as nearly as could be
to the condition in which it was when Dr. Johnson lived
therein. First, it was necessary thoroughly to repair the
structure itself. This was done without any sacrifice of
original features: modern partitions were removed —
these were found in the hall, on the landings, and in the
Dictionary Attic. The plasterwork throughout the house
had fallen into such a condition of rottenness that most
of it had to be replaced. The window sashes were renewed: those found in the house at the time of the purchase
were modern, flimsy, and unsuited in style to a house of
the early eighteenth century. The staircase was strength-
ened by the introduction in one or two places of iron joists.
But regarding the house as a whole and as the visitor
sees it to-day, it is satisfactory to note that almost every
original feature of importance has survived. The paneling of the two rooms on the ground floor, of the grey room
to the right of the staircase on the first floor, and of the
two rooms on the second floor, is as old as the house. The
room to the left of the staircase on the first floor seems
never to have been paneled throughout, and there is no
indication that the Dictionary Attic was paneled or intended to be partitioned. The staircase, with its stout
balustrade (not of oak, as has frequently been stated, but of
pine), is perhaps the most interesting feature of the house: it
is entirely original. Three of the fire grates found in the
house have been left *in situ*, but according to the best opinion
it is unlikely that any of them go back to Johnson's time.

In the decoration of the house no pains have been
spared in the selection of paints and distempers suited to

its age and style. In the case of the paneling in the two rooms on the first floor and on the stair landings, resort has been made to what is unquestionably a somewhat daring but successful experiment. When the many layers of paint had been removed from the paneling, it was found that the wood had been dyed, by the pigments composing the paint, a motley brown. The wood has been left bare, with the application only of so much staining, here and there, as was necessary to produce a uniform effect. The same principle has been adopted in regard to the balustrade of the staircase, except that in this instance no stain has been used. There is no doubt, however, that the wood-work throughout the house was painted in Johnson's time.

It is, I think, only fair to Mrs. Cecil Harmsworth to state that her good taste is everywhere apparent in the selection of carpets, curtains, and in such simple furnishings as there are. RESTRAINT was from the first insisted upon: it would have been an easy matter, indeed it was difficult to avoid not turning the house into a curiosity shop, but it was felt that miscellaneous antiques had no place therein. As Mr. Harmsworth himself says: "I feel that a few good paintings, half a hundred choice prints, some autograph letters, and a good collection of books — not much more is necessary. Furnishings do not add but rather detract from the interest of memorial houses; the illustrious person whom it is sought to honor is lost sight of in a wilderness of dry-as-dust impedimenta." The visitor to the Johnson House will not fail to observe the stout chain at the hall door with which, as we cannot doubt, he often barred out furious publishers and importunate duns, and the staircase that has so many times creaked to his footstep as he made his way up to the Dictionary Attic; nor the paneled walls that have resounded to his elephantine laughter and perhaps to his touching prayers. What more, or better, can the most enthusiastic Johnsonian desire?

We have traced, however imperfectly, the history of the Gough Square House from the time when Johnson took it, through the days of its neglect to the time when an ardent Johnsonian bought it, restored it, — if the word may be permitted, — and then pondered over the next step. To own and maintain a public museum is a glorious hobby, but it entails not only expense but continuing responsibility. Caretakers were necessary, and a house on a plot of ground that had been an adjoining garden "somewhat larger than a bed-quilt" — to quote Carlyle again — was built for them. Three better Johnsonians than Mrs. Dyble, and her daughter Mrs. Rowell, and her daughter Betty, it would be hard to find. It is a pleasure to listen and to talk to them. For years no admission fee was charged, but the increased cost of everything, due to the War and its *sequelæ*, made the small charge of sixpence, which goes into a pension fund, desirable.

During the twenty years that the Gough Square House has been open to the public, it has established itself as one of the minor show places of London. Visitors have come to it from well-nigh every country in the world, especially from America, and all who have visited it have found it a pleasant refuge from a noisy world that is growing noisier every day. The easy way to get rid of the burden of the Johnson House would have been to convey it to some existing public body, state department, corporation, or to the National Trust, but the easy way never appealed to Mr. Harmsworth, and the creation of a Board of Governors was decided upon. Here at least there was no

THE RECEPTION ROOM IN JOHNSON'S HOUSE, GOUGH SQUARE

The open door leads to the powdering closet

difficulty, only too many were ambitious for the honor, which carries with it little or no responsibility; for behind the Governors are the Trustees, who are the actual owners of the house. I have no means of knowing, since I am one, the principle upon which the Governors were selected; except that in the case of Mr. R. B. Adam, of Buffalo, Mr. Harmsworth chose one who is the ranking Johnsonian of America. Yale University has just confirmed this judgment by giving him an honorary degree upon the publication of the *Catalogue* of his Johnson Library, in three large volumes, entirely the work of his own head and hand.

The formal passing of the house from private to public ownership was accomplished at a dedication dinner given by Mr. Harmsworth on Wednesday evening, December 11, 1929. It was "a dinner to ask a man to." The old house, could it speak, might have much to say. It has seen the Great Man in the pride of his accomplishment and in the agony of his depression; it has seen Goldsmith and Reynolds sitting in the drawing-room, and it has heard bailiffs knocking upon the door, but never had a more distinguished company assembled than that brought together by Mr. and Mrs. Harmsworth to do honor to the occasion.

The dinner was given in the Dictionary Attic, the scene of the Doctor's most important literary labors; its only drawback was its limited accommodation. This drawback was overcome by Mrs. Harmsworth, in characteristic fashion. She secured accommodation in the near-by Cheese for her distinguished party of ladies, with here and there a lord to squire them, and after *our* party had dined in the Attic and *her* party had dined at the Cheese, her party joined our party to hear the speeches. Was the ghost of Dr. Johnson there? It must have been, and it must have been particularly pleased to see hospitality and kindliness so much in evidence. Before we were permitted to work our way to the Attic, our gracious host insisted that certain formalities be complied with: there were documents requiring many signatures, and, of course, a photograph of the Board of Governors made for the newspapers. I was sorry, indeed, that Mr. Adam was not present, but his name led all the rest, and this was something more than an alphabetical coincidence, for, as one of our number remarked, "Everyone has something good to say about Adam."

The dinner could not have been better had "a whole Synod of cooks" been employed thereon, as perhaps there were. To serve an elaborate dinner to a large group of hungry men on dining bent, — for all Johnsonians love a good dinner, — in a relatively small room, up three flights of winding stairs, is not easy of accomplishment, but an efficient staff of well-trained servants under competent direction made the job seem relatively simple.

> Come what come may,
> Time and the hour runs through the roughest day —

and the same may be said of the smoothest dinner. There came at last the removal of the cloth, chairs were pushed back from the table, Mrs. Harmsworth and her party arrived and were accommodated; Mr. Harmsworth rose: "Gentlemen, charge your glasses. The King." All rose, and a murmur went round the table: "The King, the King"; there was a pause, and we resumed our seats. "Gentlemen, I give you the immortal memory of Dr. Johnson." We rose again: the health was drunk in silence, and then we settled back comfortably in our chairs while Mr. Harmsworth spoke with brevity and characteristic modesty of his gift and what prompted him thereto.

Sir James Barrie, prevented by an earlier engagement, forgotten when his acceptance was dispatched, was unable to attend, but sent a characteristically whimsical message. Not to litter up this paper with such notable names as those of the Lord Chief Justice of England, Lord Charnwood, and others, let me at once come to that of Augustine Birrell, the Right Honorable of that Ilk, our Senior Trustee, whom death has recently taken from us. Like a bottle of sound old port which gives no suggestion of its flavor by its rather gritty exterior, "Old Birrell," as he was affectionately called, was one of the best after-dinner speakers in London; he never suffered fools gladly. Indeed, it may be said that he did not suffer them at all, and in accepting the rose which he occasionally passed you it was always well to look out for its accompanying thorn. To Mr. Harmsworth, however, he handed, very gracefully, a whole bouquet of roses, entirely minus thorns; and then, to my horror, I was called upon. To speak before (in advance of) Lord Hewart, Chief Justice of England, is an honor which needs be explained, and I accounted for it by saying that I had come further for my dinner and had further to go to get home — and little else. Speeches read after the occasion which gives them birth are like the dregs of a bottle of wine — to be avoided. There was good speaking, good wine, good comradeship, and a general feeling that

> God 's in his heaven:
> All 's right with the world.

How sad it is that such feeling cannot last forever! But the Johnson House in Gough Square is not ours. It has been given by Cecil Harmsworth to the English-speaking world. For us, for all of us, it is a delightful backwater, a resting place in life's march. There is a to-morrow —

it was already here.   Once again had history been made
in the old house: it was time for us to move on.

How long will the Johnson House in Gough Square
remain a place of pilgrimage?   Just as long as we respect
learning and modesty, courage and tenderness, honesty
and wit; for these are the qualities which made Johnson
beloved in his own time and in ours.   And in thinking
of Dr. Johnson, it is well to remember that we know more
of him than of any other man, and less, much less, to his
disadvantage.

VIII

FRANKLIN AND JOHNSON MEET AT MR. STRAHAN'S

On September 20, 1930, upon the celebration of the 221st birthday of Dr. Samuel Johnson, Mr. Newton was elected President of the Johnson Society, and in the Guildhall of Lichfield (England), Mr. S. C. Roberts, of Cambridge, the outgoing President, introduced Mr. Newton, who took the chair and thereupon read a portion of the following paper, which was subsequently very handsomely printed for the Book Club of California by John Henry Nash. It is here reprinted with the permission of the Book Club.

SIR, THE GREAT END OF COMEDY IS TO MAKE AN AUDIENCE MERRY.

— DR. JOHNSON

PROLOGUE

(In this little skit it suits the author's purpose entirely to disregard chronological accuracy, and we are to imagine ourselves in Dr. Johnson's House in Gough Square, London, early one afternoon on a dull November day in the year seventeen hundred and — no matter what. The Doctor has just come downstairs in a very untidy state and, upon observing his friend Mr. Boswell, calls out to his servant.)

JOHNSON. Frank, I see Mr. Boswell is here; let us breakfast in splendor. Bozzy, I'm glad to see you. (*Holding out his hand*)

BOSWELL. And I you, Sir. But I breakfasted early: I finished mine two hours since.

JOHNSON. Then, Sir, sit with me while I have mine. I love not to come down to vacuity. You will have a cup of tea. I know you will: one does not like to drink alone — not even tea. But what brings you here at this hour?

BOSWELL. Among other things, I came to inquire if you had accepted Mr. Strahan's invitation to dinner on Thursday next. I would, in that case, be glad to accompany you.

JOHNSON. I have not, Sir, I believe, received an invitation from Mr. Strahan . . .

BOSWELL. Oh, Sir, there must be some mistake. I saw Mr. Strahan only yesterday, and he then told me he had firmly decided to take his courage in both hands and ask you to dine with him. It is to be a small but distinguished gathering, prologue to opening his new house to the vulgar.

JOHNSON. But why, Sir, should it be necessary for Mr. Strahan to "take his courage in both hands"? We are old friends. I know few men whom I esteem so highly as Strahan.

BOSWELL. It may be that upon further reflection he decided that the company might not be entirely to your taste. He might be having some of his democratical friends.

JOHNSON. Well, Sir, and what then? What care I for his democratical friends? Pooh!

BOSWELL. I beg your pardon, Sir, for wishing to prevent your meeting people whom you might not like.

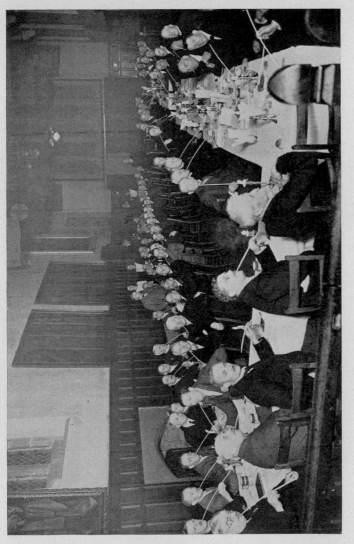

MEMBERS OF THE JOHNSON SOCIETY

Celebrating the 221st birthday in the Guildhall of Lichfield

JOHNSON.   Sir, I am a man of the world and take in some sort the colour of the world as it moves along.

BOSWELL.   I should not be surprised to meet Dr. Franklin there: he is an old friend of Strahan's, and a great man in Pennsylvania.

JOHNSON.   A great man in Pennsylvania, perhaps, but insignificant in London.   And what if he should be there! What is that to me?   My dear friend, I am sorry to be angry with you; but, really, it is treating me strangely to talk to me as if I could not meet any company whatever, occasionally.

BOSWELL.   Pray, forgive me, Sir.   I shall, with your permission, inform Mr. Strahan that an invitation will not be displeasing to you.   It will be a great pleasure to him to know this.

(*The curtain falls, is immediately raised, and the Play begins.*)

SCENE I

(*We are looking into a comfortable, if newly furnished, room, in which two men are sitting by an open fire.   Mr. Strahan, the host, is about sixty years of age.   Dr. Franklin, his guest, is ten years older.*)

STRAHAN.   So you have never met Dr. Johnson!   He is the finest Englishman living — and the most violent in his opinions.   His manners are uncouth, but his head is stored with learning; his heart is pure gold; and his hand is open as the day.

(*The door opens and Dr. Johnson and Mr. Boswell are announced.   They are accompanied by the French Ambassador and General Paoli.   Introductions follow.*)

SCENE II

(*A small dining room.   It is about four o'clock.   The dining table is laid for six: lighted candles in handsome silver candlesticks are reflected many times in the heavy plate with which the table is*

*decorated. Evidently, "a dinner to ask a man to" is in prepara-
tion. Presently six men file into the room, led by Mr. Strahan.
He takes his place at the head of the table, graciously directing
Dr. Franklin's attention to a place on his right. The French
Ambassador is conducted to Mr. Strahan's left. Dr. Johnson
takes his position next him. General Paoli is waved to the end of
the table opposite Mr. Strahan. Mr. Boswell stands by his
chair. Dr. Franklin looks around complacently. There is little
conversation, and that little is carried on by General Paoli and
Mr. Boswell, who regards the appointments of the table, particularly the number of wineglasses, with approval. Mr. Strahan
bows and the gentlemen take their seats. A moment later another
door opens and a tall servant enters carrying a large bowl of steam-
ing hot turtle soup. Dr. Johnson smiles his approval.)*

STRAHAN. Gentlemen, it is a pleasure to welcome you.
This is my first dinner party in my new home.

JOHNSON. It is a pleasure to be with you. I begin to
feel the need of the repairs of the table.

STRAHAN. I think I shall not disappoint you, Dr.
Johnson. An occasion such as this demands the best that
an honest printer can supply.

FRANKLIN. Honest printer! Do I hear my name
called? You and I, Mr. Strahan, have risen to the head
of our profession: no journeyman printers ever rose higher.
You are a member of Parliament and I represent the
happily United States of America.

JOHNSON. Sir, let us hear no more of it. I regret that
you did not confine yourself to your early occupation,
which was, at least, honest. I, myself, was bred a bookseller and have not forgotten my trade.

FRENCH AMBASSADOR. We, in France, do not regard
trade so highly as you English do. It would be impossible,
in France, to sit down in so small a company as this with
three distinguished men all of whom had been in trade.

JOHNSON. An English tradesman is a new species of gentleman: there are, I think, few ways in which a man can be more innocently employed than in getting money.

FRANKLIN. It is better that a man should be an honour to his family than that his family should be an honour to him.

BOSWELL. I shall not take that remark personally.

FRANKLIN. It is not meant personally. I was merely voicing what I believe to be the general opinion. (*Addressing General Paoli*) General, I hope that we in America are soon to have the honour of a visit from you. President Washington has several times expressed the desire of making the acquaintance of the liberator of Corsica.

JOHNSON. Do not mention the name of Washington in my hearing. He has a head to contrive, a tongue to persuade, and a hand to execute any mischief.

FRANKLIN (*ignoring the interruption and still addressing Paoli*). Not far from where I live, in Pennsylvania, we have named a town after you.

PAOLI. The name of Washington will live in history as one of the greatest . . .

JOHNSON. Sir, do not attempt to usurp the function of history, which is to record what has taken place, not what may. The difference between a patriot and a traitor depends upon his success: if he is successful in his treason he becomes the Father of his Country; if he fails, he is hanged.

FRANKLIN. Just so. As I remarked at the time of the signing of the Declaration of Independence, "Now, gentlemen, if we do not all hang together, we shall all hang separately."

JOHNSON. That, Sir, was a pernicious document. It taught — it sought to teach the doctrine of equality: that

all men were created equal.   There is no such thing as
equality, no, Sir.   I agree with the Roman Emperor who
said, "If I am only a man, my subjects are something less:
if they are men, then I am something more."

FRANKLIN.   That was a saying of Caligula.   He also
expressed the pious wish that the Roman people had but
one head that he might cut it off.

JOHNSON.   He would have known, Sir, how to deal
with the Americans.   We were much too lenient with
them and they took advantage of our clemency.   The
time will come, Sir, when you will regret the separation
from the Mother Country.

FRANKLIN.   I can quite understand your thinking so.
My dream was the union of the Colonies and their incorpo-
ration into a British Empire.   But different political groups
in this country could scarcely understand what was going
on in America.   It was so far off, and the problem was
so vague.   America had a bad press.   She was noisy and
bothersome.   Your politicians considered her future independence as certain, and wanted to get as much out of
her as they could before it was too late.

JOHNSON.   Those who did so were right, as the event
proved.

FRANKLIN.   For years I laboured to prevent the separation: I am not yet entirely convinced that a republican
form of government is the best.

JOHNSON.   Sir, it is the worst: a republic is a nation
governed by a mob.   A mob is a monster with many
heads and no brains.

FRANKLIN.   We have some brains in our heads.   I
wish that there had been such brains, in high places, in
England.

JOHNSON.   Sir, we have brains . . .

FRANKLIN.   Not in high places.   You would not, I

think, accuse Lord North or Lord Sandwich or Alexander Wedderburn of brains.   The brains, Sir, were on our side. But we were unable to get the English people to see that with our immense areas and our rapidly increasing population . . .

JOHNSON (*with a roar*).   I know all about your population, Sir.   We have been told that the continent of North America contains three millions, not of men merely, but of Whigs, of Whigs fierce for liberty and disdainful of dominion, prejudiced against the standing order of nature, that they multiply with the fecundity of rattlesnakes and . . .

BOSWELL.   I believe, indeed, that the rattlesnake is emblazoned upon the flag of one of the Colonies . . .

FRANKLIN.   It has hardly come to that dignity, but I remember that I have seen a flag somewhere on which is depicted a rattlesnake and under it the significant words, DON'T TREAD ON ME.   This is our way of quoting Shakespeare.   Like the camomile, the more we are trodden on the faster we grow — a warning which this country saw fit to disregard.

STRAHAN.   Gentlemen, we are all philosophers here. I would be glad if our conversation took a more philosophical turn.   You, Dr. Franklin, have, I understand, been conducting some interesting experiments in the physical sciences in Philadelphia; perhaps you will tell us about them.

FRANKLIN.   You may well call them experiments. Do you refer to my effort to prove that lightning and electricity are one and the same thing?

JOHNSON.   I, too, have made some interesting experiments . . .

FRANKLIN (*annoyed at the interruption*).   With orange peel, I believe.

BOSWELL. Dr. Johnson believes that he has found in orange peel a most useful physic, which he takes regularly.

STRAHAN. It is an interesting subject. Perhaps in the next edition of Dr. James's Dictionary he will favour us with an account of his discoveries.

FRANKLIN. Dr. Johnson can scarcely add to his very great achievement in the production of his own Dictionary. I know no other book, the work of any one man, which so well deserves the acclaim with which it was received. I chanced to be in London when it first appeared and at once purchased two copies: one I dispatched to our College in Philadelphia, the other I retained for my own improvement.

FRENCH AMBASSADOR. It is an amazing work, especially, Dr. Franklin, when you consider that it is the work of one man. Completed in so short a time, too — eight years, I believe. Consider that it took the French Academy, which consists of forty members, forty years to complete our dictionary.

JOHNSON (*smiling*). This, then, is the proportion: forty times forty is sixteen hundred: as eight is to sixteen hundred, so is the proportion of an Englishman to a Frenchman. But, Sir, I beg your pardon. My work was undertaken in order that we might not, in perpetuity, resign the palm of philology to the scholars of your nation. It is a large volume — in fact, two large volumes of small essays: each a trifle in itself.

FRANKLIN. Who shall say what is a trifle? Any trifle may become important. A nail is a trifle, but for want of a nail the shoe is lost; for want of a shoe, the horse is lost; for want of a horse, the rider is lost; for want of a rider, the nation is lost; all for the want of a horse-shoe nail. Dr. Johnson, in the little leisure which my public duties permit me to enjoy, your *Ramblers* have frequently been an inspiration to me.

JOHNSON. I wish, Sir, that my political writings had been an inspiration to you. But, Sir (*generously*), this is not the place for political discussion. The business of the moment is for us to discuss Mr. Strahan's excellent dinner. Are you not of my opinion?

FRANKLIN. My motto is frugality. I eat not to dullness nor do I drink to elevation.

JOHNSON. Sir, for my part I mind my belly very studiously, for I think that a man who does not mind his belly will hardly mind anything else.

BOSWELL. And, Sir, *in vino veritas*, you know.

FRANKLIN. I do; but I also know that the median way is best in all things: the truth, as the Romans said, is always in the middle.

BOSWELL. How wise you are. I wish I were, but I am always running into excess. I have such a gust for life; I think sometimes that a duchess or a drab equally appeals to me. Like Macheath I can sing: —

> How happy could I be with either,
> Were t'other dear charmer away.

JOHNSON. Bozzy, you are talking nonsense, which does not particularly offend me because I am accustomed to it; but Dr. Franklin here, who does not know you as well as I do, is likely to draw erroneous conclusions.

FRANKLIN. I am able to make allowances for youth, as do you also, Dr. Johnson: and then Mr. Boswell is Scotch, and I am prepared to forgive a Scotchman . . .

JOHNSON. You, Sir, have not suffered from the Scotch as much as we English.

FRANKLIN. I think I may say that the densest happiness of my life was the six glorious weeks I spent in Edinburgh. I had the pleasure of meeting all the notabilities: Hume, Robertson, Lord Monboddo, Adam Smith, Lord Kames . . .

JOHNSON. Hume, Sir, is a man without principles: he is a Tory, to be sure, but he is a Tory by chance. And (*laughing*) Lord Monboddo! He is still engaged in searching for his own tail, I presume. Robertson is a good and wise man of respectable abilities. I like Robertson.

FRANKLIN. I was going to add that these six glorious weeks were crowned by the University of St. Andrews conferring upon me an honorary degree.

JOHNSON. I have no doubt you deserved it, Sir. But you must consider, also, that a degree costs the university which confers it very little. Universities get rich by degrees.

FRANKLIN. I never look a gift horse in the mouth.

BOSWELL. Did you go to Scotland well provided with letters of introduction?

FRANKLIN. I did not: I never present letters and I am loath to give them. Indeed, I have a formula which I frequently employ in which I request the recipient to do the bearer all the good offices and show him all the favours which on further acquaintance he shall find him to deserve.

FRENCH AMBASSADOR. Excellent! I shall remember that the next time I am called upon to recommend a man of whom I know nothing.

PAOLI. Dr. Johnson, I have just had an opportunity of visiting St. Paul's Cathedral under very distinguished auspices. What a magnificent fabric it is! And how suitable that the first person to be buried in the great fane should be its architect; and how true the inscription to his memory: *"Si Monumentum Requiris Circumspice."*

JOHNSON. Sir, St. Paul's is magnificent; and the inscription to Sir Christopher Wren is as brief as it is true — which is more than can be said of most epitaphs. In general, it may be said that in lapidary work a man is not under oath.

PAOLI. Have I not heard, Dr. Franklin, that you have already prepared the epitaph which will be cut upon your own tomb?

FRANKLIN. You may have done so. It was merely a piece of youthful folly, composed in what I thought at the time was a species of wit.

BOSWELL. Will you not give it to me, Dr. Franklin? I am constantly taking note of the good things I hear in conversation.

JOHNSON. It seems horrible to me that a man should jest on such a subject. But these things are matters of taste. *"De gustibus non est disputandum."* (*Complacently*) I have no objection to hearing it.

FRANKLIN (*with much gravity*): —

THE BODY OF
BENJAMIN FRANKLIN,
PRINTER,
(LIKE THE COVER OF AN OLD BOOK, ITS
CONTENTS TORN OUT, AND STRIPT OF ITS
LETTERING AND GILDING),
LIES HERE, FOOD FOR WORMS,
YET THE WORK ITSELF SHALL NOT BE LOST,
FOR IT WILL, AS HE BELIEVED, APPEAR
ONCE MORE
IN A NEW AND MORE BEAUTIFUL EDITION,
CORRECTED AND AMENDED BY
THE AUTHOR.

BOSWELL. Excellent, excellent.

JOHNSON. Why, no, Sir, the wit is obscure and the impiety obvious. I cannot imagine a man approaching Omnipotence with a jest upon his lips. Perhaps, Sir, you do not believe in a future state?

FRANKLIN. I do. I do not believe that my Maker will suffer the waste of millions of minds that now exist and

JOHNSON. From what I have heard of you, Sir, I did not expect to hear you speak in favour of religion.

FRANKLIN. Since I became a thoughtful man I have never spoken or written against religion. I think the system of morals and the religion of Jesus of Nazareth the best the world ever saw or is like to see; but I apprehend it has received various corrupting changes, and I have, like most of the present Dissenters in England, some doubts as to His divinity; though it is a question I do not dogmatize upon, having never studied it, and think it needless to busy myself with it at my age. I expect soon to have an opportunity of knowing the truth with less trouble.

JOHNSON. I regret, Sir, that you are not in entire sympathy with the apostolical hierarchy of the Church of England.

FRANKLIN. It is a subject upon which I have never greatly concerned myself. I have ever let others enjoy their religious sentiments, without reflecting upon those that appeared to me insupportable or even absurd. All sects in America — and we have a great variety — have experienced my goodwill in assisting them with subscriptions for the building of their places of worship; and, as I never opposed any of their doctrines, I hope to get out of the world in peace with them all. I cannot help believing that on the last day multitudes of the zealously orthodox of the world's sects will flock together, united only in the hope of seeing each other damned. How disappointed they will be when informed that they must be content with their own salvation. Have you ever, by chance, seen a little volume of verse called *The Day of Doom*, by one Michael Wigglesworth, a teacher of Divinity at a college in Cambridge in Massachusetts?

JOHNSON. No, Sir, I have not.

FRANKLIN. It is a sulphurous poem; very distasteful to me but very popular with the masses, having passed through many editions.

JOHNSON. Is there, Sir, much or any good poetry in America?

FRANKLIN. Yes, notably in Philadelphia. The poems of Dr. Watts are greatly admired, especially those that inculcate the virtues: "How Doth the Little Busy Bee?" and

> Early to bed,
>   And early to rise,
> Makes a man healthy,
>   Wealthy and wise.

JOHNSON (*shouting*). Nay, Sir, nay, don't call that a poem, or if it is I 'll match it with another. (*After a moment's pause*): —

> When the morning riseth red,
> Rise not thou, but keep thy bed.
> When the morning riseth grey,
> Sleep is yet the better way.
> Beasts are up betimes; but then,
> They are beasts and we are men.

BOSWELL. An excellent impromptu, Dr. Johnson. I shall remember it.

JOHNSON. I understand, Sir, that the Book of Common Prayer of what you, in America, call the Protestant Episcopal Church is not greatly different from our Prayer Book here.

FRANKLIN. I do not know. I hope the Athanasian Creed is omitted, and I presume we no longer pray for the King and other members of the Royal Family. We had difficulty, you know, in carrying on what you call the Apostolic Succession. Your bishops here at first declined to consecrate William White of Philadelphia, one of the founders of the Protestant Episcopal Church, and finally a clergyman by the name of Seabury, of — somewhere in Connecticut — went or was sent to Scotland, where several Scotch bishops were found who performed . . .

JOHNSON. Scotch bishops! Sir, Scotch bishops would consecrate a yellow dog!

BOSWELL. Oh! Sir, you are too severe. Dr. Franklin, who is much at home in Edinburgh, will tell you that our bishops are . . .

JOHNSON. I do not wish to hear Dr. Franklin's opinion of bishops in general or in particular. I have my own. However, Mr. White came to London and disarmed us all by his piety and learning. I knew him well, and upon his return to America he sent me a copy of *The Prince of Abissinia*, printed in Philadelphia by a Robert Bell — I fear a Scotsman. The impression is not magnificent, but it flatters an author because it shows that the printer expects his work to be scattered among the people.

FRANKLIN. I am sorry that the printing house which I, many years ago, established did not have the prescience to print the book. It is unnecessary for me to praise it since the public has so generally done so. The opening paragraph is pitched in a particularly exalted strain.

FRENCH AMBASSADOR. Indeed it is. It has, I understand, given our translators the utmost difficulty.

JOHNSON. Why, Sir, where is the difficulty? I think, if you could understand my pronunciation, that I could do it.

BOSWELL. Oh! Sir, pray do. (*Taking out his notebook*) Let me make a copy.

JOHNSON (*after a pause*). Mortels! vous qui prêtez l'oreille à la douce voix d'une imagination séduisante et qui poursuivez vivement les fantômes de l'espoir: vous qui attendez de l'automne de la vie l'accomplissement des promesses, que son printemps vous a faite, et qui croyez que le lendemain vous donnera ce qui vous manque aujourd'hui, écoutez l'histoire de Rasselas, prince d'Abissinie.

FRENCH AMBASSADOR. Excellent! Magnificent!

BOSWELL (*who had been writing in his notebook*). What an amazing proof of your versatility. Sir, I presume you have never given the matter a thought until this moment.

JOHNSON. No, Sir. I have, I think, made a translation of this paragraph into Latin, but it did not occur to me to turn it into French.

BOSWELL (*addressing the French Ambassador*). Have you, M. le Comte, by any chance, observed how like Dr. Johnson's fable is to M. Voltaire's *Candide?* Had they not been published almost upon the same day it would have been difficult to prove that that which came latest was not taken from the other.

FRENCH AMBASSADOR. I have been much struck by the resemblance.

FRANKLIN. If you will permit me, Dr. Johnson, to say so, much as I was struck by the beauty of the opening paragraph, I was still more amazed at the chapter in which you give a dissertation on the art of flying. It is astonishing that a man of letters should forecast, and, as I believe, accurately, what the mechanical sciences of the future may perform. I believe that what you call a "sailing chariot" may be built, which will sustain itself in the air, and that it will be propelled by the impulse of its wings upon the air, which will renew itself faster than the air can recede from the pressure. I have considered, too, the effect of an army sailing through the clouds, and agree with you that neither walls nor mountains nor seas could afford any security therefrom.

JOHNSON. I am afraid, Sir, that this was the dream of a poet doomed at last to wake a lexicographer.

FRANKLIN. You have shown the value of imagination, without which nothing important is accomplished. Sometime since when I saw a balloon ascension in Paris . . .

STRAHAN. A what?

FRANKLIN. A balloon is a large globe or ball filled with inflammable gas, capable of lifting into the air the weight of several men.

STRAHAN. Of what value is a balloon?

FRANKLIN. Of what value is a new baby? When I saw this contrivance rise into the air I thought of Dr. Johnson's "sailing chariot." Five thousand balloons, each capable of raising two men, would not cost more than five ships of the line, and where is the prince who could so cover his country with troops for its defense that ten thousand men descending from the clouds might not in many places do an infinite deal of mischief before a force could be brought together to repel them? One result might be that of convincing sovereigns of the folly of war.

JOHNSON. If men were all virtuous I should teach them to fly, but what would be the security of the good if the bad could at pleasure invade them from the sky?

FRANKLIN. Mankind's progress from folly to wisdom is a slow parade: for the last three hundred years we have been almost entirely concerned with religious philosophy, out of which no good has come. Men have been so concerned about their future bliss as to neglect altogether their present comfort. For the future, men will be concerned with the sciences which will affect human life. We are on the threshold of great discoveries which will change the entire world: a happier day for humanity is dawning. I wish it were possible to invent a method of embalming persons in such a manner that they might be recalled to life at any period however distant; I have a very ardent desire to see and observe the state of America a hundred years hence. I should prefer to any ordinary death the being immersed in a cask of Madeira wine, with a few friends, till that time, to be recalled to life by the solar warmth of my country.

JOHNSON. But as that is impossible, however much to be desired, we should do what good we can while there is an opportunity.

FRANKLIN. We should, Sir, and I have invented a little scheme by which much good may be done with little. When a man seeks to borrow money from me, as many do, I lend it if I can. With the money I send a note in which I say, "I do not pretend to give you this sum. I only *lend* it to you. I hope that in time you will be enabled to pay your debts. In that case, when you meet with another honest man in similar distress, *you must pay me by lending this sum to him;* enjoin ng him to discharge the debt by a like operation, when he shall be able and shall meet with such another opportunity. I hope the money may thus go through many hands before it meets with a knave that will stop its progress." This is a trick of mine for doing a deal of good with a little money. I am not rich enough to afford *much* in good works, and so am obliged to be cunning and to make the most of a *little*.

JOHNSON. It is an excellent plan and I shall adopt it: every man should pass on the kindness he has received.

FRANKLIN. I am glad to find myself in full accord with you, Dr. Johnson. The whole civilized world is interrelated and all skill should be exerted for universal good. It has always been my habit to give to the public the result of any small discoveries I have been fortunate enough to make. As we enjoy great advantages from the invention of others, we should be glad of an opportunity to serve others by any invention of ours.

STRAHAN. Have you not by so doing deprived yourself of a considerable source of income?

FRANKLIN. No doubt, but I would wish to have it said of me that he lived usefully rather than that he died rich.

STRAHAN. I have frequently heard Dr. Johnson express the same sentiment.

FRANKLIN. What I conceived to be my duty has made it necessary for me to live for many years at a time out of my own country, hence I have learned to admire and respect other nations than my own and to seek to do them such good as was in my power. The foulness and darkness of the streets of this great city prompted me recently to submit to Dr. Fothergill a proposal for the more effectual cleaning and keeping clean the streets of London and Westminster. I would have the dust swept up early in the morning before the shops are open — a revolutionary proposal, but I am convinced that it is a practical one; for, in walking through the Strand and Fleet Street one morning at seven o'clock, I observed there was not one shop open, though it had been daylight and the sun up above three hours; the inhabitants of London choosing voluntarily to live much by candlelight and sleep by sunshine, and yet often complain — a little absurdly as it seems to me — of the duty on candles and the high price of tallow.

BOSWELL. I have always looked upon London as a particularly clean city and I am surprised to hear Dr. Franklin . . .

JOHNSON. Compared to Edinburgh and Glasgow we are clean enough, but we would not wish to be compared to Paris.

FRENCH AMBASSADOR. Ah, Paris is, indeed, a lovely and beautiful city.

JOHNSON. Sir, it is. I spent some weeks there a few years ago in the company of my good friends, the Thrales.

Your houses are very fine, and I was much struck by their furnishings and hangings, but you make little provision for your poor and your hospitals are miserably kept.

FRENCH AMBASSADOR. I am afraid that we have no hospital which would compare with St. Bartholomew's.

FRANKLIN. "Barts" is, indeed, a noble institution. When I was a printer, working at my trade, I lived in Little Britain, and I never passed its gate without hoping that we should one day have a great hospital in Philadelphia.

FRENCH AMBASSADOR. And have you?

FRANKLIN. Yes, St. Bartholomew's was the model for the Pennsylvania Hospital which I helped to create many years ago, IN THE YEAR OF CHRIST, MDCCLV, GEORGE THE SECOND HAPPILY REIGNING, as I caused to be cut upon the cornerstone.

JOHNSON. In what part of London do you now reside, Dr. Franklin?

FRANKLIN. In Craven Street, near Charing Cross. I have lived in the house of a respectable widow and in the company of her charming daughter for many years. I cannot think of any place where I should be more comfortable.

JOHNSON. I can well believe you. The full tide of human existence is at Charing Cross.

FRANKLIN. When I go home I never leave this happy island and my friends in it without regret, though I am going to a country and a people that I love. I am going from an old world to a new: I fancy I feel like those who are leaving this world for the next: grief at the parting, fear of the passage, hope of the future.

JOHNSON. No man fond of letters leaves London without regret: a man who is tired of London is tired of life. I will venture to say there is more learning and science within the circumference of ten miles from where we now sit than in all

the rest of the kingdom.   Moreover, Sir, consider how well
ordered is existence in this realm.   Life in a republic is like
life upon a raft: its course is uncertain: it has no direction;
it may be that few are drowned but all are constantly wet.
Every man gets a little but no man gets a full meal.

FRANKLIN.   If it be as you say, which I do not admit, may
it not be said that life in a monarchy is like life upon a ship?
The captain directs and is obeyed: all is well so long as the
course is kept, but should it be lost, the ship goes upon the
rocks: all are not merely wet, but drowned.

JOHNSON.   No power can long be abused; mankind
will not bear it.   There is a remedy in human nature
against tyranny.   If a sovereign oppresses his people to a
great degree, they will rise and cut off his head.

FRANKLIN.   Sir, we considered doing so, but decided not
to follow your example.   Your King, Sir, from our point of
view, was blind and wrong-headed, but from his own he
was able and industrious, honest and patriotic, and the
people tolerated him.

JOHNSON.   Tolerated!   Sir, we were proud of him.   His
ministers were to blame.   Such a bunch of imbecility never
disgraced a country.

FRANKLIN.   The King was a man of good character; if
he had had a bad one, Wilkes might have turned him out
of the country.

JOHNSON.   Wilkes was a scoundrel, Sir, always yelping
for liberty.   The fact is, the Crown has not power enough.

FRANKLIN.   Do you think Englishmen in going to the
Colonies in America renounced their rights as Englishmen?

JOHNSON.   The Colonists are the descendants of men who
either had no vote or resigned the power of voting to live in
a distant and separate government, and what they have
voluntarily quitted they have no right to claim.   The
Americans are rebels, Sir, and they have no rights.

FRANKLIN. I cannot agree with you. We, in what were the Colonies and are now the States, were taxed without our consent: we were deprived of our public as well as our private rights, of our rights as free-born Englishmen. Our petitions were . . .

JOHNSON. Pooh! Sir, petitions are nothing: most people sign them merely to show that they can write. Petitioning is a new form of distressing government. I will undertake to get up a petition against coining half sovereigns, with the help of a little wine. Had I been Prime Minister during the recent controversy concerning the Stamp Act, I would have sent a man-o'-war to level Boston or New York to the ground. I would have had no parleying with a pack of rebels, be their resentment what it may.

FRANKLIN. I take the liberty of disagreeing with you, and I am convinced you would have done nothing of the kind. Nor would you have sent hired German assassins to fight against English flesh and blood. Have you seen the recently discovered letter of a petty German prince who, with paternal solicitude for the brilliance of his court, recommended his general in America not to take care of his men, since England gave him thirty guineas apiece for each soldier killed, and he needed the money to pay for his last trip to Italy and for his coming season of Italian opera? Let me read a paragraph from a newspaper. (*Taking a clipping from his pocket. Reading*) "I am about to send to you some new recruits. Don't economize them. Remember glory before all things. Glory is true wealth. There is nothing degrades the soldier like the love of money. He must care only for honour and reputation, but this reputation must be acquired in the midst of dangers. A battle gained without costing the conqueror any blood is an inglorious success, while the conquered cover themselves with glory by perishing with their arms in their hands. Do you remember that of the three hundred Lacedæmonians who defended the defile of Thermopylæ, not one returned? How happy should I be could I say the same of my brave Hessians!"

JOHNSON. Sir, I don't believe a word of it: the newspapers are always packed with lies, even Mr. Strahan's *Chronicle*. One does not believe all that one hears, why should one believe all that one reads?

FRANKLIN. Which brings us to the old question — What is truth? How is the liar to be restrained?

JOHNSON. Every man has a right to utter what he thinks is the truth, and every man has a right to knock him down for it.

FRANKLIN. Yes, Sir, society may crush the liar but this only promotes his lie.

JOHNSON. I have given much thought to the subject and am constrained to believe that we must sit upon one horn or another of the dilemma. If nothing may be published but what authority shall have previously approved, power must be the standard of truth. If every murmurer at government may diffuse discontent, there can be no peace; if every skeptic in theology may teach his follies, there can be no religion.

FRANKLIN. Quite so. With my friend Voltaire, I would say, "If there were no God we would have to invent one."

JOHNSON. Sir, I am amazed that you quote Voltaire to me: he is a man of knowledge, but he is without principles. You may have Voltaire.

BOSWELL. Sir, do you think he is as bad as Rousseau?

JOHNSON. Why, Sir, it is difficult to settle the proportion of iniquity between them.

BOSWELL. I have never been friendly towards our conduct of American affairs: some time since I formed a clear and settled opinion that the people of America were warranted in resisting the claim of their fellow subjects in the Mother Country, and in this opinion I am confirmed by the great Earl of Chatham and the no less great Edmund Burke and Charles James Fox.

JOHNSON.   Whigs, Sir, vile Whigs.   And the first Whig was the devil!

PAOLI.   May not a Whig be what you call a patriot?

JOHNSON.   Patriotism, Sir, is the last refuge of a scoundrel.

PAOLI.   I have always looked upon myself as a patriot and a lover of my distressed country.

BOSWELL.   I think America gave the world a beautiful spectacle of a small nation fighting for its liberties against a powerful and misguided one.

FRANKLIN.   It was a beautiful spectacle, as you say, but unfortunately the spectators did not pay to see it.   I did everything in my power to prevent the war.   I was loyal to the last.   My enemies were many and powerful and abused me plentifully, in the newspapers and elsewhere, in an effort to force me to resign.   In this they did not succeed. I am afraid that I am deficient in the Christian virtue of resignation.   You remember my letter, Strahan, in which I said, "No one shall go beyond me in thinking my own king and queen the best in the world and the most amiable"?

STRAHAN.   I do, very well.   I thought that my heart would break when I heard that a battle had taken place at Boston.   Do you remember, old friend, the plans we formed to have my son, Billy, marry your daughter, Sally?

FRANKLIN.   Sons and daughters frequently take delight in thwarting the plans of their parents.   By the way, when do you intend to begin to live, to enjoy life?   When will you retire to your villa, give yourself repose, make yourself happy with the conversation of your friends, enjoy their society; or, if alone, amuse yourself with your books?   I was only forty-two when I retired from active business to devote myself to intellectual pleasures, — as I thought, — but alas! man proposes and God disposes.

STRAHAN. I do not know that I shall be able to retire. The war in America has made a vast change in my plans. Business is not as good as it was. Where shall we find another Johnson's Dictionary or a *Wealth of Nations* or a *Decline and Fall?* To say nothing of Blackstone, Blair, and Robertson. These men enabled me early to keep my coach.

JOHNSON. Do not mention the *Wealth of Nations* in my hearing. I was obliged to call its author a liar.

STRAHAN. I have not forgotten the incident. Ben, you have met the celebrated Mr. Gibbon, have you not?

FRANKLIN. No, I never met him. I once spent a night under the same roof with him: it was at an inn in France; we were both journeying to Paris. The landlord came to me in high excitement, saying it was a great day for him, in that he had the honour of entertaining Dr. Franklin and the learned Mr. Gibbon at one and the same time; whereupon I sent Mr. Gibbon my compliments and asked that he would share with me my bottle of wine at dinner.

BOSWELL. What was his reply? I never liked the man: he poisoned our Club for me.

FRANKLIN. The landlord returned, much embarrassed, with Mr. Gibbon's message: that he respected my abilities as a man, but that as a traitor to his king and country he had no wish to make my acquaintance.

BOSWELL. That 's Gibbon, out and out. And what did you say? I warrant you had the last word.

FRANKLIN. I very courteously sent him a message to the effect that when he undertook to write a History of the Decline and Fall of the *British* Empire, as he no doubt would, I should be glad to supply him with a mass of material which he might look for in vain elsewhere.

JOHNSON. A fly, Sir, may sting a stately horse and make him wince, but the one is but an insect and the other remains a horse.

FRANKLIN. I do not care to be called an insect, but your observation does you credit, Sir. You remind me of a French lady I once met who remarked, very seriously, "I don't know how it happens, but I meet with nobody except myself who is always right."

BOSWELL. You speak French perfectly, I presume, Dr. Franklin?

FRANKLIN. I think not; I speak it fluently. I had an excellent master — I should say mistress. The best teacher of a foreign language is a mistress.

BOSWELL. I do not claim to have anticipated Dr. Franklin in his discovery, but my experience prompts me to agree with him.

FRENCH AMBASSADOR. The evening wanes, gentlemen; I fear I must be going. We have all very much enjoyed Mr. Strahan's excellent dinner.

JOHNSON. Good food, good company, and good conversation afford, I think, the most lasting enjoyment that this world has to offer. Before we go, I have a word that I should like to say to Dr. Franklin. Sir, if in the give and take of conversation I have said anything offensive to you, I beg your pardon.

FRANKLIN. I wish that I might have made that speech first. It has been an honour as well as a pleasure to meet you. Sir, I am once again indebted to my dear friend, Strahan.

STRAHAN (*holding each by the hand*). I am merely an isthmus, happy in uniting two great continents.

BOSWELL. It has been a great pleasure to stretch one's legs under Mr. Strahan's mahogany, and, as Dr. Johnson says, have one's talk out.

FRANKLIN. I go reluctantly. I have the advantage of you, Dr. Johnson, in one respect: I am the elder man.

JOHNSON. An advantage of which I have no wish to deprive you.

FRANKLIN. My life has been a busy and arduous one. I feel that I am getting — nay, that I am old, and good for nothing; as the shopkeepers say of their remnants of cloth, I am but a fag end, you may have me for what you please.

JOHNSON. Let us not discourage one another. I am glad I have met you. I did not look forward with pleasure to the meeting: I accepted Mr. Strahan's invitation only that I might assure myself that I could be at home, occasionally, in any company. But, Sir, as I grow older I am prepared to call a man a good man on easier terms than heretofore. There is my hand. (*Offers it.*)

FRANKLIN (*taking Johnson's hand*). I shall not soon forget the pleasure of this evening.

STRAHAN. But, gentlemen, we have all forgotten something. Charge your glasses. I give you a toast. The King. (*All rise.*) The King, the Sun whose rays enlighten and fructify the remotest corners of the earth.

ALL. The King. The King.

FRENCH AMBASSADOR. I rise to a question of privilege. I give you La Belle France, the Moon, whose mild and cheering beams are the delight of all nations, consoling them in their darkness and making all beautiful.

ALL. La Belle France. France.

FRANKLIN. Gentlemen, I, too, have a toast which, with your permission, I shall propose. My Master, George Washington, who, like Joshua of old, commanded the Sun — and the Moon — to stand still — and they obeyed him.

All . . . is confusion.

(*Curtain*)

EPILOGUE

(The Epiloguer has a thankless part, especially if he tells the truth. I have tried to keep the conversation in key, but the fact is, the meeting of Dr. Johnson, the noble old Tory, and Dr. Franklin, the wise old Whig, is entirely apocryphal. They lived in London and they had many friends in common, one of whom was William Strahan, the King's printer; but everyone was afraid to bring the two men together. It would have been the striking of an irresistible force against an immovable body — that old problem in physics which has perplexed so many generations of philosophers. At this distance of time there seems to be no reason why an intrepid man should not rush in where many feared to tread.)

IX

ADVENTURES WESTWARD

WITH characteristic indirection we began our course westward by going south. A charming lady, a daughter of
Virginia, had been induced by someone in Richmond "to
ask Mr. Newton if he would deliver a lecture there, on any
subject which pleased him"; such profits as might arise were
to go to the "unemployed." My usual terms — smiles and
tea — being immediately agreed to, we journeyed to the
one-time capital of the Confederacy and were most graciously received. I would not seem to boast of the F. F. V.'s
who did me honor, of luncheons here and dinners there,
or of the many juleps I first sniffed, then tasted, and then,
like Oliver Twist, asked for more. I was particularly
pleased to renew my acquaintance with Ellen Glasgow,
whose novel, *The Romantic Comedians*, should be read by
every man of middle age who is thinking of getting married
and who feels that the laws of nature have been suspended
in his behalf. At her house I met James Branch Cabell, the
author of the famous *Jurgen*, of which I have two copies,
both unread — one, a first edition with a dust wrapper, and
the other, the beautifully illustrated edition published by
John Lane. I was able to tell him a story which amused
him greatly. A Richmond girl, who several years ago
married a Philadelphian and thus became Mrs. Edwin
Swift Balch, confided to me, one evening at dinner, that
only recently had Richmond indulged itself in a real,
honest-to-God public library. I expressed my astonish-

ment and said, "What did you do when you wanted to know anything?" "Oh," was the reply, "we did n't want to know very much, and when we did we just called Mr. Cabell up on the phone." Now that is what I call being real neighborly.

Our visits to Brandon and Shirley and Westover, and several others, were delightful, but the beauties of these famous houses on the James River need no description from me. They bespeak a civilization that is gone forever, and with it much that is beautiful. I have long since given over the wish I once had of living in an historic house, a house in which history — literary, social, or political — has been made. Now, fully convinced of the importance of a man to himself and to no other, what history I cannot make for myself I do without. But old places where things happened, "where the lightning once came down," as Le Gallienne has it, have always interested me enormously. When I hear of these historic places passing into alien hands, I feel sad, indignant, or amused, as the case may be. What right has a rich New Yorker to take Warwick Castle, say, for the summer? A developed sense of humor would protect him from such a blunder.

Of Jamestown, the first English settlement in America, founded in 1607 by Captain John Smith, but little remains. The tower of the church in which Pocahontas was married to John Rolfe — so the legend goes — and a few tombstones did not detain us long, but Williamsburg, the ancient capital of Virginia, is different. It is a lovely old place owing its chief distinction to the College of William and Mary, which almost ties with Harvard as being the oldest institution of learning in the United States. The original buildings, which are very fine, are said to have been erected from plans by Sir Christopher Wren. Williamsburg is a place of such peace as has to be sought for these days. It is, practically, just one long street, the Duke of Gloucester Street, which runs for a mile or more in a straight line from the campus, in the centre of which is a quaint old statue of an early colonial governor, Lord Botetourt.

The college has been the Alma Mater of governors without end and three Presidents of the United States, but it is chiefly fortunate in having attracted, some few years ago, the attention of John D. Rockefeller, Jr., who decided to buy up and re-create not only the college, but, in effect, the whole town.   The work was vigorously undertaken and has been reverently completed.   Some of the buildings which were falling into decay — for the college was not properly endowed — were pulled down and reërected, as much as possible out of old materials.   The result is delightful: a new-old village has arisen; nothing has been changed, not a false note has been introduced, but the college and the town have been given a new lease of life.   Millions have been spent — judiciously; it seems that wherever I go in my travels Mr. Rockefeller has just preceded me, writing his name as one who loves his fellow men.   And not upon the college buildings alone, but the fine old courthouse, the parish church, — famous in the annals of Virginia, — the blacksmith's and many other shops, the famous inn, even the prison for "poor debtors," have been torn down and reconstructed.   Perhaps Mr. Rockefeller is providing a home for himself in his indigent old age, which Congress is doing its best to bring about; I hope he may be happy in it — he deserves to be.   What other man since the world began has been so universal a philanthropist?   It may be said that no man should be permitted to accumulate so colossal a fortune as his; in the future it will be more difficult, — perhaps impossible, — but he did not make the times in which he lives, and, recognizing his responsibilities, he has done what he can to ameliorate them.

At the risk of wearing out our welcome we would have stayed longer in Richmond, but we were tied to an hour. My "lecture" was well attended; there were no serious casualties, and as soon as it was over we were motored to the railway station and entrained for Philadelphia, which we reached early next morning. To go while the going is good is an excellent habit; I govern myself with few rules, but this is one of them. As my old friend, Hawley McLanahan, used to say, "There is one thing I like about the Newtons: when they say they are going, they do not disappoint you."

We had heard California calling us for years, and at last had decided to heed its call. The idea was to follow the course of the empire in early February and March, there being too much weather in these months in Eastern latitudes — but things happened. In the first place, Helen Keller was to receive an honorary degree from Temple University (curiously enough, the achievements of this amazingly accomplished and useful woman had never before been so recognized), and I had been asked to present her, an honor which carried with it the privilege of entertaining her for a day or two. What I feared might possibly be an inconvenience turned out to be a delight which will long be remembered. In a census of then living Americans distinguished above their fellows, conducted, as I remember, by the *New York Times*, there were five men in the second rank and only two names, Thomas A. Edison and Helen Keller, in the first. Miss Keller has been called, and I think with truth, the most wonderful woman in the world. Many guests have been entertained at Oak Knoll, but none of such distinction as Helen Keller. So amazing is her personality that in two minutes one forgets that she has neither sight nor hearing nor speech — for her speech has to be translated. But she is so agreeable, so gay, and she looks at one so frankly with her great blue eyes, her mouth is so expressive and such a beautiful soul is revealed by her smile, that one forgets her great afflictions and instantly becomes her slave. This was the effect she had upon Alexander Graham Bell, Mark Twain, and Professor Einstein; this was the effect she had upon every member of our household.

I have said that I stayed home from California to present her for an honorary degree conferred by Temple University. Upon the platform to receive a degree at the same time was the governor of this state, Mr. Pinchot, seated by the President of Temple, Dr. Beury. The mayor of the city was to present the governor. Dr. Beury in his introductory remarks felt called upon to speak, chiefly, about Helen Keller. When the governor was presented for his degree by the mayor he was buttered, *ad nauseam*, by his orator, who then turned his attention to Helen Keller. The governor, in accepting the degree, said it was an honor to receive a degree at the same time as Helen Keller. Finally, when my time came to present Helen Keller, everything had been said. So I began by informing the audience that the three miscreants who had spoken before me had stolen my act and had been clumsy with it. "Now," said I, "if you wish to hear of Helen Keller's accomplishments eloquently presented, listen" — and I went on to repeat what had already been said. But I went further. It had originally been suggested that Miss Keller's teacher, Miss Sullivan (who later became Mrs. Macy), should also receive a degree, but she had declined the honor; she said she was not worthy, did not wish to seem to detract in any way from the recognition of her pupil. She was reasoned with, but remained firm. She would not even come to Philadelphia. Miss Polly Thomson, Helen Keller's secretary, would accompany her. I told of Mrs. Macy's obduracy. I said, and truthfully, that her pupil had had the urge to break out of the dark into the light, whereas the teacher had voluntarily entered the dark in the hope of dissipating it for the pupil; that Mrs. Macy had taught herself much in order that Helen Keller might learn more, and that it was Temple's good fortune to recognize the greatness of both women; in a word, that the English, French, German, Greek, Latin, mathematics, philosophy — all that Helen Keller knew and was, she owed to Mrs. Macy. And, I continued, occasionally one settles important matters by voting upon them, and I asked that all who agreed with me that a degree should be conferred upon Mrs. Macy, by force if necessary, should signify the wish by standing. The immense audience rose as one man — all but one woman: Mrs. Macy herself remained seated, with tears of happiness rolling down her face. Polly Thomson had spotted her in the audience. Neither Polly nor Helen nor anyone else knew that she had come over, alone, from New York to see her pupil honored. She certainly disproved the old adage that listeners never hear any good of themselves. A year later Mrs. Macy accepted a degree and we had another party, with another and a better mayor, "Hampy" Moore, upon the platform.

I cannot bear to leave this subject. Delightful Polly Thomson travels with Miss Keller everywhere. She talks into Helen's hand and Helen into hers as fast as I can dictate a letter. They can also read each other's lips. Between them they can do anything. It is well known that a person deprived of one set of faculties has others abnormally developed; especially is this the case with Helen Keller. She enjoys music through vibrations. As she walks through a garden she can name the flowers on either side from their perfume. I walked with her through a conservatory; by chance she touched a flower. "Ah," she said, "the parrot plant!" It was; I had never heard of it before. We went to a dinner; after we were seated someone asked her how many people were at the table. "How should I know?" she replied, with a smile; "I have met twenty." We were a party of twenty-three; two people had not been presented to her.

After Helen's party was over, there remained but one — two other things to keep me in Philadelphia. On the twenty-third of April, three hundred and sixty-odd years ago, one Mary Arden, in Stratford-on-Avon, was brought to bed of a boy; this boy turned out to be no less a person than the greatest of the sons of men, William Shakespeare. It is obligatory under the last will and testament of Edwin Forrest, America's greatest tragedian, to celebrate the birthday of Shakespeare in a fitting manner at the Edwin Forrest Home for superannuated actors and actresses. In these celebrations I was seriously implicated. Moreover, there was a dinner to be given to the Shakespeare Society of Philadelphia by Edgar Scott on the evening of that same day; Edgar being one of our baby members, the rest of us being mostly old codgers who, while suspecting, unreasonably perhaps, his knowledge of "The Bard," were willing — nay, eager — to show our confidence in his ability to give us a dinner "fit to ask a man to," as Dr. Johnson once said. And here and now "I 'll tell the world" (*Measure for Measure:* Act II, Scene 4) that this confidence was not misplaced. One of our members, the Honorable James M. Beck, the eminent lawyer and orator, who has denied himself the pleasure of scholarly retirement for the sake of representing a thankless Philadelphia in Congress, came up from Washington to add lustre to the occasion. I suppose the fact is that he was glad to absent himself for a few hours from the petty squabbles which make up the life of our politicians in the Capital City. It was a delightful occasion. Finally

and at last all my little chores were cleaned up and we
started westward.

Our first stop was Chicago.   John Ruskin, whom I never
much loved, says somewhere that railway traveling is really
not traveling at all: it is merely being sent to a place, and
very little different from becoming a parcel.   I had occasion
to think of this remark several times as we were speeding
over some of the most uninteresting landscape in the world,
in that section of these United States called the "Middle
West."   I could not get through this part of my journey
fast enough.   English writers on our country say that if one
would know what the United States are (they should say *is*,
but they don't) the thing to do is not to bother about New
York or Boston or Chicago or San Francisco, but go into
the Middle West and travel and live on four dollars a day.
They are quite right, of course, but, good heavens, what
conclusions they will reach!   I met a woman on a train
who told me, — as who should say, "Match this for enterprise in the East if you can!" — "There is scarcely a town
in the Middle West that has not its civic centre!"   There
are people who do not like their portraits painted with the
warts, who do not think that Sinclair Lewis deserved the
Nobel award.   Main Street has two sides, a shady and a
sunny side.   He has painted only the shady side, they say.
I find that he has, in all his books, painted us as we are.   If
we don't like his portraits, let us change ourselves.   *Main
Street, Babbitt, Dodsworth,* and *Elmer Gantry* are not greatly
written perhaps, but when this generation gets through
with them they will be regarded as exact chronicles of the
time, if not abstract and brief.   How like Sharon (in *Elmer
Gantry*) is "Sister Aimee McPherson" of Angelus Temple in
Los Angeles.   Think of Al Capone — now, at last, a guest
of the United States.   No novelist would dare to create such

characters; they are the product of what we call our civilization. Someone, a year or two ago, published a book which had for title *Why We Behave Like Human Beings*. The answer is clear — most of us don't.

Chicago is what it is, the most wonderful city in the world. That I don't wish to live there is nothing to the point. I remember Chicago when I first saw it, just after the fire; very few buildings were standing and high board hoardings enclosed great masses of smouldering ruins. At intervals in these fences were wickets towards which long lines of dejected men and women were headed, patiently awaiting their turn for small tin buckets of hot coffee and such provisions as could be secured and dispensed. That was the time to buy land; it could then be had as cheap as stinking mackerel. And now look at it! One does not expect all its streets and boulevards to be superb, as Michigan Avenue is, the wonder boulevard of the world. The difficulty in making comparisons is that people too often do not compare like with like. Chicago has its many square miles of dirty, sordid, wretched houses and miserable shops, tenements which are a disgrace — we have them in New York and Philadelphia, in all our large cities. London has cleaned itself up amazingly in the last twenty years, but Liverpool is awful, and Glasgow is worse. Berlin has, I believe, been built without slums. But I 'm for Chicago — with reservations. I am like a little boy I once knew, the son of an old friend. For some reason or other the lad, of perhaps nine, was sent to the far West to spend his summer on a ranch. On his way he stopped for a few hours in Chicago, just long enough to write his parents a postcard, on which he said, laconically, "Since I have seen Chicago it has rose in my estimation." How typical of the self-satisfied Philadelphian, "corrupt and contented," as was once said of us — and with reason. Philadelphia, on a low-lying spit of land between two rivers, has little to recommend it except its suburbs, which are beautiful, accessible, and salubrious. And with the advent of the motor car everyone lives out of town except a few hardened souls who prefer dirt and noise to quiet and fresh air. This leaves our city to the "racketeers." We are robbed unconscionably; no mayor of our town in recent years, except my old friend Ned Stuart, — who kept a famous bookstore, Leary's, — but has gone out of office unwept, unhonored, and unsung. But I forget the present incumbent, Mayor Moore, who has been elected mayor a second time after an interregnum of twelve years, a most unusual honor. He is at least an honest man, but the politicians will tie his hands if they can, in accordance with their habit. But I was speaking of Chicago.

Chicago has, indeed, "rose" — rose right out of a swamp or marsh at the bottom of Lake Michigan. What a city it is! And its people, millions of them, a mass of nervous energy! That is their chief trouble — they have no repose. They want a wide and magnificent boulevard, and pump it out of the bottom of a lake. They took an open sewer which sluggishly flowed into the lake, grandly called it a river, picked it up and turned it around and made it flow into the Gulf of Mexico, via the Illinois and Mississippi rivers. This was not done without expense and litigation, for the level of the water in the lake was lowered appreciably, it is said; other states and Canada objected. But it was done. And the buildings upon the lake front are among the finest in the world: colossal, magnificent structures, temples reaching into the heavens, given over to worship, — nowhere in the world more intense, — the worship of the almighty Dollar. Skyscrapers are a necessary evil in New York, where there are more people than there are square feet of land, but Chicago, having the whole

State of Illinois to extend into, did not need them. However, the fashion of tall buildings was set, and one might as well be out of the world as out of fashion.

I have never visited one of the most famous sights of Chicago, the stockyards, nor have I any wish to do so. I should, however, like to ask Mr. Armour or Mr. Swift or Mr. — whoever might tell me — why it is that one cannot, out of our immense supply of meat, get a good cut of roast beef, or a succulent piece of lamb, or a tender ham or a crisp rasher of bacon, such as one can get almost anywhere in England. It is "mass production," I suppose; I wish it were otherwise.

We lunched gayly with some friends who tore themselves asunder to entertain us at the Tavern Club, situated on the top of one of the tallest buildings; and dined sumptuously at the Drake, one of the best hotels in the country. We were unlucky enough to miss our friends, Mr. and Mrs. Julius Rosenwald,[1] whom it is a privilege to know; and the Walter Strongs, who had visited us at Oak Knoll only a few weeks before, were also away. Who could have supposed that that able and public-spirited man, the owner of the *Chicago Daily News*, in the prime of life and seemingly in robust health, would have passed away before we returned home? He leaves his family a fine inheritance — a noble name. But the Martin Schwabs, upon whom we dropped unexpectedly, received us cordially. Schwab's office (he is a consulting electrical engineer by profession) might well be mistaken for that of the custodian of some great archæological museum, so filled it is with rare specimens of Chinese art. After a few friends had been asked to meet us at luncheon, we were immediately taken to the newly opened Planetarium, a gift to the city from Mr. Max Adler. The

[1] Since this was written Mr. Rosenwald has passed away, but his admirable works remain.

building that houses this amazing astronomical device — the operation of which I wish I were learned enough to describe — has just been erected on a site that was pumped out of the lake. The Planetarium was operated and explained to us by Professor Philip Fox, an astronomer in whose keeping it is, and I told him that I found his explanation much more lucid than the one to which I had before listened, given in very choice Italian in Rome several years ago.

The University of Pennsylvania was, some time ago, offered one of these amazing contrivances by which the motions of the stars and planets in the heavens during the course of a year can be reproduced or suggested in the course of an hour, but the acceptance of the offer was so long delayed that it was withdrawn, and it is now installed in the new Franklin Memorial Building recently erected, largely by the gifts and energy of my old boss, the late Cyrus H. K. Curtis, who has done so much for Philadelphia. Our most public-spirited men come to us; they are not of native birth. Franklin, Girard, Curtis, are names which immediately come to mind.

Two nights and a day on a train, practically without a stop. Verily, as John Ruskin said, I felt like a parcel marked SPECIAL DELIVERY — RUSH. The while, what I am pleased to call my mind played with an idea which I should like to put into effect, and which, if effected, would certainly produce WAR. But it would not be for more than a few minutes, and the United States would be the better for it. I should like to say to the citizens of Wyoming, Utah, Nevada, Colorado, New Mexico, and Arizona, and perhaps several other "backward states": "Either relinquish your privilege of selecting two Senators each or get out of the Union. You may, if you decide to stay in, elect among you one Senator, provided he promises to be seen but not heard — often." The idea that a group of six so-called states, with a total population of only 2,700,000, the least populated area in the whole civilized world, should each of them speak with as much authority as the great states of New York, Pennsylvania, Massachusetts, Illinois, and others, is ridiculous. What good are they, to themselves or anyone else? What do they produce? What taxes do they pay? Take Idaho, Senator Borah's state: it contributes in Federal taxes $868,000, against New York's $928,000,000, Illinois's $247,000,000, and Pennsylvania's $230,000,000. The population of Nevada is under one hundred thousand. This state — it might be called a state of mind rather than a State — has as much weight in the Senate as New York, which has in its metropolitan area a population of over ten millions, and Pennsylvania, whose population is just under that figure. And what does Nevada produce? A little silver and copper, — of which we have more than enough, — cactus, rattlesnakes, and Reno divorces which are a national scandal.

I have taken my figures from an address delivered by the Honorable James M. Beck at the Union League in Philadelphia, but the conclusions, I hasten to say, are my own. The matter is a serious one. A politician, with a reputation to lose, would shrink from saying, "Turn the rascals out," but I am oppressed by no such difficulty. I know, of course, how these "backward states" got into the Union. I know why the territory of Dakota was split into two states, as do you also, Reader. I do not deny that both North and South Dakota are enormous areas, and I do not forget that Delaware and Rhode Island, too, have the same representation as have the larger states; but these states, though small, have enough intelligence to pull their weight. These miserable Western states have nothing, and they are a drain upon the entire country.

Such were my thoughts — if so I may call them — as I looked out of my car window at endless miles of dry, barren land. One gets up in the morning and looks out of one's window at the landscape. Six hours later one is, seemingly, in exactly the same place, and it has changed little at bedtime or next morning. But when it does, it is glorious. There could not possibly be better preparation for the Grand Canyon than the country one passes through to reach it. But we are not there yet.

I am so constituted that I can read for hours on end in my library, but to read all day long on a train is fatiguing; so, after a time, I put my book aside and began to muse (I prefer this word "muse" to "think," for thinking implies labor and I am not good at it). "Whither are we going?" I mused. I knew that *we* were going to Santa Fe — but this nation, of which I am so small, so insignificant a unit, whither is it going? I know nothing of Russia (who does?), but, Russia aside, where else in the world can one travel for days and see nothing new, nothing strange? The same faces, the same ugly, disorderly towns, the same deadly monotony of landscape. The inheritors of a continent of practically unscratched resources, what have we done with it? Are we, as I suspect, a nation of grafters and killjoys? Working like the very devil — for what? To get to the end of our lives without having lived a single minute. Was it to build up such a nation as this that our ancestors (not mine — mine were on the other side) fought the English and the Hessians a hundred and fifty years ago, and, with the invaluable aid of the French, won our freedom? Freedom, forsooth! There are a thousand small towns and cities — to mention one would be invidious — in which no man in his sober senses would live if he could help it, if he knew any better. Of recreation we know nothing; golf is for the few — it is a rich man's game. A few boys play baseball, but more prefer to see it played, and not one man in ten thousand could make a home run without dropping dead. We do not know how to sing, and walking against the noise of a saxophone is not dancing. We are a nation without tradition, without legend or folklore, without any of the quaint and homely sayings which illuminate and abbreviate conversation. I have seen husbands and wives sitting opposite each other for hours without opening their mouths except to yawn. Three things only interest us: Business, which has largely passed into the hands of a group of ignorant and wicked men who confess and call themselves bankers, against whom the individual has no chance whatever; Religion, which in the Catholic sect, the only one that takes it seriously, is too frequently a form of politics, and in the Methodist is a form of intolerance out of which that great evil, Prohibition, sprang — this is the sum.

As we rolled through the endless wheat fields of the Middle West, I thought of the ignorant farmers wondering why Europe refuses to take her wheat from us if she can buy it elsewhere. The great vineyards of France and Italy produce what is just as much a staple to them as wheat is to us. We shut our doors upon their wine and think it strange that they will not take our wheat and cotton. When will our politicians have the courage to tell us the truth, or, better still, when shall we have the intelligence to think for ourselves? We, a crime-swept nation, deserve the scorn in which we are held in Europe. What is our chief contribution to the world? *Democracy*, that horrid farce which thoughtful men fear. How curious it is that the only nation in which, by an election, a proper person may possibly be elected to high office — England — should still be governed, at least nominally, by a king!

The operations of democracy are everywhere the same: men without experience or knowledge are placed by the

WESTWARD THE COURSE OF EMPIRE TAKES ITS WAY

A Currier and Ives print

mob in positions of responsibility and power — only the
ignorant need apply.   Hence the mess in which the world
finds itself.   As I think of the history of my country I find a
steady deterioration, in civic, state, and national government alike.   It used to be said that the Presidency was an
office which should not be sought and which could not be
declined.   In the light of present-day politics such an
aphorism makes one smile: it is too naïve.   The founders
of our country were, almost to a man, men of education, not
infrequently men of ideals.   When I was a boy one knew
the names of many of the men in our Senate and had an
idea, at least, what they stood for; the office was an honorable one.   In order to make the Senator more immediately
responsible to the will of the people, the selection was
taken out of the hands of a group who could at least read
and write and given to that great beast — the mob.   What
shall be thought of a nation which, after one hundred and
fifty years of the greatest material prosperity that the world
has ever seen, is so governed that its entire banking system
collapses, that every bank closes its doors?   Only one
small group of men, the Supreme Court, stands before the
world as respectable; when that goes, all goes.   And what
reason have we to suppose that it will escape the general
trend?

From these musings I was interrupted by my wife, telling me it was time for lunch.   We were on a famous train
on a great railway, renowned, as we had been told, for its
luxury, speed, and safety — or perhaps I have stated these
important items in reverse order.   But at the thought of
that dining car I shuddered.   That the meal would be
expensive I knew; that it would be eatable I doubted.
Soup!   Bought by the hogshead, warmth and wetness its
chief characteristics; I could see and taste it in imagination.   Meat and vegetables!   The art of dining was dealt

a body blow when dining-car chefs discovered the wonderful possibilities which lurked in what they call "minute steak" — which, with fried potatoes, cost a dollar and a quarter. The worst bread in the world, a slab of pie "baked on the train," — as if that were a recommendation, — and for forty cents a bottle of ginger ale, sold upon the distinct understanding that it was not to be mixed with anything to drink, which was contrary to the law of the state through which we were traveling, and the United States!

I wonder how many of my readers remember the Raines law sandwiches which, twenty or thirty years ago, we used to have to buy when, under certain conditions, we wanted to get a glass of beer in New York. Few made any pretense of eating these sandwiches; indeed, they were not intended to be eaten: they were merely served to comply with the law which said that drink could only be served with food. They were served time and again, until they were worn out in service and discarded. Indeed, I think toward the last something resembling a sandwich in appearance, but indestructible, was invented, and this I prophesy and hope will be the fate of the "minute steak." It is generally made of a small piece of tough meat which has been parboiled and subsequently fried or grilled and put away; under favorable conditions it will keep indefinitely. When an order reaches the kitchen for one of these delicacies, it is merely heated for a moment over a quick flame, "garnished" with a dab of butter and a sprig of parsley, and it is ready to serve. Such is the efficiency of our train service and of too many of our tourist hotels.

"Last call for dinner in the dining car," a colored brother sings out, and we rise and go to the shearing. "Now don't make a scene," my wife tells me as we make our way through the train. "Remember we are traveling for pleasure."

Mrs. Basil Hall, in her interesting book, *The Aristocratic Journey*, being outspoken Letters written during a Fourteen Months' Sojourn in America (1827–1828), Mrs. Trollope (Anthony's mother) in her better-known *Domestic Manners of the Americans* (1832), Charles Dickens in his *American Notes* (1842), all make the same comment, that we Americans have no conversation, that we take no joy in life. They say, all of them, that we have good intentions, but that we are deadly dull.

Reader, the next time you have an opportunity of looking over a lot of American men (to say "business" men would be tautological), count the number of contented faces you see. Then try the same experiment in any other country in the world. It will be perfectly obvious that "the American standard of living" and "our great national resources" and "Democracy," about which our politicians are constantly talking, have given us, those of us who have survived the strain of these blessings, in general a haunted look. It was of Americans that Thoreau spoke when he said, "Most men lead lives of quiet desperation." So we were, and so we are, only more so since his day. If we no longer use knives for forks and no longer use forks to pick our teeth with, we are, indeed, a dreary and unhappy lot. "Mamma, you order," says the head of the family, handing his wife a menu; whereupon he subsides, eats what is put before him, pays for it, lights a cigar or a cigarette, and stalks away from the table. A foreigner, if one comes to your table at a hotel, and frequently on a train, will make a little bow and exchange a word; if it is well received, conversation follows, perhaps a discussion. A story is told of three men, apparently strangers, meeting at a hotel table in France. They engage in conversation; presently it becomes animated, intense. Voices are raised; a quarrel seems imminent; an onlooker thinks it well to

X

THE COURSE OF EMPIRE

SANTA FE. The end of a long, long trail and the beginning of another. I am bound to confess that my first sight of the historic city of Santa Fe did not give me the thrill which may have been the experience of those who, eighty years ago, came upon it at the end of a journey which was packed with almost unbelievable hardships. In the early days there were two historic westward trails, both starting at Kansas City, one ending, for a time at least, at Santa Fe, the other with a sight of the Pacific Ocean — which, according to one observer, disappointed because it did not look larger than any other ocean. There is, no doubt, a certain amount of romance attending the settlement of any new country, but our Mid-Western states were largely political creations, and while of squabbles there were plenty, of romance there was little. But as the early settlers trekked westward, pushing Indian tribes before them, a bivouac became a trading camp, and a trading camp grew into a village, and a village into a city, frequently on the banks of a river, — and some authority has remarked how curious it is that rivers flow, almost invariably, alongside great cities, — until finally the West was won and we settled down to digest our winnings. To push from Virginia into Kentucky and Tennessee was doubtless difficult enough, but it was a very different matter to push from St. Louis to Kansas City and thence into New Mexico and Utah and finally into California. The

pioneers confronted their journey of more than two thousand miles full of hope, and continued it — those who
survived — in despair, keeping on, perhaps, because it
seemed no more difficult to go on than to turn back.   Only
in the summer months were the plains of the great West
passable, the mountains scalable, and the rivers fordable.
The average distance covered each day by the caravans
seems to have been from fifteen to twenty miles, deadly
difficult miles for the most part, the journey punctuated
only too frequently by encounters with Indians, Mexicans,
half-breeds, and Mormons.   There is record of the slaugh-
ter of one hundred and twenty men, women, and children,
members of an emigrant party, ordered by a Bishop of the
Mormon Church who was subsequently convicted of the
crime.

Annoyed by flies, devoured by mosquitoes, their progress
was further interrupted by encounters with reptiles and
wolves, bears and buffalo; and, above all, they had to
fight disease.   But all their troubles could have been
borne, perhaps, but for the burning sun of the day and the
bitter cold of the night, together with the sufferings from
hunger and from thirst.   The hardships increased as
resistance to them lowered, and were almost unbearable
upon the desert.   Think of the miles of alkali desert with
dust as fine as flour, dust which blistered the lips, burned
the eyes, and destroyed the clothes and what remained of
the shoes of the weary and exhausted pilgrims.   Water!
Water!   There was water to be had occasionally in plenty,
but it was "poison water" or "bitter water," about as
refreshing to man and beast as the water of the Dead Sea.

Of the two historic trails across the continent, the Santa
Fe is the older and more dangerous, because nearer to the
corrupting influence of Mexico.   Known from the earliest
times, even before the days of Columbus, it formed a

natural highway — if the word may be permitted — between the valley of the Mississippi and the far West. But it must not be supposed that this highway was always well defined and always in the very same place. It was a "trail" merely, in some places very narrow, in others wide enough to be lost in the trackless, treeless prairie which it traversed. It changed from season to season and from year to year as short cuts were taken and abandoned; it was blazed, so far as it was indicated at all, by natural markers: mountains and hills, rivers and springs, and the graves of those who had fallen in their tracks, the bleaching skeletons of animals, and the wreckage of traveling and household gear which, for one reason or another, had been abandoned.

What caused these men, women, and children to set out upon this hazardous adventure? In brief, the desire to improve their condition; to seek better conditions for themselves and their families — to find GOLD. And in these groups of men and women brought together from all lands the passions which arise wherever human beings are assembled found full play, so that there were murders and marriages, births, deaths, and robberies — all the events which go to make up the "news" of our daily grind. How many fell by the wayside? Nobody knew, or cared much, or for long. What proportion of the horses and mules and cows and sheep with which one set out reached their destination? Perhaps only a moiety; it was a matter of luck and skill. At Hangtown, which later changed its name to Placertown, near the end of the California Trail, an egg cost fifty cents, and a chicken, a pound of powder, or a bottle of champagne brought sixteen dollars. A man's life or a woman's virtue brought less.

Is it any wonder that, after months of such experiences, the sight of Santa Fe was a sight for sore eyes? And not for the eyes only — it brought relief to every bone and muscle in the body. It is only within comparatively recent years that the odysseys of these groups of adventurers have taken — if indeed they have yet taken — their picturesque and important place in our history.

We do things quickly in this country. Only forty years later such a toilsome pilgrimage as I have described was no longer necessary. The journey was made by train, of which there were two kinds — emigrant and express. Horrible as was an emigrant train, it was luxurious compared with the covered wagon of a generation before. It is just about fifty years ago that Robert Louis Stevenson was ferried from New York to Jersey City, there to take an emigrant train to California. His short narrative, *Across the Plains*, is literature, and no writer, I think, of equal skill has attempted to depict the exquisite discomfort of such a train journey from New York to Chicago, Ogden, and San Francisco. A shrewd observer, he complains of the monotony, of the "huge sameness" of the country, and the dullness and sullen lack of manners of our people. "At North Platte," he says, "where we supped, one man asked another to pass the milk jug. . . .

" 'There 's a waiter here,' was the reply.

" 'I only asked you to pass the milk,' explained the first speaker.

" 'Pass! Hell! I 'm not paid for that business, the waiter 's paid for it. You should use civility at the table and, by God, I 'll show you how.'

"The other man very wisely made no answer, and the bully went on with his supper as though nothing had occurred."

I am happy to record that such rudeness is now a thing of the past. In the matter of manners we are, I think,

while distinctly inferior to the English, about on a par
with other nations.   People in the mass are neither interesting nor interested.   How should they be, leading, for
the most part, as Thoreau has it, "lives of quiet desperation"?

There is, I suppose, in the express train of to-day as
much superiority over the emigrant train of fifty years ago
as there was in the emigrant train of that day over the
covered wagon.   And the expense is not proportioned to
the luxury.   In the early days it cost about sixty dollars
to cross the continent in such a train; and Stevenson says
— and I agree — of joining the two sides of the continent
together by the railway, "If it be romance, if it be contrast, if it be heroism that we require, what was Troy
town to this?   But, alas! it is not these things that are
necessary — it is only Homer."   If the Song of the Iron
Horse was thought worthy of Homer, who shall sing our
recent conquest of the air?

Santa Fe is very old, probably the oldest continually
inhabited spot in the United States.   New Mexico had a
prehistoric civilization of which *we* know little and *I* nothing.   There were mound builders and cliff dwellers long
before the Mexicans, working their way north from Old
Mexico, who found it a desirable spot in which to establish
a mission and build up a trading settlement.   As a city, it
may be that St. Augustine is older, but Santa Fe has all
the marks of age.   Situated in a depression entirely surrounded by hills, it is protected from the sand storms
which render life in some other parts of New Mexico disagreeable, if not impossible.   Its climate is said to be
pleasant all the year round, and it boasts a society of
literary and artistic folk, with which largely — and naturally — I, a tourist, failed to connect.   The city is built

around a small plaza or square, and it has several good hotels and at least one that is luxurious, under the direction of the ubiquitous Harvey. Many of the buildings in Santa Fe are very old for a "new" country, but adobe houses characteristic of an older generation are now giving way to American types of architecture, and this trend will, unless checked, soon spoil its original character. This would be a great pity, for there is so little that is individual and characteristic in this country that what there is should by all means be retained.

The most interesting building in the city is the old Governor's Palace, a low spreading adobe structure, erected early in the seventeenth century, partly destroyed and reërected after the massacre of four or five hundred Mexicans by Pueblo Indians in 1680. Another "massacre" occurred when the Indians were, in turn, expelled. Much fighting took place in and around Santa Fe between United States troops and Mexicans during the American and Mexican War, until finally the United States flag was raised by General Kearny in 1846, since which time, with the exception of sporadic rows between Mexicans, Indians, half-breeds, and whites, the city has had, happily, no history.

Sixty years ago, I lived in Fort Scott, Kansas; since that time, until I reached Santa Fe, I had seen no Indians except at Wild West shows, nor had I wish to see any. I have no doubt that we treated them abominably: the way only to be expected when a few thousand, or even a million, untutored savages, armed with bows and arrows, attempted to defend themselves and their property — a continent — against superior numbers armed with guns, Bibles, and fire water.

> Lo, the poor Indian! whose untutor'd mind
> Sees God in clouds, or hears him in the wind.

To me, the Indian appears to be a dirty, lazy, and ugly creature, and I believe his reputation for treachery is deserved. He may be none of these things, but I well remember when, in the Centennial year, the news of the defeat and destruction of Custer and his gallant little army by the Sioux confirmed the generally held belief that the only good Indian is a dead Indian.

We, in Philadelphia, have for many years celebrated New Year's Day in a unique manner. We have what we call a Mummer's Parade. It is an elaborate spectacle, and immense crowds congregate along its line of march. Parading clubs, many of which have been in existence for years, dress themselves up in every conceivable manner and march to the music of many bands past a reviewing stand. After it is all over, substantial prizes are awarded the clubs which have provided the most original, amusing, or costly spectacle. There is intense rivalry among the clubs, and much ingenuity is shown and money spent. The story goes that some years ago a German prima donna, Frau Lilli Lehmann, was staying at the little old Bellevue (of blessed memory), along the line of march, when, hearing a terrible racket outside her window, she looked out to see a band of wild Indians — as she supposed — dancing a war dance, waving their tomahawks, celebrating, apparently, some bloody victory. It made a great impression upon the diva; she thought she was seeing real savages, and she wrote home about it. In this way is history made, by "eyewitnesses." The lady was much chagrined when she was told that she had seen only a part of a harmless and picturesque pageant.

Such Indians as these I am familiar with; the Indians I saw in Santa Fe — there were a good many about — were different. They were the descendants of Hopi, Pueblo, and Navajo tribes who had suffered from the extortionate attention of our Indian Agents — a race now, happily, almost extinct (like the Indian), who some years ago found it almost as profitable to be appointed Agent to an Indian tribe as it now is to be a Councilman in New York, Philadelphia, or Chicago: the qualifications — ignorance and cupidity — being the same.[1]

But we were eager to take the next step in our journey, and the desert which surrounds Santa Fe contains nothing to break its monotony; the mind becomes relaxed, so that when one of the greatest sights in the world unfolds itself one sees it with a fresh eye. All my life I had wanted to see two things especially — the Grand Canyon of the Colorado and the great trees of California. The Grand Canyon was, as distances are known in the West, not far away, and the Santa Fe Railway manages these things well. Trains are timed so as to arrive at a convenient hour in the morning, and they leave for East and West in the evening, so that one may spend one day or many days and nights in what I believe must be the most fantastically beautiful spot in the world.

Almost everyone who has seen the Grand Canyon has attempted to describe it, in words or in paint — and all

[1] I shall let the above paragraph stand just as it originally appeared in the *Atlantic*, where it surely started something. I received half a dozen letters from people who usually began by saying, "I have always read what you have written with interest, but . . ." and then followed several pages of vitriolic objections to my strictures upon the Indian. "You are old, ignorant, and prejudiced," writes one. I am coffin-ripe, I admit it, I reply. "You may know something about first English editions, but you know nothing about first-edition Americans," writes another. You are half right, I say, very politely. "Why repeat that vile slander that 'the only good Indian is a dead Indian'?" I did n't know any better, I say. "Do you know what the Indian thinks of us?" I don't, but I can make a pretty good guess, I suggest, as I can as to who taught him to murder and steal and lie and get drunk. I never thought very much of the human race, white, red, brown, or black, anyhow. We are very complicated inside — any physician will tell you so and give you pills for it. If I say that I 'm sorry I spoke disrespectfully of the Indian, I hope my critics will be satisfied.

have and will forever fail; highfalutin writing should especially be avoided.   The Grand Canyon is a national park
(since 1919), through and at the bottom of which flows a
river, the Colorado.   Geologists tell us (and a geologist,
like an astronomer, will say anything) that the action of
this river in cutting its way through a hundred miles of
stone for millions of years has created a canyon, a gorge,
a valley, so immense in size and so beautiful in color as to
be unlike anything else in the world. I have seen it
described as "a mountain chain reversed"; that is to say,
if this great work of nature were to be used as a mould
and a plaster cast made therein, when it was taken out
and set up it would be like a chain of mountains a hundred
miles long, from one to ten miles wide, and, in places,
one mile high; then all you would have to do would be
to paint it in every color you could conceive of, and you
would have the Grand Canyon *in reverse*.

As one stands upon the rim of this Canyon — and a
canyon is a gorge with a stream at the bottom of it — one
looks across to the opposite rim and, upon a clear day, is
amazed when told that it is ten miles distant.   You are
urged to spend several days at the Canyon, that you may
see it at sunrise and at sunset — when it is lit by the moon
and when it is filled with clouds or under a blazing sun.
But the glimpse of an instant is better than a volume of
description.   I am susceptible to color, and as I think of
the Grand Canyon as I saw it, some months ago, it seems
to have been a deep valley ablaze with color in which
purple was predominant.

And the river, that thing which lies seemingly motion-
less at the bottom of the gorge, is — should I not say was?
— responsible for all this beauty!   I do not believe it.
The movement of the river can scarcely be discerned; the
water looks like a dirty, narrow, winding road, and it

drains three hundred thousand square miles of territory! Did I not say that a geologist will hurl figures at you like a student of the stars? How long, or wide, or deep is the Colorado River? I neither know nor care. I simply do not believe that the river had anything to do with the creation of the Canyon, or that it took millions of years to produce this beauty. I believe that it was done in a day of twenty-four hours. I am, for the moment, a fundamentalist. I believe that God moved upon the face of the water and said: "Let there be Light" . . . and the dry land appeared, and so on and so on, until finally He saw that the work which He had made was good and He rested on the seventh day. This explanation has the merit of simplicity — it is understandable; no other explanation is.

We had a motor and a guide, and we walked and sat and talked, just as other people did, with this magnificent spectacle spread out before and beneath us. We stopped at another Fred Harvey hotel — I forget the name. It makes no difference; there are several. We ate and drank and slept, and the guide told us that just in front of where we stood there was a sheer drop of three thousand feet, and below that two thousand feet more, and that "one or two such drops after dinner is enough to settle the most squeamish stomach." This sounds as though it had been said before. It then occurred to me to ask a question: "How does one get water up here?" The answer: It is brought by a train of tank cars every other day during the season from Flagstaff, a hundred and forty-five miles away, at a cost of three hundred dollars.

A few days later I was in Los Angeles. What is one to say to this amazing city? The late Henry E. Huntington said to me some years ago, when I asked him why he placed his wonderful library and picture gallery in San Gabriel, a suburb of Los Angeles: "Because I am a fore-sighted man. I believe that Los Angeles is destined to become the most important city in this country, if not in the world. It can extend in every direction, as far as you like; its front door opens on the Pacific, the ocean of the future; the Atlantic is the ocean of the past. Europe can supply her own wants; we shall supply the wants of Asia. There is nothing that cannot be made and few things that will not grow in Southern California. It has the finest climate in the world: extremes of heat and cold are un-known. These are the reasons for its growth." I thought of this remark when I was dining with some friends. My hostess, a charming lady, much younger than I, told me she had been born in Los Angeles. "I remember," she said, "when we had a population of ten thousand."

"And what is it now?" I inquired.

"One million, six hundred thousand," was the reply.

A city that has grown as fast as this is like a boy who has suddenly grown to six feet: the city has, in a way, outgrown its strength. It needs filling out; there are many spots filled with sordid and miserable shacks, but they are no worse than — not, indeed, as bad as — similar spots were in New York, on Fifth Avenue, where the magnificent shops and palaces now are. I remember when, fifty years ago, the district above Fifty-ninth Street was a rocky waste, with here and there a disreputable shanty, where nanny goats, tethered by a rope, were expected to thrive, or at least survive, upon a diet of ashes and tin cans. Let those of us who criticize Los Angeles remember this.

Of filling stations there are more than enough. The Sherman Antitrust Law has outlived its usefulness — if it ever had any. The greatest economic waste in this country of colossal waste is the oil business. A man who makes two ears of corn grow where only one grew before does more essential service to his country than the whole race of politicians put together, says Dean Swift. Very true, but what shall be said of the politician who makes ten service stations grow where one would serve? These horribly garish, smelly, and noisy establishments occupy and temporarily ruin strategic corners everywhere. But can anyone say that these crimes are peculiar to Los Angeles? In this respect, as in many others, we are setting a bad example which the world is quick to follow.

If rapid growth is desirable, — and I am sure it is not, — it should be blamed upon the automobile. Not elsewhere in the world is its use so common: in California it is quite impossible to get along without one. You get an invitation for luncheon, which you accept, and you find you are going seventeen miles out in the country. In some trepidation you tell your hostess you have an engagement for tea. "Where?" she inquires. You tell her and she says, "Oh, very well, I 'll send you in my car," and you find you have a thirty-mile drive ahead of you. You dash back to your hotel, get into a dinner jacket, and again are whisked out into the country and again into a city, the magnificence of which amazes you. Of the hospitality of California I had heard much, but, as the Queen of Sheba said of the glory of Solomon, "the half was not told me."

We were in Los Angeles so short a time, and out of it so many times, that I lost all count of where I went, but I shall never forget the magnificence of the scene when one night, coming home from a party, our course took us over a very high hill. Beneath us lay Los Angeles, surrounded by its satellites, each glowing with the blaze of what seemed to be millions of electric lights. I was reminded of a night up the Nile, some years ago, when, after spending an hour in the gloom of the Temple of Abu Simbel, I came out into the night to see the dark blue dome of heaven lit with millions of stars. Now, as then, the stars were above us, but beneath us were Los Angeles and her surrounding cities with their gorgeous display of lights sparkling in the clear dry atmosphere. *Sic itur ad astra*, "Thus to the stars," might well have been the motto of Thomas A. Edison. One thinks of the New York Edison, the Boston Edison, the Chicago Edison, the California Edison, and bows — or should — in reverence at the thought of the great inventor. What a testament of beauty to leave the world! "Let there be Light," and there *was* light — and power, too, and heat.

Hollywood. We think of it as a place of dissipation, filled with movie actors and actresses more or less raising hell all the time. I did not find it so; some people do, I think. Does any sane man with a knowledge of the world think that the achievements of Douglas Fairbanks or Mary Pickford, or the amazingly versatile Jean Hersholt, are attained by days and nights of dissipation? My guess is that there is as much hard work — and more disappointment — in Hollywood as in any city of its size in the world. A suburb of Los Angeles, which is a city of suburbs, Hollywood is a thriving town, largely created by moving-picture interests, to be sure, but having many other interests drawn to it by its beauty and its climate. Two of the most charming and cultivated people I met on my journey lived in Hollywood — in it, but not of it. At a dinner table, at which no wine was served, my host said, "I want to pick a crow with you."

"Go ahead and pick it," said I.

"You quoted in one of your books Dr. Johnson's remark about Burton's *Anatomy*, that 'it was the only book that ever took him out of bed two hours earlier than he wished to rise'; you said it had the effect of putting you to sleep two hours earlier than — something foolish. Now, for an intelligent man to make a remark of that kind — or do I flatter you? . . ."

Sometimes, when in a jam, the truth will serve better than anything else; so I said, "I know the book very slightly. I have a good copy of the first edition — 1621, as I remember. It is an ugly, dumpty book, badly printed in small type, with anywhere from three to ten Latin quotations to the page. Gibbon, as you know, conceals his naughty stories in a 'learned language'; I suspect your Burton of doing the same. I don't read Latin and the book exasperates me." To which my friend replied: "Burton's *Anatomy* is to me what Boswell's *Life of Johnson* is to you, and some of these days I will send you a book about Burton, that 'old great man,' as Charles Lamb used to call him, which may cause you to change your mind."

To finish this subject while I am on it: some months later I received in the mail a book, *Bibliographia Burtoniana*, written, as its author says, for devout Burtonians. In this book I discovered that my friend had, with the help of another, edited and published an edition of the *Anatomy* in which every Latin word had been translated. I immediately bought a copy; it is on my table as I write, and I here and publicly withdraw and renounce my former opinion and pronounce it silly. The book has been handicapped, for this generation at least, by a misleading title. Its author, who called himself "Democritus Junior" (Democritus the Elder was a Greek philosopher who lived four hundred years before Christ; he was a man of ample

means, which is a great help to one who sets up as a philosopher, and he spent much of his time in laughing at
the frailties and follies of his fellows), in his *Anatomy* pro-
ceeds at great length to give advice to and make fun of
the men and women of his day, justifying his remarks by
quotations from the ancients. Burton was one of the
most learned men of his time, and not wise only, but witty,
as a truly wise man should be. He never married —
shall this be set down as wisdom or cowardice? "A
question not to be asked," as Falstaff says.

The bookshops of Los Angeles are certainly worthy of
a city possessing culture of more than two or, at most,
three generations. One might travel far to find a better
shop than Dawson's. It may be that I owe my introduction to it to Gaylord Beaman (I owe so much to him); I
should have found it anyway, as I did Jake Zeitlin's.
From Jake I bought a copy of my own book, *Mr. Strahan's
Dinner Party*, published by the Book Club of California.
I wanted to give it to a friend. From Mr. Dawson I
bought nothing, but on his shelves I found a slender book,
published in London, which I had been looking for for
years. It seems curious that I should have found it in
far-off Los Angeles. I was not permitted to purchase it,
but I found it again, at my hotel, as I also did a copy of
The Subtyl Historyes and Fables of Esope, translated by William
Caxton, and printed by the famous Grabhorn Press of San
Francisco. This archaic publication, admirably printed,
and bound in full niger morocco, bore on its flyleaf an
inscription signed by every member of Mr. Dawson's staff,
eighteen in all. I should like to print it, but modesty
forbids — and I am overtaken by modesty much less frequently than Mr. Samuel Pepys was by liquor. The gush
of the "hands" and the "heads" which Mr. Dawson has
gathered about him suggested to me what, I fancy, must

have been the enthusiasm in a sixteenth-century shop when it first became the fashion to sell and buy books.

And it certainly is the fashion in Los Angeles. A few days before my arrival, to do me honor, a large collection of first editions of books recommended by A. E. N. had been placed on sale at Dawson's, but a lady, Mrs. Edward L. Doheny, — whose husband has just given to the University of Southern California a much-needed library building, — happening in, had bought *en bloc* the whole collection, so I was invited to see it in that lady's house. I could not resist the invitation, and as my eyes traveled over her well-filled shelves I found a book, of value, which I had long wanted and lacked in my own collection. I mentioned the fact, quite casually, and nothing more was said; but upon my return to my hotel I found this book, also, on my table, with an inscription which once again modesty prevents my transcribing. Am I wrong in thinking that the influence and example of the late Henry E. Huntington are still — and will ever be — at work in this community?

In Mrs. George M. Millard — whose house in Pasadena was designed by Frank Lloyd Wright — I found an old friend whom I had last seen in London. Shall I say that Mrs. Millard makes a living selling books? Perish the thought. But in a tiny palace, one of the loveliest homes it has ever been my privilege to enter, my friend has a collection of books, prints, manuscripts, rugs, and similar articles, any one or all of which may be acquired if one has the taste — and the means. The people of Los Angeles and its unsurpassed and unsurpassable suburbs are under a heavy debt to Mrs. Millard for assembling, displaying, and dispersing such a wealth of treasures as are usually seen only in museums or in the bookshops of the great merchants of New York, London, Paris, and Florence —

for there is more than a touch of Italy in La Miniatura, as Mrs. Millard has named her villa. Not one, but many a man and woman of means has entrusted to the knowledge and exquisite taste of its chatelaine the task of making a whole library or of furnishing an entire palace, for Mrs. Millard spends much time abroad and knows how to acquire and transport "museum pieces" in profusion. Were Mr. Huntington alive he would endorse this statement. My friend Mr. William Andrews Clark, Jr., both can and will. Where, west of Chicago, would it be worth your while to ask to see a first folio of Shakespeare or an old French tapestry or an old refectory table, save at La Miniatura? Did I say west of Chicago — why lug in *west?*

I was unlucky in finding that Mr. Clark had left for Paris, where he spends much time, on the very day that I arrived to pay my respects to one who has been sending me, for many years, his annual Christmas publications. Book lovers as fortunate as I know that Mr. Clark's facsimiles of first editions, famous in English literature, not only are costly and beautiful in themselves, but contain in the essays that accompany them an amount of bibliographical and critical matter which is hardly accessible elsewhere. Hence it is that the Clark reprints of *Tamerlane*, Gray's *Elegy*, *The Deserted Village*, *An Essay on Criticism*, *Sonnets from the Portuguese*,[1] and many another, never fail to bring increasingly high prices when, on rare occasions, they come up at auction. They have another merit: they are splendid examples of the printing of John Henry Nash, of whom I shall say more elsewhere.

Mr. Clark's library, housed in a small marble temple in the back yard of his beautiful estate, filled me with delight

[1] It has recently been discovered that the Reading 1847 edition of the *Sonnets* is a forgery.

and envy. I say "envy" merely to round out my sentence;
I felt nothing of the kind. As Dr. Johnson remarked to
Boswell when they were being conducted over Chatsworth,
the seat of the Duke of Devonshire,

"My admiration only I express,
No spark of envy lingers in my breast."

The library is the playhouse of a rich and scholarly man
who knows and loves his books. He honors them and
they are an honor to him. With his librarian, Robert E.
Cowan, and his assistant, Miss Cora Sanders, I spent some
pleasant and profitable hours. Mr. Cowan, always referred to as "Sir Robert," is an authority on and has a
fine collection of Californiana, but I was unable to avail
myself of an invitation to see it; this I much regretted. I
shall go back — indeed, all during my stay in Los Angeles
I found myself promising what I should do on my next
visit. California is a beautiful woman — with a history;
of no other state is this so true. Of my paper on "The
Format of the English Novel," read before the Zamorano
Club (Zamorano was the first printer of California), I shall
say nothing, except that the casualties were unimportant.

The Huntington Library and Art Gallery have been so
many times described and their priceless books and pictures so many times referred to that praise is not construc-
tive, and I shall venture a criticism which I hope may be.
I am in entire sympathy with the reasons which prompted
Mr. Huntington to build in Southern California. There,
chiefly, he made his fortune, and in San Gabriel, a suburb
of and much older than Los Angeles, on his own magnificent estate and only a stone's throw from his mansion, he
erected his world-famous library. The West needs books,
a great many books, but even more it needs intelligent

readers, as we in the East do. In the East we have the Boston Public Library which is admirably managed by a small board of trustees, all of whom take their duties seriously (large boards do no work — think of the board of "Directors" of the Chase National Bank!), and who have that unusual Hungarian scholar, Zoltán Haraszti, functioning among English books as though to the manner born. We have the John Carter Brown Library of Providence, the New York Public Library, and the magnificent libraries of Harvard and Yale; we have, too, that "shrine frequently called a library" created by the late J. Pierpont Morgan and endowed and given to New York by his son, and we have the Library of Congress — its name is a misnomer. What use has Congress for a library? There are magnificent reading rooms for Members of Congress and for Senators in which no living man has ever seen a reader; indeed, it is doubted whether many of them can read — they give no evidence of it. This library should be called what in fact it is — the National Library. Some day it will be, and then it will attract to itself treasures of incalculable value, as now does the most useful and most ably directed of all libraries, that of the British Museum. Have I a right to refer to the William L. Clements Library of Americana in Ann Arbor, which my friend Randolph G. Adams directs so admirably, as being in the East? Probably not, but I am permitted to sing a hymn of praise to the magnificent Folger Shakespeare Library in Washington. The building was dedicated two years ago — on April 23, 1932, Shakespeare's birthday. It is a relatively small building, seemingly of one story only, but so perfectly proportioned by its architect, Paul Philippe Cret, as not to be overwhelmed by its great neighbors, the National Library (I insist upon so calling it — I am in debt to no Congressman) and the new Supreme Court Building, where im-

THE ELIZABETHAN THEATRE IN THE FOLGER LIBRARY

portant guessing matches of the nation will soon take place, and which is ten times larger than it should be. But the Folger Library! Its beauty is overwhelming. One doffs one's hat instinctively, it is so exquisitely beautiful and harmonious. Think of all that has been said and written in praise of libraries; Mr. and Mrs. Folger have listened to the world's enchanters and have turned their words into reality. How tragic that Mr. Folger did not live to see his dream realized! When one enters, one sees at once beauty and books, and when its treasures are finally catalogued and arranged, — it takes years to get a great library functioning properly, — it will be valued for what it is, the finest library in the world devoted to the memory of one man: Shakespeare.

> Thou art a monument without a Tomb,
> And art alive still, while thy Book doth live,
> And we have wits to read and praise to give.

With all this wealth — and much more — in the East, Mr. Huntington was well advised when he placed his library on the Pacific Coast, but unfortunately he erected a building which is entirely devoid of architectural merit: it might be a suburban railway station or the administration building of the General Electric Company; it certainly gives no suggestion of being — what it is — one of the great libraries of the world. The main entrance not only is unimposing, it is positively ugly; and, unluckily, the Library is only one of several attractions — I use the word "unluckily" advisedly — which Mr. Huntington created. There are Japanese Gardens and Rose Gardens and Cactus Gardens and a Picture Gallery, each wonderful in itself, but the whole suggesting unlimited wealth rather than discrimination and taste. Such surroundings, however magnificent, are not the proper setting for a great library. And the entire lack

of that all-important, intangible thing called atmosphere is
even more noticeable upon entering the building. Who
that has entered for the first time the Morgan Library in
New York, or the Bodleian at Oxford, or the Rylands at
Manchester, or the great Reading Room of the British Museum, will ever forget his feeling of reverence? No such
feeling overcomes one in San Marino.

Dr. Max Farrand, Director in Chief, was in the East at
the time of my visit, but I was most courteously received by
my old friends, Mr. Leslie E. Bliss, the Librarian, and Mr.
Robert O. Schad, the Curator of Rare Books. These men
I had known years ago, in New York, and it was a pleasure
to see them again, as it was to renew my acquaintance with
Captain Haselden, the Curator of Manuscripts, with whom
I had last dined and wined in London. Nor must I forget
the Curator of Art, who devoted an entire afternoon to
showing me the pictures in the Art Gallery, which is in the
Huntington residence. One and all did everything in
their power to make my visit pleasant and profitable. I
had long looked forward to my visit, but I could not overcome my feeling of keen disappointment. When it is
realized that the books themselves were purchased by one
man, in a few years, at the end of a busy life, one is lost in
amazement, and his achievements and not his shortcomings
should be remembered. Many of the books are unbeliev-
ably rare, but they are books for the scholar, and the library
contains little or nothing to interest the average citizen of
Los Angeles or the average tourist; yet both throng the
exhibition room. What went ye out for to see — the
famous Ellesmere Chaucer or the *Book of Privileges* granted
to Christopher Columbus by King Ferdinand and Queen
Isabella of Spain, or a unique *Hamlet*, or the manuscript of
Franklin's *Autobiography*, or a Great Bible, or a First Folio
of Shakespeare? Few people are really interested in these

things, priceless and wonderful though they are. I realize that it is a difficult matter to exclude people from a public institution which has been greatly overadvertised. Perhaps, after a time, when the novelty wears off, a smaller and more select attendance will be attained; let us hope so. The Library was not planned by Mr. Huntington for *hoi polloi:* it was intended for students; they use it, no doubt, but the books are not sufficiently accessible, and the custodians, overwhelmed by the crowds, are unable to differentiate between an idle and ignorant gazer and the man for whose use the books were assembled. To make the exhibition room interesting to the casual visitor the items displayed are too miscellaneous in character, and many are altogether trivial; they are not mutually self-supporting and of such educational value as they should be.

And it must be remembered that the Huntington Library is, not, in Sydney Smith's phrase, ten miles from a lemon, — lemon and orange trees abound, — but several thousand miles from other like institutions; hence the custodians have little opportunity of seeing and learning how other great libraries are administered. They should constantly be sent East, and from time to time to Europe, to consort with their fellows. To expect a librarian to live in Los Angeles and keep up the *esprit de corps* of his profession is like expecting a man to be brave in the dark. Everyone needs the inspiration of travel — Shakespeare has it, "Home-keeping youth have ever homely wits." The fact that the Library is crowded means nothing: the crowds only exhaust the custodian. They make a heavy draft upon his energies and do nothing to refresh and stimulate him. I doubt if any one of the Trustees has the faintest conception as to how such an institution should be manned or managed. A grave duty devolves upon them; they may be excellent men of business, bankers, lawyers, or what not, but they

certainly have no idea as to the direction of a great library;
a bibliographical tour is earnestly recommended.   I hope
they will ponder this matter; Mr. Huntington died too soon.
There is a portrait of my old friend, a bas-relief in marble,
which looks to be the work of William Blake in one of his
least inspired moments; this should immediately be removed and forgotten.

Los Angeles has been settled very largely by farming folk
from the southern Middle West; these people, many of
them Methodists and Baptists, go to their respective
churches not for worship only, but for breaks in the deadly
monotony of their lives that might otherwise be unendur-
able.   Temperamentally opposed as I am to the injection
of any kind of "pep" into religious services, whether the
merrymakings take the form of revivals, camp meetings, or
what not, I looked with aversion at a large poster outside a
theatre in which religious services were being held on a
Sunday evening by a smug evangelist depicted as standing
with outstretched hand above the legend, "He greets sinners
with a smile."   And still greater was my disgust with the
colossal effrontery of Aimee Semple McPherson — almost
invariably referred to as Sister Aimee.   How much longer
will this woman be able to hoodwink the immense congregations, audiences, crowds, which pack her Angelus
Temple? Nobody dare prophesy. The stories one hears
of her escapades are, even to one who is not easily shocked,
appalling, but one has to watch one's verbal step in discussing with a stranger the lady's conduct, for she has a
host of believers still, and they are quick to take offense.
Yet people say that Sinclair Lewis exaggerates his characters; the fact is that no one would dare put the true Aimee
McPherson into a book.   I am told that the lady is a book-
collector and that her favorite book is *Gentlemen Prefer*

"Mr. Hearst," said I, — for my companion was none other, — "do you object to my reciting a short poem?" I thought I saw him start as though stung by a wasp, but I may have been mistaken; then, before he could recover himself, I proceeded to "paint the home" for him as my old uncle used to paint it for me. When I had finished my recitation we both burst into laughter.

"Where on earth did you get that?" said Hearst. "I 've heard it somewhere. It 's Claude Melnotte to the Lady of Lyons, is n't it?"

"Yes," I replied, "and what Bulwer-Lytton saw in imagination you have created on this mountain side overlooking the Pacific. It is well named — La Cuesta Encantada: The Enchanted Hill. It is — it is like Monte Carlo, with that churchlike palace of yours instead of the Casino, and the exquisite quiet of your surroundings instead of the laughter and motion of the ribald crowd."

"It is lovely, is n't it?" said Hearst.

"Do you spend much time here?" I inquired.

"As much as I can," was the reply. "I am a busy man, but I try to spend about half the year here. It was a favorite spot of my father's, and I love it. I used to come up here with him as a boy. In those days we had a little cabin just about where we are now sitting. He used to be very fond of that tree," — pointing to a fine old oak, — "and so am I; that's why, when I found it interfered with the view from one of my windows, I had it shifted so carefully that it never knew it was being moved. I never destroy a tree."

Something within me said, "But would you show the same consideration to a man?" and I could, in fancy, hear my host's reply, "Not if he stood in my path."

"Would you like to hear some music?" Mr. Hearst asked. And upon my reply an order was given, and presently from a tower high up in the air came the most delicious music, mechanical, no doubt, and "amplified" into heaven, and returned as though by angels. But let me get down to earth — such flights as these are wearisome.

John Henry Nash, the great San Francisco printer, had met me according to arrangement at San Luis Obispo in a high-powered car, and after motoring for several hours said to me, "We are now on Mr. Hearst's ranch." We had entered no gates and there was nothing to suggest that we were in a private estate; we were just speeding along a country road. "That is the port of San Simeon and there is the railway station," said my friend. "When Mr. Hearst sees anything he wants, he buys it and sends it here. If it fits into his scheme, he uses it; if it does n't, he puts it in storage. Those are his warehouses."

Presently we came to a wooden gate, one of those "grass-hopper" gates which leap sideways into the air by the pulling of a rope. I did the pulling, taking the opportunity to read a sign on the gate, "Beware of the wild animals." I did n't see any, but, knowing where I was, I promptly bewared and, quickly closing the gate, hurried into the motor. After a mile or two we came to another gate with a similar sign, and then another gate, this time guarded by a man who came out from a small cabin. "Are you expected?" he said. "What name?" I saw wires leading from the cabin, and no doubt our names were telephoned to the mansion. Permission to enter was soon accorded.

A few moments more and, high up on a mountain side, we saw a huge pile of superb buildings which seemed to be dominated by a Spanish cathedral. "That is La Casa Grande, and believe me that's what it is," said Nash. "Do you see that black mass down there? Buffalo." The deer,

By Burton Holmes

Ewing Galloway

THE ENCHANTED HILL

Mr. Hearst's Ranch at San Simeon, California

zebra, and giraffe seemed to be living on intimate terms
with herds of cattle and the Arabian horses — but I may be
mistaken about this; I care little about such matters.   I
was all eyes for the castle, which soon began to unfold itself
in all its magnificence.   Soon we were motoring in a park,
more properly a superb garden, and presently we drew up
upon a side terrace which led to a small door.

A lady came out, a chatelaine, who welcomed us in Mr.
Hearst's name.   She said we were expected and that Mr.
Hearst would meet us at lunch, which would be served at
one o'clock.   She hoped we should like our rooms and
should find all that we required; if we did not, we had only
to ring.   We did not ring; it was not necessary: our every
want had been anticipated.   The Venetian suite, I believe
it was, had been allotted to us.   I wanted to sit down and
write someone about it — but I could n't think of anyone to
write to.   And I remembered how Lord Macaulay, spending a day and a night with Queen Victoria, had written a
letter on Windsor Castle stationery, and how his friends had
never ceased making fun of him; subsequently I told this
story to Mr. Hearst and it made him laugh.   "Maybe
you'd prefer to telegraph or telephone," he said; "the wires
are at your service."

Someone knocked on my door and asked if I wanted to
ride, motor, shoot, golf, swim, or play tennis, and he seemed
very much surprised when I said, "Not if I can help it."
He bowed, as who should say, "This is liberty hall," and
presently I began to wander over the mansion, castle,
palace, — call it by what name you will; they all apply, —
seeking what I knew I should find — the library.   I came
upon it at last, a noble room about a hundred feet long and
thirty wide, with a magnificent ceiling which had once
adorned an Italian palace.   It was filled with books —
not collectors' books, but just such books and magazines as

one would expect to find in the house of a country gentleman; I read in Frazer's *Golden Bough* for an hour. Later
Mr. Hearst told me his books were in New York, that the
library here was very largely the creation of his mother —
but it had been kept up to date by someone who knew what
books to buy.

Afterward, having somewhat explored the castle, I turned
my attention to the grounds. One feels in retrospect how
perfectly impossible it is to give any idea of the setting of the
castle without the use of almost meaningless superlatives.
A magnificent and far-reaching panorama unfolded itself
on every side, but with the exception of the mountains and
the sea it was all "made work," giving employment to a
small army of gardeners and caretakers. There are extensive lawns and almost equally extensive flower gardens,
connected or divided by broad walks or terraces on many
levels. There are fountains and pools, both for beauty and
for use, and the skill with which the eye is carried through
or along some vista to some interesting antique or beautiful
modern statue is beyond all praise. And it is, with me, an
undecided question whether these lovely and flower-per-
fumed gardens appear at their best by daylight or when
illuminated by concealed flood lights and by long lines of
alabaster lamps.

I forbear to comment, as so many have done, on Mr.
Hearst's waywardness in building a room, or a wing containing many rooms, and then tearing it down because he
had changed his mind, having seen or thought of something
he liked better. Castles in Spain are his long suit, and he is
said to have one in storage in New York City waiting until
he finds a place to put it, and in St. Donat's he undoubtedly
owns one of the finest castles in Wales. If one were presum-
ing enough to ask him why, I can imagine his instant reply,
"Why not?"

That Mr. Hearst is an enigma is known to all men. The only son of an enormously rich father, inevitably a Senator, and an idolizing mother, he has had from his youth his own way, not in one thing but in everything, except possibly in his political aspirations. When, as a young man, he first came to New York to dispute with Joseph Pulitzer of the *New York World* the domination of a certain section of the newspaper kingdom, someone told his mother that her "Willie" was losing money at the rate of a million dollars a year. "Is he?" replied his mother. "Then he will only last about thirty years."

Pulitzer to-day is merely the echo of a name connected with certain "prizes" which are more or less of a nuisance; his newspaper has become a mere tradition. Hearst's are still to be reckoned with. Let it be understood that I do not care for Mr. Hearst's newspapers or his methods, but then I doubt if their owner himself likes his newspapers; and as for his methods, he might, possibly, condescend to ask you what other methods would give him what he seeks? He wants "circulation," for the reason that it gives him power and wealth. The commoner his papers are, — he owns twenty-five or thirty of them, — the more people he can bend to his will. Mr. Hearst could run for his own edification a newspaper which it would delight me to subscribe to and read, but what would its influence be? Absolutely nil. Such ventures in the newspaper world are not uncommon. The last tried was with the *New York Evening Post*. After a year or two its owner, having lost several million dollars, was glad to dispose of it to the late Cyrus H. K. Curtis, whose estate, in turn, was glad to pass it on to another venturesome publisher.

The stories one hears of Hearst are positively fantastic and invariably contradictory. For example: His ranch extends for miles along the Pacific Coast; there is a high-

way approaching it which may some day extend from
Alaska to Cape Horn — long stretches of it are now completed from Seattle to San Diego. Quite naturally, Mr.
Hearst did not wish a public highway cut through his estate;
he therefore opposed it and was held up to obloquy by his
detractors. Finally, bowing to public opinion, — which
he seldom does, — he yielded. Was he applauded for so
doing? Not at all; he was immediately accused of using
his influence to have a great thoroughfare cut through his
estate in order to increase its value. It is a case of be
damned if you do and be damned if you don't.

It had in some way been made clear to us that life on
the ranch was governed by certain rules: PUNCTUALITY
at lunch and dinner is one; QUIET is another. Breakfast
is served until eleven; after that hour I doubt if anyone can secure anything to eat until luncheon, which
is served punctually at one o'clock. Dinner is at seven-
thirty.

It was about one that guests began to assemble upon the
broad tessellated plaza in front of the castle. There are,
in addition to the main building, several small palaces,
called guest houses, dotting the mountain side and connected with the castle by winding paths. It was soon
evident that these were occupied by young gods and god-
desses of the screen. Our host finally made his appearance,
and those of his guests who were not known to him were
presented. Mr. Hearst seemed a reserved, not to say a shy
man. There flashed through my mind the scene in Trollope's *Doctor Thorne* of the entertainment at Gatherum
Castle, of which La Casa Grande is the American equivalent, and Mr. Hearst's many qualifications for the part of
the Duke of Omnium, except that Mr. Hearst was as polite
and courteous as the Duke was rude.

WILLIAM RANDOLPH HEARST AND MRS. BURTON HOLMES

On one of the balconies of the Ranch

Presently we entered the great hall from a vestibule which opened upon the plaza — I insist upon calling it a plaza — and found ourselves in a lofty apartment the same size as the library, which is immediately above it. The ceiling was magnificent, and around the room was a range of old choir stalls taken from some Spanish or Italian cathedral. On one side, in the centre, opposite the entrance, was a magnificent fireplace in which great logs were burning, while on either side of the fireplace a door gave entrance to the dining hall. Above the choir stalls, between the windows, were magnificent tapestries. The hall was in fact the great living room of the mansion, comfortably but not oppressively furnished.

I had, however, only a moment to look around, for we were informally making our way to the dining hall, which extends lengthwise from the great room, resembling it in size and character. Here were more choir stalls and tapestries and banners and flags. I had the feeling that we were about to regale ourselves in one of the lesser halls of Windsor Castle. By a judicious arrangement of tables I suppose two hundred or more people could dine in this room, but our party was directed to a long table extending down the centre, formed by placing three or four refectory tables end to end. Mr. Hearst took his place in the centre, and opposite him sat Miss Marion Davies. There were perhaps forty in our party, but this number would be increased at dinner. It was like a scene on the stage.

Mr. Hearst always refers to his establishment as "the ranch," but it is a ranch in which magnificence is intermingled with simplicity. On the great table there was an array of bottles extending down the centre, containing condiments of all kinds: sauces, pickles and olives and catsup, in the utmost profusion, and *paper napkins* at one's place, to which one was directed by a major-domo; and I should instantly refer to the beautiful old English silver plate, of which it pleases me to think that I know something, and the bowls of rare and beautiful flowers — for, be it remembered, flowers are as common in California as people are in London, to distort Oscar Wilde's famous remark.

I have seen printed menus which suggested that food might be expected, menus which promised much to the eye but which broke the promise to one's stomach. Mr. Hearst's menu promised little and performed much. It was an ample, delicious, but not elaborate luncheon, beautifully served. Someone once told me that Mr. Hearst was a heavy drinker, and that he always drank a quart of champagne at lunch. I watched him narrowly and observed that he drank two small glasses of excellent claret; wine and spirits were to be had, but the guests, like their host, drank very little.

After luncheon we wandered about, had coffee, and presently went about our respective affairs. Someone remarked that it would be nice if a new picture play, in which Marion Davies had a prominent part, might be given in the theatre in the evening, only the reels were in Los Angeles — whereupon a young Apollo said he would "hop into his plane and go fetch them." He did so; we saw the picture in the beautiful and luxurious theatre that evening, after dinner. That all this should go on quite without effort — automatically, as it were — seemed quite what might be expected from one's surroundings, but that it should be going on around me! That indeed amazed me at the time, and in retrospect seems almost unbelievable.

Such preconceptions as I had of Mr. Hearst were invariably wrong. I had been told not to mention certain subjects to him; I mentioned them frankly and he as frankly talked upon them.

As I have said, I owe my introduction to Mr. Hearst to John Henry Nash, whose acquaintance with him grew out of the printing of the Life of Mrs. Phœbe Hearst, our host's mother, whose memory is perhaps one of the few things Mr. Hearst reverences. It is an admirable book, printed from type especially cast, on paper especially made, and bound simply but superbly in white vellum — in Germany. The book was not made without a tussle. Hearst wanted it made one way and in a hurry. Nash does not work in a hurry and wanted it made in another. Nash had his way, and Mr. Hearst was so pleased with the result that he said, "John, you will always be welcome at the ranch, whether I am here or not — and bring your friends." It was the Life of Mrs. Phœbe Hearst that suggested the format of Nash's famous edition of *Dante* which the King of England placed in the Royal Library at Windsor, where I saw it a year ago. Mr. Hearst was not displeased when I told him of this, and said, "John, I think Mr. Newton ought to have a copy of our book. Will you see that he gets one?"

It was after dinner one evening that I recited the well-known lines from *The Lady of Lyons* and lived to tell the tale. Not many men have recited poetry to Hearst and survived. Mr. Hearst is a man of emotions. He can be cruel and remorseless, yet he is fond of animals and loves to feed them. He has a large menagerie — of what? Of all the animals one sees at a circus, but exceptionally fine specimens. The ranch is alive with subtropical birds. They were originally kept in cages so large that they thought they were at liberty; now that they are, they have no wish to leave a spot where their every want has been anticipated. Expert game-keepers and bird fanciers are among the small army of employees always at work.

The house is not finished, and it never will be. Its owner, like Queen Elizabeth's friend, — or was it enemy? — Bess

of Hardwicke, feels perhaps that if he should stop building
he would die.   And he has no wish to die.   He lives in an
earthly paradise.   The dinner was informally magnificent;
evening dress is taboo, though Mr. Hearst explained to
me that once when President and Mrs. Coolidge visited the
ranch he was obliged to relax this rule.

More guests had arrived during the afternoon.   I found
a lady sitting next to me who seemed to know everyone in
London;   I asked her who she was, and she told me she
represented Mr. Hearst's magazine interests in England.
She had been at the ranch for some time, but Mr. Hearst
had not yet told her why he had sent for her.   "But he
will when he gets ready," she said.

The Hearst property at San Simeon extends to about two
hundred and fifty thousand acres.   Senator Hearst began
to buy land sixty-odd years ago, and his son is an acquisitive
man: to see a thing is to want it, and to want it is to buy it.
I remember once that Mr. Hearst and I wanted some books
at an auction sale in New York; when I found whom I was
bidding against I stopped, thereby displeasing Mr. Hearst,
who would have preferred a battle royal — with the same
result.   When I reached San Francisco I was telling some
of my friends of my experience and was told by them that
Hearst's purchases are so large that even he, after the manner of many very rich men, does not always pay promptly.
A few months later I was in London, whither Hearst and a
large party had preceded me.   Talking to a friend, a bookseller, I asked him if he was doing any business, and he said,
"Yes, I sold some fine books to William Randolph Hearst
only a few days ago, and look at this" — and he took from
his pocket a letter from a secretary, which read: "Acting
on Mr. Hearst's instructions, I enclose a draft on New York
for the books recently purchased.   I presume they have
already gone forward."   Unluckily, for me, Mr. Hearst's

taste in books is not unlike my own, and I smile to think
how many times, years ago, at book auctions, I found myself being bowled out of the game by one who proved to be
"Mr. H.," as he is known in the auction rooms.

I am writing this in Menton, in France. I have an engagement to dine this evening in Monte Carlo. Outside
my window I can hear the gentle splashing of the Mediter-
ranean Sea, darkly, deeply, beautifully blue; overhead a
cloudless blue sky. I began by saying that Mr. Hearst's
Cuesta Encantada reminded me of Monte Carlo, and each
time I visit the place, which is almost every day, the feeling
grows upon me that Mr. Hearst must have drawn some of
his inspiration therefrom. The principality of Monaco is
very tiny — all that Mr. Hearst can see for miles, and much
more, is his, and he shares it with his friends.

At Monte Carlo I cannot escape the feeling that there is a
very sordid world just around the corner; one has no such
feeling on the terrace of La Casa Grande. The walks, the
fountains, the flowers, the climate, all are perfect. No
thought of the outside world intrudes upon one; one is
loath to leave so perfect a spot, and has the feeling that he
might stay forever without inconveniencing anyone — and
is not this the height of hospitality?

Late one evening we sought our host and tried to tell him
how much we had enjoyed our visit. We said we should
be gone early next morning. Very simply we were asked
to come again. I think we never shall; such a visit is not
to be repeated, and it certainly is not to be forgotten.

It is, I think, generally agreed that a "petting party"
(which I cannot believe is, as some claim, a discovery of the
present generation — I think I saw traces of one in a tomb
in Egypt) is at its best when composed, as a honeymoon is,

of but two people. Be this as it may, four people is the
ideal number for a long motor ride. Two is not enough —
there is no one to act as referee in case of the almost certain
dispute; three throws the whole thing out of balance; four
is just right. And this was the number which early one
fine morning left San Simeon in a motor car capable of
doing one hundred miles an hour, but throttled down, at
Mrs. Nash's desire, to less than half that speed.

The distances, the excellent roads, and the fact that everyone in California has one motor, and most people two or
three, must have played and will continue to play havoc
with railway travel. Railways, except for the hauling of
heavy freight, have largely had their day, and magnificent
and costly terminals are an extravagance which they can no
longer afford. San Francisco was our objective, and our
ride, if long, was a pleasant one.

When, late in the afternoon, we entered the rooms which
had been engaged for us at the Fairmont Hotel, we found
them so banked with flowers that my first impulse was to
exclaim, "Where are the remains?" Prima donnas and
matinée idols are, no doubt, accustomed to such things, but
for a mere book-collector our reception was a head-turning
experience. The first thing I did on my return home was
to add a codicil to my will: "Please omit flowers; I had
mine in San Francisco." One hates an anticlimax, even
when one is dead.

Twenty minutes after our arrival, the telephone began to
ring, and it kept on ringing steadily until — and, no doubt,
after — our departure. When, in the providence of God,
I again go to the Pacific Coast, I shall take with me a telephone operator and a private secretary.

XII

ADVENTURES IN SAN FRANCISCO

FOR many years the very name of San Francisco was distasteful to me: it came about this way. At the advice of some wise banker friend, — I now know that there ain't no such animal, — I bought, paid for, and put away five hundred shares of United Railways of San Francisco preferred. Then, one fine day, when the news of the great disaster which destroyed that city reached us, I, believing that reports of the disaster were greatly exaggerated, sat idly by and watched my investment go to — well, I won't say where it went, but, as I have said, for some time afterward the name of that city gave me a severe pain. I had no wish to see it. Ultimately, my losses in other directions made me feel that my experience in San Francisco Railways was one of my happiest investments, and I yielded to the seductive invitation of my oldest friend, Willie Van Antwerp, — as he used to be called sixty years ago when we both lived in Rahway, New Jersey, — and trekked westward.

The first thing that strikes the visitor to San Francisco is the hills. The mountains that skipped like rams in the Bible having decided to settle down by the Golden Gate, the lambs — the little hills — naturally did the same thing, and in due course San Francisco resulted. The old city, before the earthquake and the following fire, is said to have been the most foreign, that is to say, the most picturesque city in the United States; most of this quality now has

departed, and what was less than a hundred years ago
merely a collection of huts and tents known as Yerba Buena
(good herb), and in 1906 was a ruin following an almost un-
paralleled disaster, in which fifteen hundred lives were lost
and a money damage of half a billion dollars inflicted, is
now a flourishing and finished city, so far as any American
city may be said to be finished. I suppose that if I had to
live in a finished city — like Bath, England, for example —
I should not like it for long; I know I should not. But
San Francisco, it seems to me, has struck the happy medium
between quiet dignity and the horrible turmoil of New
York.

I found at my hotel letters of greeting, invitations, and
cards giving me the privilege of several clubs. My hotel,
the Fairmont, being near the Pacific Union Club, I was
glad to avail myself of the courtesies of that magnificent
institution. The clubhouse is of cut brownstone which
came round the Horn years ago to form itself into the
palatial residence of a once famous citizen, "Jim Flood,"
as he was always called. But there is another club, even
more exclusive than the Pacific Union, although identified
with it, of which I promptly became an honorary member,
the "Hook and Eye Club." It is usually called to order at
five o'clock in the afternoon, with the following ritual:
"*Who can I* get to give me a drink?" Everyone feels personally addressed and gives the expected answer. Late
comers invariably put the same question as they enter,
receive the same answer, and presently all is as one would
have it in this, the best of all possible worlds. There is,
naturally, a long waiting list, and I was told of a sort of
Ladies' Auxiliary or Dorcas Society called the "Hook and
Ladder Club" — climbers, hoping to break in; but, verily,
it would be easier for a camel to go through the eye of a
needle. When I was in Los Angeles it affected to be "dry";

there was no affectation about San Francisco: it was, frankly, "wet," with liquor of the best. Prohibition there, as elsewhere, was an empty word, and, between the vintages of France and the excellent wine of the country, prohibition officers had no difficulty in making ends meet and, indeed, lap over. I never expected to live to see the tragic and expensive farce called prohibition legally ended; but this curse ended gives us hope for the amelioration of other political ills.

I lift my eyes unto the hills from whence cometh, not my help, but my fear. I shall never forget my first ride around the city in a motor car; we climbed a hill as steep as the wall of a room, reached the top, shot down to the bottom and up again, and so on for hours. I sat on the edge of my seat, my heart in my mouth, expecting every moment to be dashed to pieces. If I prayed, — and I fear I did, — my prayers were answered, for nothing happened; nothing ever did happen, Mrs. Willie Van Antwerp, who was at the wheel, assured me, but this must have been said to quiet my fears. Accidents must happen; perhaps, like hanging, one gets accustomed to them. Taxi drivers, I feel certain, delight in the anguish of their fares. Noticing a sign which read, THIS HILL IS DANGEROUS WHEN WET, — such signs are common, — I inquired, "Do you have many accidents?" "Oh, yes, frequently," was the reassuring answer, "but we don't mind 'em out here."

Few American cities have an atmosphere essentially their own, and for the most part those which have are not much to be envied. San Francisco has its own, and is proud of it; perhaps before the fire it had excess of it. Its location is superb, just within the Golden Gate, a narrow strait only a little more than a mile wide, over which a bridge is now being flung; this gives entrance to a bay of great extent. It is not curious that explorers cruising the Pacific missed

the entrance to the bay and that the site of the future city
was first discovered from the land side. What I knew,
chiefly, of the city up to the time of my arrival, I had
gathered from reading, many years ago, the sea classic,
Two Years before the Mast. It was not quite a hundred years
ago that Richard Henry Dana, then a student at Harvard,
for his health's sake shipped as a common sailor on the brig
Pilgrim bound round Cape Horn for California. The
book contains some of the earliest and best descriptions of
the state that we have, and although Dana's observations
were rather upon the southern than upon the central portion, — he seems not to have gone inland at all, — he
observes, prophetically, "If California ever becomes a prosperous country, this bay [of what is now San Francisco]
will be the centre of its prosperity."

Gold had not yet been discovered in California when
Dana made his voyage, and the chief products of the country
were hides and tallow, which were plentiful and cheap;
these were swapped for the manufactures of New England,
brought round the Horn in clipper ships, and the fortunes
of some of the best people in Boston were made in the trade.
Dana's experiences in curing and packing hides, his com-
ments upon the Catholic missions established by the
Spaniards, the crimes committed by the Indians, the
Mexicans, and, indeed, by all the peoples of the then Wild
West, make most interesting reading. Viewing California
to-day it is difficult for one to realize that in less than a
century lawlessness has been banished and magnificent and
prosperous cities have arisen in what was not long ago a
wilderness.

The word "California" aroused my curiosity, and, seeking information without conspicuous success in such books
of reference as I have, I finally wrote my friend Robert E.
Cowan, who is the great authority on the state's history, and

was enlightened, as I knew I would be. The origin of the word is obscure, but it is believed that when Balboa — "stout Cortez," as Keats called him in his famous sonnet (he should have said Balboa, for it was he who first saw the Pacific) — discovered Lower California in 1535 there was, in all probability, on board his vessel a romance, then of great popularity, but now wholly forgotten, one chapter of which was devoted to a description of a fabulous island called California, an island filled with Amazons, griffins, and the like, and of course with a plethora of jewels, gold, and silver. After his long cruise, Balboa, full of the romance of his expedition, is likely to have said, "This is indeed California." At all events, such are the facts first presented in an article which appeared in the *Atlantic Monthly* in 1864 by Edward Everett Hale, which have since that time been generally accepted.

Californians are justly proud of their state, which is the second largest in the Union, and in romantic interest stands first. We took it in whole or in part from the Mexicans, whom we thought either too lazy or too incompetent to administer it. It is not, and never was, what some of our Western states are: mere geographical expressions kicked into the Union for political reasons, as the King of England sometimes makes peers — for their votes. It came in as an empire and it remains a magnificent one. Inevitably it was destined to form the greater part of our Western frontier, extending as it does along the Pacific for almost a thousand miles. San Francisco looks through the Golden Gate upon the ocean and even more upon its great bay, on the opposite side of which are the cities of Berkeley, Oakland, and Alameda. On its own side of the bay and connected with it by superb motor roads are a dozen or more suburban towns down to Burlingame, all these tending to form — I hope I do not offend them — one great city, for it is as

certain that San Francisco will ultimately absorb them all
into herself as that Los Angeles will become a great seaport
or that London has already swallowed up a dozen or more
small villages.

A seaport has an advantage which no inland city, however great, can ever overcome.   As New York may be said
to be an outlying gate to Europe, so San Francisco, Los
Angeles, and Seattle may be said to be the frontier of Asia.
What may not the future hold in store for these great cities?
It was because Mr. Huntington asked himself this question
and answered it to his satisfaction that he gave so liberally
to Los Angeles.   He took stock of its climate, which, if you
like it, — and it is a form of treason not to, — he found
better than that of San Francisco.   San Francisco has rain
and fog; but these are responsible for the enormous fertility
of the vast valleys which extend for hundreds of miles to the
south and east of the city and are connected with it by rail,
road, and boat, so that San Francisco is indeed the heart
of the state, the more so since a range of mountains, the
Sierras, forming practically its eastern edge throughout its
entire length, keeps the climate where it belongs.   Beyond
the mountains is the desert state of Nevada, with its population of less than 100,000 people chiefly employed in watching the growth of wild cactus and the intellectual antics of
still wilder Senators.   No one ever hears or thinks of Nevada
unless one of its Senators lets out a yell to "do something
for silver."

Why should I bother myself and my reader with these
details?   Everyone knows them; but not everyone has
motored or traveled by train, as I have, mile after mile
through orange groves of California, hundreds of thousands
of acres of them interspersed with orchards of peach and
plum and apricot and other fruit-bearing trees, all in such
perfect cultivation and order that one from the East has

almost a longing for that miserable and disgraceful stretch of country which is the hinterland of Hoboken and Jersey City and forms the approach to Camden, New Jersey. And the fertile areas of California can be extended indefinitely; water will do it, and the scientific management of water is not difficult these days. "By their fruits ye shall know them" — yea, verily, but what about trees that have no fruit on them? My visit to California was chiefly to see two men: one my oldest friend, William C. Van Antwerp, and another my next oldest, Canon Laurence B. Ridgely, a dignitary of the Church ("believe it or not") — and one other thing: the great trees, the redwoods, which are perhaps the oldest living things on this planet. If Van Antwerp had not, by good chance, happened to be hand in glove with A. Stanwood Murphy and Donald Mac-Donald of the Pacific Lumber Company, I should not have been able to see them so abundantly. As it is, I feel that the great trees are my personal friends — if an atom of my size and age may have for friends giants of the age of five or six thousand years. I have heard it said that individual specimens of the eucalyptus in Australia are taller and that some of the cypresses of Mexico are older than our own redwoods, but I have seen the redwoods and am content.

I am a worm, — a bookworm, — I know nothing of trees; and this paper, when published in the *Atlantic* a year ago, brought down upon me a flood of letters in which pretty much every statement I then made was challenged. I confused, evidently, — many people do, — the *Sequoia gigantea* with the *Sequoia sempervirens*. Someone writes to tell me that "the former is the larger and more colorful of the species, the latter is the more graceful and presents a more massed forest effect." Good! I 'm glad to know it. Someone had previously told me that, owing to the aromatic quality of the wood of these trees, birds and insects shunned them; I did not see any insects or hear any birds, and I repeated what I had been told; whereupon Mrs. Emerson Wallace, of Wheaton, Illinois, promptly sent me a list of twenty-seven birds which she had observed in a few hours, adding that there were more. I said that the groves belonging to the Pacific Lumber Company were better cared for than the groves belonging to the nation, and instantly the Superintendent of the Sequoia Parks was in my hair. He is very proud of the manner in which the Big Tree groves of the Yosemite and Sequoia and General Grant National Parks are cared for. More good news! He extends me a very courteous invitation to be his guest the next time I visit California. (Thank you, Mr. John R. White; I shall hold you to this. No doubt Mr. A. Stanwood Murphy, President of the Pacific Lumber Company, will be glad to release me.)

I hope I am safe in saying that we had only been in San Francisco a few days when an invitation arrived from Mr. Murphy to go with him by train to Scotia, a night's ride to the north, there to spend a week-end in the Director's Cottage, where men and motors would be placed at our disposal. How glad we were to accept this invitation I need not say. We were a party of six, and our hosts were men who had spent their lives with and among the trees. First let me say that there are two — there may be more, but we saw two — famous groups of trees: one then belonging to the Pacific Lumber Company, several hundred miles north of San Francisco, and another, the Sierra Grove, a national park about a hundred and fifty miles almost due east of the city, through which one may pass as one enters the Yosemite; this latter contains the largest and oldest trees.

As with the Grand Canyon of the Colorado, everyone who has seen these great trees has described them, and yet

one feels how futile one's attempt must be.   I have already
referred to their great age.   When I was a boy I was taught
that the world is about fifty-seven hundred years old.   If
my early training was correct, these trees, then, may be
older than the world, which adds greatly to their interest.
They grow to thirty-odd feet in diameter, a hundred in
circumference, and three hundred and fifty feet high, and
perhaps two hundred and fifty feet to the first branch.
But such figures mean nothing, and if my reader hates
them as much as I do he will be glad to have done with
them.   I asked a question.   By what known means in
mechanics is the sap lifted to the tops of these trees?   I put
this question to Mr. Murphy, who gave it up and told me
he would inquire from one who ought to know.   As a
result, a gentleman unknown to me developed a number
of interesting theories, wrote learnedly to me of "transpi-
ration pull and water cohesion" and even so far forgot the
ignorance of the man to whom he was writing as to describe
a process which he called "osmosis," finally confessing that
authorities differed — as is the invariable rule with experts
in every walk of life.   It has been said that if all the economists were laid end to end they would reach round the
world, but not a conclusion.

For their immense size the roots of these great trees are
small and do not extend many feet into the earth, so that
they are easily overturned.   The trees are, for the most
part, as straight as an arrow and their bark is thick and
rough, almost ragged; one knows, of course, that they are
"evergreens."   There is an almost unearthly quiet in these
noble forests; the trees stand close together like the col-
umns of a cathedral of endless extent; the branching
boughs, far overhead, form the roof of the great basilica in
which there is absolute silence — it is a place for reverie.
"The groves were God's first temples," and these trees may

be His last, for they are growing still, and, seemingly, can withstand anything except fire. Against this they have no protection, and it is sometimes pitiful to see a grand tree or group of trees which has been almost destroyed by that element. I think I am safe in saying that the wood of these trees is free from decay. This is proved in many ways. For example, a tree for some reason falls to the earth; presently, by some means, a sapling gets astride of it and takes root; finally the sapling becomes a tree, growing one half on one side of the fallen giant, the other half on the other. Does the fallen tree decay? No fear. After centuries — for the age of a tree can be told to a nicety by its rings (a ring for every year of its life) — the wood of the fallen tree is as sound as ever, and some day, maybe, foresters will come along and saw away the fallen log on either side of the standing tree. Several such examples or specimens were pointed out to me. Of what good is the lumber? Well, in one town through which we passed we saw a good-sized church built of the timber cut from one tree. Where great strength is not required the redwood may be used for any purpose for which lumber is suitable; it is especially good for clapboards of houses, for shingles, and for cigar boxes.

I have said that the largest trees, the Grisly Giant and others named after our famous men, are not those of the Bull Creek Flat through which I was conducted under such distinguished patronage, but in another grove southeast of San Francisco. While I was in Scotia, negotiations were just about completed by which a portion of the holdings of the Pacific Lumber Company were being taken over by the "Save-the-Redwoods League," to be preserved for the public forever. Towards the fund necessary to obtain a tract of over thirteen thousand acres, John D. Rockefeller, Jr., with his usual generosity, contributed two million dol-

THE REDWOOD HIGHWAY

lars, and various organizations, including the Garden Clubs of America, gave or pledged substantial sums, and finally the great object was achieved. My friends of the Pacific Lumber Company were in a difficult position; they had, as officers of a corporation, a duty towards their stockholders, and they had also a duty towards the public, who insisted that no more trees be cut. The "Save-the-Redwoods League" was much helped by public declarations of men in every walk of life. It is never difficult to get a man to declare that another man should surrender his property; our legislators in Washington spend most of their time in so doing. Much eloquence was expended over the big trees; Sam Blythe said this, and Professor Campbell said that, Dr. Crawford this and Joe Hergesheimer that, until finally the effort was successful and the redwoods were saved. Joe, who is a neighbor of mine, and slings a very flowery pen upon occasion, let himself go very effectively. He said: —

Standing in this grove of redwoods, I thought of the bitter and vain resentment that the future — when it had learned that commerce was not enough to keep the heart alive — would hold against the past, our present. The grace of the towering trees masked their gigantic span; the ground, in perpetual shadow, held only flowering oxalis and emerald ferns. It was raining very softly. The fallen trunks of an utter remoteness, too great to see over, were green with moss. The whisper of the wind was barely audible, far off, reflective; the gloom in the trees was clear, wet, yet mild. It was the past. And this was the redwoods' secret, their special magic, that they absolved, blotted out, the fever of time, the wasted years, the sickness of mind, in which men spend the loneliness of their lives.

It was a long pull and a strong pull and a pull all together, but after ten years' effort the thing was done; the redwoods were saved and the world is the richer therefor.

Nothing on this continent is so well worth a visit.   I shall
never forget the great trees of California.

The Yosemite is, roughly, one hundred and fifty miles
east of San Francisco.   One uses the phrase, "*seeing* the
Grand Canyon," but one refers to "*going into* the Yosemite."
Both phrases are properly descriptive.   There are indeed
two Yosemites — the *park*, which contains about eleven
hundred square miles, and the *valley*, which may contain
ten.   It is the valley which people usually refer to as the
park.   Through this valley flows a turbulent stream, but
this stream, drawing hundreds of little rivulets into itself,
finally becomes the Merced River, which is responsible for
the magnificence of the surrounding scenery.   Look at it
to-day and one would not suppose that it was once capable, with the assistance of an earthquake or two, of cutting
its way to the depth of thousands of feet through hundreds
of miles of the toughest granite.   The valley which it has
scooped out and the meadow which it has formed are now
level and park-like.   The broad and well-kept lawns are
interrupted by drives and walks bordered with flowers.
There are several excellent hotels, hundreds of cottages,
and several well-patronized camps which, under government restrictions, may be enjoyed by the public.   The
lovely and beautiful oasis, this modern tempe, was discovered as recently as 1851, when a small military force in
pursuit of some marauding Indians was unexpectedly led
into it.   Its great magnificence, however, is the granite
walls which enclose the valley on all sides except where the
river has its outlet, by the side of which a road has been
made.   One *enters* the Yosemite after a long day's motoring; a turn or two in the road, and through a great portal
of towering rock one comes upon a scene of unexampled
peace and beauty.   The craggy rocks which encircle the

valley are of such stupendous size as to form individual mountains of granite, sometimes worn smooth by the action of the elements, elsewhere forming lodgment for great trees which are so far above the spectator that they appear to be mere shrubs.   Who that has seen the great sheer silvery mass, El Capitan, over three thousand feet in height, or the Three Brothers, or Sentinel Rock, or the Bridal Veil Fall, nine hundred feet high, will ever forget its beauty?   I visited the Yosemite in the spring when the vegetation was rich and luxuriant;   I should like to visit it in the winter: I should like to see the immense dark fir trees when covered with snow.   Our national parks are a magnificent inheritance.   They are each year enjoyed by thousands and they will be enjoyed by increasing thousands as the years roll on.   California — the whole nation — is singularly blessed in having such noble recreation grounds.

Upon our return to San Francisco a life of dissipation was inevitable.   The hospitality of California is famous; one has, perhaps, some claim upon one's friends, but I was constantly meeting a stranger whom I left a friend.   Californians have a genius for friendship;   the names of Albert Bender, the distinguished, kindly, and generous art patron, and Alfred Sutro, a busy lawyer who "knocked off" an entire day to drive me down to his home in the country, instantly occur to me.   Van Antwerp devoted to us an entire week;   would a stockbroker in New York have done so?   His kindness can only be acknowledged, it can never be repaid.   I think of Flodden W. Heron, a kindly man named after a battle, but why mention individuals when so many were ready and seemingly anxious to show their boundless hospitality and goodwill?   I can quite understand the hospitality of "the Coast" overwhelming the visitor from a foreign land.   Not knowing how to account for it, he finally comes to accept it as his due, whereas it is merely the spontaneous expression of kindliness which he probably does not deserve.

Everyone knows, I take it, of the Bohemian Club; its "high jinks" are famous the world over. In the summer these take place in a grove of immense trees some distance from the city; at other seasons the clubhouse is the scene of its hospitalities. It honored me with a dinner at which over three hundred men were present, Edward F. O'Day, Sire of the Club, in the chair. The Bohemians are presumed to be interested in literature, art, music, and the drama; and men possessing among them all the talents brought them forth for my amusement and edification — but modesty forbids that I should enlarge upon the gayety of the evening other than to say that, had not Father Time screwed my head on pretty tight, it would have been turned. Richard O'Connor, a man then unknown to me, read what purported to be a characteristic letter from Dr. Johnson to me, and there was a clever skit in which Dr. Rosenbach was seen in a new light — that is, *giving* valuable books away, something he very seldom does. The menu was a work of art, the humor of which was supplied by Jimmy Hatlo, whose sketches burlesquing the titles of several of my books I shall never look upon without a smile. Towards midnight an old friend of the Lambs, in New York, whom I had not seen in years, came up and, grasping my hand, said, "Well, Newton, it was a rotten, highbrow evening and I hope it will be a long time before we have another. The next time you come, come in the summer and we 'll do something to entertain you."

The Book Club of California, of which Alfred Sutro is president, cut out a small job for me which I hope I did creditably. My Eastern complacency was sadly disturbed by the range and intensity of the interest shown in everything that concerns itself with literature and with books; this goes far to explain why it is that printing is an art that flourishes in California as it hardly does elsewhere in our country.

And this leads me to speak of the Grabhorn Brothers, printers of books which are works of art. I had known of their work, of course, but the men themselves I had not met until I reached San Francisco, and I was especially pleased to renew my acquaintance with John Henry Nash, whom I had entertained at Oak Knoll. Nash is an Old World craftsman whom chance has let fall into the City of the Golden Gate, and the text "A prophet is not without honor save in his own city" does not apply to him — he is honored of all men.

Some years ago the Book Club of California asked me if it might not print for its members some essay of mine not before printed, and I, conscious of the honor done me, replied that if and when I had anything I thought suitable I would present it to the Club, provided John Henry Nash would print it. And so it happened that when I had to read a paper at Lichfield, England, upon the occasion of my election as president of the Johnson Society, it at once occurred to me that my address might be suitable for publication by the Club. So, immediately after reading the paper in the Guildhall at Lichfield, I sent it to Flodden Heron, the fine Scotsman whom I have already referred to, and in due course a large, handsomely printed volume of not too many pages appeared, *Mr. Strahan's Dinner Party.* I have the permission of the Book Club of California to reprint this paper in this volume, but my diffident nature will not permit me to print the much too flattering introduction by Mr. Edward F. O'Day.

I was, of course, greatly pleased to be printed by such a man as Nash, and the correspondence about the book led

to our better acquaintance. It is characteristic of Nash's
thoughtfulness and generosity that he had two copies of the
book sent to a famous binder in Germany and there bound
in royal white vellum, in such a manner that the binding
will never warp, as vellum bindings usually do. One copy
he presented to me; the other, also signed by him, he gave
to the library in the Johnson Birthplace at Lichfield. I
must not say that Nash's sole interest in life is printing, for
he has a beautiful wife and a home in Berkeley than which
nothing could be lovelier. It is situated on the brow of a
high hill; from the front porch one overlooks the wide bay
with San Francisco in the distance, while from the back
terrace one looks down into a valley with a range of mountains beyond. It can hardly be that because all my life
I have longed for a view, and have been obliged to content
myself with looking upon a bank on the top of which
runs the Pennsylvania Railroad, I think Nash's site so
superb. He had, however, two ideas in mind when he
selected the spot and erected his house: one was to make
it a home for the time being; ultimately it was to become
a small and intimate museum to house his collection of
printed books, of which any man might be proud. These
books are now housed in an exhibition room adjoining his
printing house, and it was in this room and the room adjoining that he gave us a reception to which many of the
important people in the city were invited — and came, not
so much to honor us as to show their goodwill to John,
who is more an institution than an individual.

Nash is now engaged upon a printing venture which will
tax all his resources, financial and other; it is no less than
a magnificent edition of the Vulgate, the Latin text, which
will be carefully read under the direction of the Roman
Catholic Bishop of California, for John, though not himself a Catholic, stands high in the favor of the Catholic

Church. This great Bible, in Latin, has not found a proper printer in a century. It will be a magnificent publication in several volumes, superbly bound: the price is a thousand dollars per set. When I heard of the launching of this noble enterprise I sent in my subscription by telegraph; not because I feared I should get left, but because such a venture should be encouraged — especially in times like these. It would not be fair not to mention the fact that Nash owes much to the scholarship of Eddie O'Day and to the high artistic ability of William Wilke, who designs his exquisite borders, his illuminated letters, and occasionally etches a portrait.

Dr. Johnson once spoke highly of a man because he never passed a church without raising his hat. I am moved by no such impulse, but I never, if I can help it, pass a library without having a look, and the Library of the University of California pleased me greatly. I have no knowledge how the library itself compares with that of Stanford University. I was told that the standard of scholarship at Berkeley is not as high as it is at Palo Alto, but I have also been told that scholarship at Palo Alto is not as high as at Berkeley; I know nothing about it. Certainly the atmosphere at Berkeley is delightful and I was glad to meet once more my old friend Dr. Richard T. Holbrook, whom I used to know so well when he was professor of Romance languages at Bryn Mawr. By chance Holbrook was dining with us on that fateful Sunday in August, 1914, when news came that the German armies had entered Belgium and that Liége was being bombarded. We were all very much excited; he spoke of a pronouncement of Gaston Paris, a famous French savant, on science, which occurred in his lecture on *La Chanson de Roland* delivered in Paris on the eighth of December, 1870, and subsequently

gave me a translation of it.   The city was at the time being
shelled by the Germans, and patriotism had once again
fallen into one of its frequent conflicts with truth.   The
passage is Holbrook's creed and should be that of every
scholar: —

In general, I do not believe that patriotism has any cause for a
conflict with science.   University chairs are not rostrums; it is
turning them away from their real destination to make them serve
for the defense or the attack of anything outside of their intellectual aim.   I profess absolutely and without reservation this
doctrine, that science has no other object than the truth, and the
truth for its own sake, without any care as to the consequences,
good or bad, regrettable or fortunate, which that truth might
have in practice.   He who through a patriotic motive, religious,
and even moral, allows himself in the facts that he is studying, in
the conclusions that he draws, the least concealment, the slightest
alteration, is not worthy of holding his place in the great laboratory where probity is a claim for admission more indispensable
than skill.   Thus understood, the studies that we share, carried
on with the same spirit in all civilized countries, form, above
nationalities which are restricted, diverse, and too often hostile, a
great fatherland which no war soils, which no conqueror threat-
ens, and in which men's souls find the refuge and the unity that
the City of God has given them in other times.

I was interested to see this passage in its original French,
illuminated and framed, hanging over my old friend's desk
at Berkeley.   The attitude of the two score or more German college professors was very different — this group of
donkeys who at the crack of the Emperor's whip set down
their names to a silly document to the effect that Germany
did not begin the War, that the Fatherland was invaded
and they were only fighting in self-defense.   They had
completely forgotten the often-repeated doctrine to which
they had once subscribed, — the doctrine of Bernhardi and

of Treitschke, — that "war is the supreme expression of the energy of the state, and that nations owe it to themselves to create enemies whom they must fight in order to perfect and develop their own characters."

The University at Berkeley is fortunate in its location. From its wooded hills it overlooks the fine Bay of San Francisco, and the architecture of its buildings suggests considered growth rather than sudden creation. At Leland Stanford, I found the yellow stone walls and the red-tiled roofs of its buildings, under a glaring sun, monotonous and fatiguing. Stone walls do not a prison make — nor universities, and all our universities are too large by half. We used to believe that education was the solution of all our difficulties; we know now that it too frequently augments them. When one looks at the news in our papers one feels it is a pity that so many boys and girls have been taught to read.

There is much to be seen in San Francisco; it is a real, self-contained city, not so much in size or population as in character, in individuality. I do not speak of its night life, of which I know nothing, or of its Chinatown, which does not interest me. Its streets and shops and people have a metropolitan character which seems to be lacking in Los Angeles. In one shop I saw an exhibition of sculpture which had only recently been brought from French Indo-China. Where else in the world, save in London, and perhaps in New York, could such a collection be seen? For delicacy and sheer beauty I have never seen anything lovelier than the sandstone heads and busts and figures which date from the twelfth century, or earlier, and in no museum in the world could such art objects be more admirably displayed. I visited the bookshops, of course, and bought from John Howell a silver teapot which had once

been Charles Dickens's, with an unexceptional provenance
— and in such matters I bring to bear an amount of skep-
ticism which is not easily quieted.   I had hoped to see my
friend Mr. Templeton Crocker, to whom for many courtesies I am indebted, but he was making a scientific cruise
around the world in his yacht, the *Zaca*, and his magnificent apartment, which my daughter tells me is alone worth
the journey across the continent to see, was closed to me.

The City by the Golden Gate has suffered or enjoyed
one bonanza after another, each very different in kind, but
all money-producing; it is the centre of an empire of its
own.   A century ago it was hides and tallow.   Wild or
half-broken horses roamed the plains and were practically
valueless; a man caught or borrowed one, rode it till it
dropped, and then for a dollar got another; later they
were practically exterminated to make way for cattle.
Then came the gold rush, with its evils and its romances.
This was followed by an era of cattle-raising on such a
scale as only we in America (and perhaps Australia) know
anything of.   In 1876, California had over seven million
sheep alone.   Then came wheat and barley, and now
FRUIT, including grapes and nuts.   "God smiles on California."   It is her boast that she can supply the entire
world with fruit, and as one rolls for hundreds of miles over
matchless roads through orchards devoted to growing, under seemingly ideal conditions, every fruit one can put a
name to, and many that one (this one) cannot, this boast
would seem to be well founded.   The climate of California,
which enables one to grow practically anything, makes the
people, women as well as men, an out-of-doors, pleasure-
loving folk.   Men go fishing and hunting to an extent unknown to us of the East.   Life seems much more generous,
much less complicated than with us.   Golf clubs desired to
extend their hospitality and I was obliged to confess that

I loathed the game.   As I look back upon an afternoon at the Cypress Point Golf Club at Pebble Beach I begin to feel that in my busy life I have neglected two important things: golf and cards.   "To play cards is to speak an international language" — so says my friend Ellis Ames Ballard; and, by the way, he speaks it very fluently.   I have no smattering of it and am too old to learn.

I now understand the objection that Californians have to being called Westerners.   They want to be Californians and I don't blame them.   The illiterates of the middle states would impose their crudities upon the world.   Despite the evidence of science, there are people in Kentucky who believe that the account of the creation of the world in Genesis is the correct one.   Do they care that as a result of the "noble experiment," prohibition, — as to the merits of which Mr. Hoover, who hails from Iowa, was never able to make up his mind, — neither life nor property is safe in this country, and that civilized Europeans look upon our lawlessness with horror and amazement?   Not they.   It does not move them that the most popular plays in London are those which depict, and on the whole not unfairly, our life over here.   *Late Night Final* shows the workings of a tabloid newspaper in New York.   *On the Spot* is a melodrama of the rum ring in Chicago.   *The Shame of a Nation* I have not seen.   I do not have to — it is only too evident; we are three thousand miles of disorderly monotony relieved by crime.   Self-satisfaction and intolerance are, I had almost said, a national characteristic.   Listen to this bit of evidence: —

The Automobile Club of Southern California recently called attention to the minutes of a meeting of the leading citizens of Denison, Iowa, in 1906, at which the "horseless carriage" was loudly denounced and owners of such vehicles were warned to keep off the highways.   It was stated that "the object of the

meeting was to organize and agree not to trade with anybody who
owned an automobile nor anybody who drove one or hired a man
who used one, and further that they should not vote for any man
for judge or legislator who would not agree to use his influence to
abolish the machines from the highways."

It is just one hundred years ago that George Bancroft,
in his monumental *History of the United States,* wrote: "It is
the object of the present work to follow the steps by which
a favoring Providence, calling our institutions into being,
has conducted this country to its present happiness and
glory." Would a historian writing to-day refer to our
present happiness and glory? Hardly. But it is folly to
generalize, as I am prone to do, about so large a country
as the United States. Edmund Burke has said the last
word on the subject, in a famous remark usually mis-
quoted: "I do not know the method of drawing up an
indictment against a whole people." A cultivated European gentleman remarked to me, in speaking of the Middle
West, "Make no mistake: I have never heard more stim-
ulating conversation than in the small city of Topeka."
And there drifts to my desk, as I write, the programme of
a celebration of the two hundred and twenty-fifth anniversary of the birth of Samuel Johnson, held in the Kansas
State College. Where in the East was such a celebration
held?

XIII

VIENNA AND I

MANY years ago someone inquired of the wisest man in
England, Mr. Punch, whether or not to marry. Punch's
reply is brief and historic: "DON'T." But it is not of
record that there were fewer marriages that year, and it
may well be that in some form or other marriage has come
to stay. Now, were a man to come to me for advice, I
would say, "If you are marrying for the long pull, look the
girl's mother over carefully, and if you like what you see
and can't possibly control your emotions, go ahead."
This, at any rate, is the advice I gave myself, and I do not
regret taking it. A more amiable, generous, and charming little woman never lived than my mother-in-law —
and she was a Viennese. She was always planning some
little pleasure for me or my friends, and someone had early
told her, or she may have discovered the fact for herself,
that the way to a man's heart is through the stomach. Be
this as it may, from the day I became engaged, almost to
the day of her death, she fed me with toothsome dainties
which seemed especially designed to destroy a good diges-
tion and to distort a once faultless figure.

Thus emotionally predisposed to Vienna, I first went to
that city many years ago — and I hated it. It was in mid-
winter and the weather was awful. I went to the Bristol,
a very expensive hotel; it was almost deserted, for the
court was in half-mourning owing to a scandal in which
some demirep relative of the Emperor had been discovered.

The streets of Vienna are not crowded at night as the streets of other great cities. There is plenty of "night life," but it goes on behind closed doors; how the people get from one place to another I have never discovered.

In some way or other I had caught a bad cold in the Liechtenstein Gallery — which I remember as a palace with miles of concrete passages carpeted with cocoa matting, full of pictures of doubtful authenticity — and one evening I left my hotel to go in search of a drug store. I found one, but it was closed. I did not then know, what I have since been told, that it is customary in Vienna, when a drug store closes, for the proprietor to affix to the door a small sign, giving the address of the nearest shop likely to be open. But I saw no such sign, nor could I have read it if I had. And incidentally I might say that in foreign cities a chemist shop is by no means a small department store and a "quick lunch" establishment, as with us, but a small and dignified place where drugs are compounded and sold, the proprietor of which looks upon himself, not as a tradesman, but almost as a gentleman of science. I looked elsewhere, wandering here and there, and lost my way; it came on to rain, there was no one on the streets to direct me, and I could not find a cab; at last, drenched to the skin, I reached my hotel, went to bed in a huff, and the next morning I took a train direct to London!

It is quite a jump from Vienna to London, and by the time I got there my cold was better, my anger had cooled, and I was not exactly proud of my behavior. I had intended to break the journey home (to London, that is) by short stays in Munich, Frankfort, Cologne, and Antwerp, but in my disgust I went right slapdash through to the Hook of Holland and Harwich. And so it was that whenever I heard Vienna mentioned — coupled always with a glowing description of its interest and beauty, the charm and hospitality of its men, and the beauty and style of its women — I felt that I owed it to myself to go back to Vienna and behave like a human being.

And in this frame of mind on a fine spring morning I found myself riding, in a comfortable taxi, along what the guidebooks call Vienna's "Girdle of Splendor" — the Ringstrasse — to my hotel, this time the Imperial.

And now I am going to set down, rather to clarify my own mind than to enlighten my reader, what I seem to remember of the history of what came to be called Austria. When Gibbon's Roman Empire came to an end, — whenever that was, — ultimately another Empire came into existence, called the Holy Roman Empire; it was, as some historian has taken pains to point out, neither holy, nor Roman, nor an empire, but let that pass. It sought to rule what we now call Holland and Belgium, a part of what is now France and Germany, and all of what was, until the World War, Austria and Spain. And be it remembered that at that time Spain, except for a narrow strip bordering upon the North Atlantic, dominated the New World. It was some empire! There was then no Italy; what is now Italy was a mess of small kingdoms or republics fighting merrily among themselves, the Popes seeing to it that they never were at peace for long. The Hapsburgs of Austria were at this time one of the oldest families in Europe "already," as a German would say. The founder, Rudolf, a German Count out of Switzerland, had been elected back in the twelve hundreds King of the Germans; this entitled him to the crown of Austria. The Pope looked complacently upon this election, and the Pope then was the ruler not only of the spiritual but also of the temporal world, which interested him most. I am looking back to the time when Henry VIII sat upon the throne of

England, when Francis I ruled France, and Charles V the
rest of Europe. I think of Charles V as the greatest emperor of modern times.

Dr. Johnson, in his *Vanity of Human Wishes*, says, —

> Let observation with extensive view
> Survey mankind, from China to Peru, —

to which I, not being a poet, would observe: "He will sur-
vey chiefly water." But Charles V observed mankind
from the Danube to Peru from his youth until his fifty-
sixth year, when, in disgust, he gave up the job, remarking
that as he was unable to make *men* go as he wanted them
to, he intended to devote his declining years to seeing what
he could do with *clocks*. Presently the Hapsburgs ceased
to be warriors as we understand the term, and sought and
succeeded in dominating Europe by marriage rather than
by war. To be sure, a few hundred thousand people —
common people — were destroyed annually for the amusement of their rulers, but what of it? They were but can-
non fodder, anyhow. Enter now Napoleon. Up to his
time war was the summer sport of kings. With cold
weather the various armies went into such hiding as they
could find and devoted themselves to vice; but he changed
all that. The Austrian generals, to whom he devoted his
attention for some years, complained, bitterly, of his methods. "It is magnificent," they said, "but it is not war."
Their idea was to strut around on foot or on horseback in
the most magnificent and costly costumes that could be
designed by men who devoted their entire lives to the study
of contrast in color and in material. Officers were fitted
out like targets, not for bullets, but for women's eyes. So
it is that Austria has few generals of distinction — her
greatest soldier was an Italian, Prince Eugene of Savoy.
Except his, she has few victories to celebrate; her tri-

umphs were the triumphs of diplomacy — that is to say, of chicane. One exception there was to all this: Maria Theresa. She was magnificent; she was Austria's Queen Elizabeth.

We are taking our history at a hop, skip, and jump; come we now to the last real Austrian statesman — Prince Metternich. He completely dominated Continental politics from the overthrow of Napoleon to the revolution of 1848. Napoleon, after fighting and practically conquering all Europe, — except Britain, — had divorced Josephine and married Maria Louisa, the daughter of the proudest man in Europe, the Austrian Emperor. By her he had a son to whom the title of King of Rome was given. But Napoleon had come to the end of his tether; all Europe rose against him; and in 1814, in Paris, practically surrounded by enemies, he threw up the sponge and retired to Elba, being allowed the sovereignty of that island.

Then came the Congress of Vienna. It was a magnificent affair. Rulers from petty kinglets to truly royal Emperors came and brought their friends — especially their lady friends. Balls and parties were continuous and superb. For twenty-five years Europe had lain under the shadow of Bonaparte; he had fought all Europe, in his own original manner; now he had abdicated and was practically a prisoner on the Island of Elba. All was going swimmingly when, suddenly, he returned, and the Congress broke up in disorder; the delegates ran to their homes like rabbits. Then followed the "Hundred Days" and Waterloo, after which the great man, in a letter which I have seen framed and hanging in the library of Windsor Castle, "surrendered to the King of England, the most powerful and generous of my enemies." Powerful, yes; generous, hardly. At any rate the English took no further chances with their distinguished prisoner; they packed him off to St. Helena and he disappears from the record, and Metternich became practically Prime Minister of Europe. What did he want? First of all, he wanted peace, and, second, he wanted to destroy Italy. "Italy!" he cried. "There is no such country. Italy is merely a geographical expression!" The thorn thus planted with such care rankled for over a century until, at the comparatively recent Congress of Versailles, Signor Orlando extracted it and poured in oil and wine, in the shape of provinces which had long been a part of Austria.

Next Metternich wanted to dominate Germany, and as far as possible to dictate the policies of Russia and Spain; for France he made as much trouble as he could — he was for fifteen years virtually her ruler. There remained the son of Napoleon; what to do with him was a problem. Taught to play with toy soldiers from his babyhood, he looked forward eagerly to the time when as a man he could play with armies, as his father had done. As soon as he was old enough Metternich decided that he was to be fed to the ladies, or ladies fed to him; they were many, beautiful and amiable. For the sake of Europe it was probably the best thing that could have been done. At twenty he died — of consumption, it was said. Metternich smiled when he was told. One of the ladies with whom the boy fell passionately in love was the Archduchess Sophia, wife of the Archduke, who was successor to the throne. She was a beautiful young woman only three years older than he, but childless. Soon after it was observed that their relations were cordial she became the mother of a son, and this son became our old friend, the Emperor Franz Josef, and it was whispered that the father was the young Napoleon. This is gossip, not history, but accidents will happen in the best-regulated families — and the Royal House of Austria was one of the worst.

THE DUKE OF REICHSTADT

From a miniature by M. M. Daffinger

The young Napoleon — Napoleon II, as the Bonapartists called him, christened Napoleon Francis Charles Joseph, subsequently called the King of Rome, who died the Duke of Reichstadt and whom we know best, perhaps, as L'Aiglon, "the Eaglet" — grew to be one of the handsomest young men in the Austrian court. His death was a great relief to all Europe, and I am told that some of these days the small bronze coffin which contains his ashes will be given by the Austrians, in exchange for something valuable, to the French, who will put it in a proper sarcophagus which will be placed in the Invalides at the foot of the porphyry tomb of his great father. If this comes about, there will be another magnificent state funeral — another *Second Funeral of Napoleon* which will call for the pen of another Thackeray. It will be remembered that the author of *Vanity Fair* described the placing of the ashes of the great Emperor "upon the banks of the Seine in the midst of the French people whom he loved so dearly." That neither the father nor the son was French makes no difference to the French people, who dearly love a spectacle.

To a thoughtful man a place of sepulchre is always interesting, whether it be a simple country churchyard, magnificent Beauchamp Chapel in the parish church at Warwick, or the Poets' Corner in Westminster Abbey. The crypt in the Capuchin Church, which for several hundred years has been the burial place of the Hapsburgs and their consorts, is entered from a court which runs off a busy thoroughfare in the heart of the old city. Passing up the court, one comes upon what appears to be a dignified entrance to a cellar. A group of people are standing about as though waiting for something to happen. Presently it does — a door opens, people come out; a line forms and a number of people pay a shilling to a monk, file in, and descend a flight of stone steps. At the bottom is a large vault or series of vaults or chambers, irregular in size, shape, and decoration. As one becomes accustomed to the dull light, one observes bronze sarcophagi standing all around one, in well-ordered confusion. Some are merely bronze boxes, others are of immense size like gigantic inkstands, elaborately wrought; the effect is very curious.

The stone coffins of the Kings of France, in the Church of St. Denis, in Paris, are empty shells; the French mobs have wreaked their vengeance upon them. The coffins in the Capuchin Church contain the remains of Emperors, good and bad, — if any good there were, — of Empresses and Archdukes, undisturbed, awaiting what? The last trumpet, it is customary to say. The most elaborate sarcophagus is that of Maria Theresa, Austria's greatest ruler, next to Charles V, who is buried in Spain. But to me the most moving of all is the small plain bronze box in which reposes all that is mortal of the Duke of Reichstadt. And one remembers that Napoleon said that "he would rather see his son strangled than brought up in an Austrian court." How constantly the romance of the Corsican rushes in upon one! A few weeks before, I had visited, for the first time, his birthplace in Ajaccio. In a few weeks I shall again see the magnificent tomb in Paris of the greatest and most contemptible man of modern times, in the Invalides. Where is Josephine, his first wife, buried? I wonder. Here is the coffin of his second wife, Maria Louisa, who, born an Archduchess, became Empress of France and died the wife of her chamberlain, Count Neipperg, after having been his mistress. Here, too, is the sarcophagus of the Emperor Maximilian, — of Mexico, of all places, — and that of the murdered Empress Elizabeth and her son, Crown Prince Rudolph, whose suicide, if it was suicide, is still discussed. As one ascends the steps and comes out into the street to be buffeted by the traffic of to-day, one murmurs to

oneself, "The boast of heraldry, the pomp of power,"
and the rest of it.   How true it is!

From Waterloo to 1848 there was such peace as Europe
is accustomed to; then came the revolution which drove
Metternich into exile and unseated a weak and vacillating
Emperor, Ferdinand; and Franz Josef, a young and handsome boy, ascended the throne which he was to occupy,
uneasily, for sixty-eight years.   His reign, one of the longest
in history, was packed with horrors, and when he died, in
the midst of the World War, the Austrian Empire practically came to an end and a part of Gibbon's magnificent
prophecy came true.   "The romance of *Tom Jones*, that
exquisite picture of human manners, will outlive the palace
of the Escurial and the Imperial Eagle of the House of
Austria."

Vienna is a very large and beautiful city, almost as
beautiful as Paris, but it is off the beaten track and it is not
gay in the same way that Paris is; it is much more leisurely
and seemingly sedate; that is to say, it is gay (or was), in its
own way, but it seems unable to advertise its charms.   In
the old days it had no wish to; to-day it needs the tourist,
but does not seem able to "sell itself" to the world, to use an
advertising phrase.   I never met a man or woman who had
spent any time in Vienna who did not love it and its people.
The way Vienna came to be so beautiful is this.   It
is very old and for centuries was a walled city, and its
people found the wall useful, for it was frequently besieged.
The wall extended right around the city, and outside it
there was a wide open space or glacis on which no buildings
were allowed within eighteen hundred feet of the wall.
This open space became a parade ground.   After the Emperor, whom we shall always think of as old Kaiser Franz

Josef, had been upon the throne for ten years, he caused the wall, which was no longer of any protection and had become a nuisance, to be removed. There arose, of course, the question: To whom did this great space belong — to the city or to the nation? The Kaiser decided, wisely, — perhaps it was the only wise decision he ever made, — that it belonged to the nation and to the city, fifty-fifty, as we would say. A magnificent boulevard, which all the world knows as the Ringstrasse, was then constructed, and the open space not required for that purpose was sold for enormous sums, and with the money thus obtained some of the finest modern buildings in the city, some of the finest I have ever seen, were erected. I entered few of them; public buildings, museums, and picture galleries are very fatiguing.

But one building, in the centre of the old city, interested me enormously — the Hofburg. It is a colossal, shapeless pile, about as unimposing from the outside as the Vatican in Rome. Whenever an Austrian Emperor wanted to build anything, no matter what, — a library, a church, a stable, a conservatory, or a theatre, — he just built it on to and made it a part of the Hofburg, so that in this great sprawling palace there is, or was, accommodation for man or beast in whatever might happen to be his mood. The theatre and the church are pulled down now; there remains, however, "the Hofburg," one of the show places of Europe. The library, which interested me most, is one of the great libraries of the world. The building itself is the work of the famous Fischer von Erlach, an architect to whom Vienna owes some of its finest buildings. The great hall is one of the most superb rooms in Europe. It is baroque at its very best and is so placed that the doors at one end can be opened; it then becomes a part of a great ballroom. We first visited it, under very distinguished patronage, by way of the great balcony which extends around the entire room,

THE IMPERIAL LIBRARY IN THE HOFBURG

after having been shown some, and only some, of its magnificent bibliographical treasures. The books are those which originally formed the Imperial Library, together with those of Prince Eugene of Savoy, who was not only a great soldier but a collector as well. The National Library in Paris is the most unhospitable institution in the world; the British Museum holds out a welcoming hand to the scholars of all nations; but for sheer beauty the Hofbibliothek of Vienna surpasses anything I have ever seen.

Not very far away is something very different — the Spanish Riding School, it is called. It was once a plaything of the imperial family, where a special breed of magnificent white horses are trained to dance and otherwise keep time to the music of an orchestra. The riding school, together with a small stable where the exhibition horses are kept, was formerly very private indeed. Since the fall of the Empire, however, it is open to the public every Sunday upon the payment of a small fee. I had an amusing experience on the Sunday that I visited it. I wanted to smoke while the horses were going through their paces, but a sign, NICHT RAUCHEN MACHEN, warned me not to. When I got into the open, I took a cigar from my pocket and then found I had no match. I sought a shop, found one, — two, half a dozen, — all closed. I wanted to smoke; presently I saw two taxi drivers on a street corner smoking cigarettes, but I could not for the life of me think of the German word for "match." All I could think of was Kreuger, that Napoleon of the match business who, all too late for the world, had just blown his brains out. So, very politely, I went up to the taxi drivers and in my sweetest tones said, *"Bitte sehr, hast du ein Kreuger?"* There was for a moment a look of amazement, and then a hearty laugh — and I met my match.

The conservatory and rooms containing the crown jewels and other insignia of office, imperial plate, glass, and china, are much visited. I protested that I would not look at any of these things, but I was overruled and almost fainted when I saw such a display of wealth in gold and jewels as (if they are real) would almost suffice to put Austria financially upon her feet again. I staggered by case after case of magnificent robes and crowns and sceptres from the time of Charlemagne (Charlemagne maybe?) down to the present. After all this I was not surprised to see a complete solid-gold dinner service for one hundred and forty persons and a similar service of silver for a thousand. One born and brought up in a republican atmosphere cannot possibly understand the feeling of divinity that doth hedge a king, the feeling that he is the Lord's anointed, the belief that he can do no wrong. And all this gear, all these trappings, passed too frequently from scoundrel to scoundrel, until at last the whole scheme blew up and the last Emperor died in exile in the Island of Madeira.

About three miles away from the great mass of the Hofburg is another palace, Schönbrunn, the summer palace, originally designed by Maria Theresa to be larger and finer than Versailles, but this idea was not completely carried out. Here it was that the Congress of Vienna, a gathering of all the wasps and butterflies of Europe, was held. Twice after successful battles Napoleon made it his home, and here, in a magnificent apartment once occupied by his father, died the Duke of Reichstadt. There is also another palace, the Belvedere, right in the heart of the city in a lovely garden, one of the finest in Europe. This palace was built by Prince Eugene of Savoy and became the winter home of the Crown Prince, Franz Ferdinand, whom the Emperor, his uncle, and everyone else hated. It was his murder, twenty years ago to-day as I read this proof, that started the World War. But these palaces were not enough. Some years ago two more were planned — one actually erected. It was not

entirely completed when the War broke out, and, now that
there is no one to occupy it, it has been turned into a
museum.

There are, of course, many other palaces and châteaux
scattered all over the country, and while this life of luxury
was going on the condition of the poor of Vienna was something pitiable.   It is said that *thirty thousand families lived in
one room each*, and if the room happened to be a large one,
two families occupied it, it being divided by a clothesline.
But the people were for the most part uncomplaining; they
had plenty of excellent music for little or nothing, and few
actually starved.   The court was haughty, cruel, and corrupt, and into it no modern idea ever penetrated; modera-
tion was a word nonexistent in the lexicon of the Hapsburgs.
One would suppose that some thoughtful aristocrat would
have said, "Times are not what they were; we must watch
our step.   Indifference to the sufferings of the poor brought
on the French Revolution.   If we are not careful we shall
lose our fortunes, if not our heads."   But no, right up to the
outbreak of the World War, *Wein, Weib, und Gesang* was the
motto of the aristocracy — taken from Luther, by the way.
A tourist in Paris is accustomed to see more than traces of
the luxury of the Kings of France and of Napoleon, but it
came to an end more than a century ago — and it seems
longer.   In Vienna, luxury lasted until the end of the Great
War, which left Austria prostrate, and what had been once
the richest Empire the world had ever seen — save Rome —
came to an end.   The corpse was buried while it was yet
breathing;   four men — Clemenceau, Orlando, Lloyd
George, and Woodrow Wilson — were the pallbearers.
What happened to Austria is unbelievable — positively
fantastic.

The old Empire was composed of many nations, all
of whom hated one another;   there were differences of

language and of religion.   Into this mess Woodrow Wilson threw a phrase which was like a firebrand in a barrel of gunpowder.   With his fatal facility of speech he spoke of the "necessity for the self-determination of small nations," and the damage was done — but not entirely completed; it was completed at the Congress of Versailles.   Hence it is that Vienna, one of the largest cities on the continent of Europe, is isolated — has no hinterland.   Before the War, the Dual Empire, Austria and Hungary, had a population of fifty millions.   Hungary is now a kingdom without a king, and Austria is, or was until the advent of Herr Doll-fuss, a socialistic republic, with a population of about six millions, of whom more than two millions live in Vienna — two millions of people with nothing to do.   They are patient, kindly folk accustomed to poverty, but they must eat occasionally.   The question is how are they to get food. Vienna produces practically nothing.   Its mechanics and craftsmen are the best in the world, but they must have materials with which to work;   materials cost money, and they have none.   One cannot live on music, or scenery, however grand.   Vienna, when I saw it, was a ruined and deserted city, deserted not by its population, but by trade. It is curiously amusing the way different nations take their troubles.   The American says much and does little;   the Englishman says little and does much.   In Berlin they say the situation is serious but not hopeless;   in Vienna they say that it is hopeless but not serious.

All my life (all my married life, that is — all that counts) I have been hearing of the court of Kaiser Franz Josef, how exclusive and aristocratic it was, how different from the vulgar court of the German Emperor and from the demo-cratic court of the King of England.   I did not dare tell my dear little mother-in-law how rotten it was, nor would she have believed me if I had.   One of her brothers, whom I

learned to love and call "Uncle Louis" (he was a tall, dis-
tinguished-looking man, and what a gentleman! — had
been an officer in the Austrian army), was represented, in
the family, as having been something of a favorite of the old
Kaiser. He left Vienna because his rank in the army would
not permit him to marry a lady with whom he was in love,
who had no fortune. I never met Uncle Louis without his
making a little almost unconscious motion of bringing his
heels together and saying, "*Servus, Eduard,*" and I never
knew him to greet my wife without, "*Küss' die Hand,
gnädige Frau.*"

The Kaiser himself was a good, busy, and respected man
of simple tastes. He slept on a camp bedstead — you see
them in half a dozen palaces in Austria. He was an early
riser, and, neglecting everything important, made himself
a master of petty detail. It is said that when he and his
friend Edward VII, King of England, went together to one
of their favorite spas, they usually met at the same hour, —
five in the morning, — the Emperor just beginning his day's
work, the King on his way to bed. Franz Josef's wife was
the beautiful Empress Elizabeth, with whom he did not get
on well. She was greatly beloved by the Hungarians,
whereas they had small regard for him and he none for
them. There was no crime or misfortune that did not come
very near to his heart. A revolution placed him on his
throne; almost immediately there was an attempt upon his
life. His brothers — he had several — were so mean and
degenerate that, even in a court in which degeneracy and
vice were the distinguishing marks of nobility, they could
not be tolerated. His favorite brother was Maximilian,
whom the French sought to make Emperor of Mexico,
whereupon the Mexicans promptly and properly shot him;
what right had he in Mexico? Presently he became involved in a war with Prussia which he lost, and with it he

was forced to yield much territory. The Empress Elizabeth was stabbed to death by a lunatic in Switzerland.
But his great grief was the romantic suicide or murder of his
only son, the Crown Prince Rudolph; the details of his
death are still obscure.

A Hapsburg, one of the proudest men in Europe, —
compared to whom Kaiser William was but a weed of
hasty growth, — he was forever concealing or attempting
to conceal some fresh disgrace which had fallen upon some
member of his family, but he could not bring himself to
permit anyone not of aristocratic birth — however useful
to himself or his Empire — to enter the charmed circle of
his court.   He was, himself, a man of simple tastes; in addition to his iron cots one sees tall desks at which he used to
stand reading reports, signing papers, and no doubt thinking of himself as the flywheel of a colossal machine, whereas
he was in effect merely a nut which kept the wheel on.
When, in the midst of the World War, it fell off, the wheel
came with it, and a seven-hundred-year-old machine fell
quickly to pieces.   But long before the World War the old
man had practically withdrawn from the direction of forces
which he could no longer control, and this was the condition
of affairs when, at the cracking of the Emperor of Germany's whip, he declared war on Serbia, knowing — he
must have known — that his action would bring about the
general war for which one section of Europe was hoping
and the other fearing.   The rest is the history of yesterday.

I let this paragraph stand as it originally appeared in
the *Atlantic Monthly*, where it brought forth the following
letter from a gentleman in London :—

I take leave to differ with you as to the responsibility you lay
on the Austrian Emperor's shoulders in respect of foreknowledge
of the result of the declaration of war by Austria against Serbia,
and in support of this would tell you the following story, which,

in view of the Emperor's advanced years and the position occupied
by the narrator of the story, may be true.

In 1926 I sailed for New York from Southampton with a gentleman who occupies a distinguished position in Vienna and controls
an important industry. Getting to know him very well, he said
that all Austria was aghast when they realized they were fighting
against England, whom as a nation they knew and liked, and told
me the following story, which to the best of his belief was true.
"That the Emperor, after the burial of the murdered Archduke,
stayed at Ischl, his summer palace, for some time, and in the
middle of August returned to Vienna, the War having been in
progress at that time for over two weeks. His two A. D. C.'s —
old men of seventy-five — became much perturbed for fear the
Emperor might accidentally learn from some lady-in-waiting or
by picking up a newspaper that his country was at war. They
drew lots as to who should tell him, and the next morning one of
them approached his Imperial Master and said he had with much
regret to inform him that his Government had found it necessary
to declare war. The Emperor was much shocked by this statement and said at his time of life, after all his troubles, he hoped
to go down to the grave in peace, but, rising from his chair, he
said: '*Well, if we do have to fight those damn Germans, I hope to God we
lick them this time.*'"[1]

All his life long the Kaiser had enjoyed the company of
very charming ladies, but for the last thirty years of his life
he was devoted to one, Frau Kati Schratt, an opera singer,
whose portrait might be seen in the royal box, otherwise
decorated with the insignia of the House of Austria. She
had a small palace in Vienna near the Hofburg and a villa
near Schönbrunn opposite a small green gate — to which
the Emperor and the lady alone had a key — in the wall of
the garden surrounding the palace. More than this, she
had houses dotted all over the Empire — and her jewels are

[1] For obvious reasons I withhold the name of my correspondent and his
friend. — A. E. N.

said to be magnificent. The lady, she is an old woman now, knows more scandal than any person living, and it is said she has declined a large fortune from an Austrian publisher to tell it. Perhaps her "recollections" will some day be published.

Too much cannot be said in praise of the Austrians. They are from top to bottom an amiable, polite, and considerate people. If the aristocrat in his heart of hearts despises you, as he undoubtedly does, he conceals it. *"Bitte," "Servus,"* and *"Küss' die Hand"* are not idle words. The French have the reputation of being polite, but their politeness is as nothing compared to that of an Austrian. Make this test. Go to a café in Paris and order something to drink. You drink it and immediately the waiter will take your glass away, ask if you will have another, and, if you won't, begin to wipe off your table with a dirty towel and ultimately wipe you out of your chair. Not so in Vienna. Go to your café and order a drink. You drink it slowly; presently the waiter comes up, very politely removes your empty glass, and brings two other glasses — two, mind you — and fills both of them with water; this so that you may not feel embarrassed at having nothing before you to drink. In all probability he will bring you a newspaper, making a faultless guess as to what language you read with the greatest facility.

And now I have come to the thing for which, after their music and medicine, the Viennese are most famous the world over — the café. England has its public house, commonly called a pub; we have had the saloon and the speak-easy; the café is the essential Vienna. There are over a thousand of them. Every man and many women have their café to which they resort daily to drink coffee — and the best coffee in the world. Austrians are frugal; their wines are not much to boast of; substantial food in a café is usually a sandwich. But their *Kuchen!* Curious and bewildering names ring in my ears, meaning the richest and most delicious shape-destroying individual rolls, buns, and cakes that can be conceived of. One does not so much eat them as let them melt in the mouth.

In a Viennese café hurry is unknown; a "quick lunch" — that abomination — is unthinkable. One goes to his café, — I soon discovered mine; it was the Herrenhof, — gets, if he can, a seat by a window, and takes no note of time. But one observes everything else. The air becomes warm and agreeable, if one likes the smell of tobacco. The place is or becomes crowded with quiet men and a sprinkling of women who talk by the hour in tones so low that they can scarcely be heard, even if one understands the language — which I do not. Small ices and a cooling drink, resembling raspberry shrub, are in demand. Have these people anything to do? Seemingly not. But they are intensely interested in conversation. I presume that there are political and professional and musical and literary cafés. The Café Herrenhof is distinctly literary — perhaps journalistic would be a better word. With a pleasant companion I can imagine no more delightful place in which to pass an hour or an evening than the Herrenhof in the Herrengasse.

There is a ritual in ordering and receiving supplies in a Vienna café which it is most important to observe, and I have no doubt that in my ignorance I did many things that distinctly were "not done." If you take the *Besitzer* (or proprietor) for a *Herr Ober* (head waiter), you are done for. If you call a common or garden waiter *Herr Ober*, he knows you for a fool. The *Herr Ober* takes your order and ultimately your money and your tip, but a *Speisenträger* (waiter) brings you your food and drink, and expects a tip too, naturally. There is also a *Kuchenträger* (cake waiter), who brings a big tray of cakes and expects to be paid and tipped.

It is all very simple when you know it — as most things
are — and very complicated when you don't. But one
may read or write or play cards or flirt by the hour, quite
undisturbed, with two glasses of cold water before him after
he has had his, for the *Besitzer*, more profitable drink. It is
sehr gemütlich, and if you ask me what that means I would
reply that is something conspicuous in our country by its
absence.

I know little and have no wish to know much about the
several political parties in Austria. There are all kinds of
Socialists, and Communists, who take from those who have,
to give to those who have not. This creed will always have
the approval of the majority. The first revolution in
Austria was accomplished without the shedding of a drop of
blood — of that there had been enough during the War;
there was no fight left in anyone. There were misery and
starvation, of course, but they were nothing new, nor was
misgovernment. The last Emperor, Charles, abdicated in
November 1918 and fled the country, and the printing press
completed the ruin of the Empire. Whoever was in power
at the time gave the fatal order. They began to print
kronen until they became worthless, fourteen thousand
paper kronen to one gold one. Such a process is like drinking sea water to quench thirst. By this time my daughter,
who is a fluent German scholar, was doing relief work in
Vienna under the guidance of the "Anglo-American"
something or other — for which the "Anglo" took the credit
and the "American" put up the money. I remember that
she came home for a little respite, and, as she was packing
to return, I noticed a large bundle of "money" of which
she seemed very careless. When I upbraided her, as is a
father's duty, she said, "Pooh! I'm not going to take
that back. I have n't the room for it and it would n't buy
a newspaper, anyway."

And then came the permanent tragedy, compared to which war is merely an opportunity to show heroism. Wealth is, generally speaking, of two kinds — paper evidences thereof, such as bonds and stock, as we should say, and real estate. These billions of millions of paper kronen put into circulation made all other paper evidences of wealth not relatively but absolutely worthless. A man who by thrift had saved up ten thousand kronen as a solace for his old age now found himself the possessor of a questionable fifteen cents, or, to put it another way, of two loaves of bread. If, on the other hand, he had real estate to sell or to rent he received paper kronen with the same result — RUIN.

Come we now to another experiment in government. The Social Democrats by a simple twist of the wrist had acquired the physical assets — all that was left of the Empire. These they proceeded to distribute. By a form of legal robbery they found themselves possessed of immense areas of land; then, securing the services of the best architects, they proceeded to build the finest apartment houses, flats, community dwellings — call them what you like — that have ever been erected for the laboring classes. These buildings are at once the despair of the economist and the delight of the social worker, the architect, and the engineer. Securing the services of an excellent guide, with proper introductions and a wife whose mother tongue is the pleasant patois of Vienna, I spent several days in studying these buildings and their occupants.

The immensity and substantial character of these model tenements are beyond belief, and their exterior beauty is hardly excelled by the great apartment houses in New York or Chicago. The gardens in which they are placed, or which have been constructed around them, have well-kept lawns, dotted with trees and beds of flowers with artistic fountains or statuary here and there for the solace of age, and playgrounds which are the joy of children. From having been born and bred in slums, Viennese children now have the care and amusements of the children — I was going to say of the very rich, but I know no rich children whose wants, real or imaginary, are so studied. A pool for wading in summer automatically becomes a skating or sliding rink in winter. But have they skates and shoes? I do not know. I was there in the spring, when everything was abloom.

I think few blocks of buildings are more than five stories high, although I noticed some of nine stories, this height being employed, I fancy, to break the monotony of the sky line, and there are miles of streets of small "detached" cottages. The flats are of one, two, three, five rooms each, open to the sun, frequently with balconies looking out into the gardens. The cooking, toilet, and laundry arrangements are amazingly complete. In some of the largest of these flats the laundries are equipped with the most modern electrical apparatus, which in size would admirably serve a modern hotel. I know something of the cost of electric equipment, and I can tell when money has been thrown away with both hands. To operate a laundry completely furnished with the most modern and complicated electrical devices takes skillful operators and not such folk as have been, in the past, accustomed to washing their clothes on a smooth stone laid flat on the bank of a stream. And of what use can a mangle be, which at one operation will smooth a tablecloth six feet wide, to a group who have nothing to wash? I protested vigorously against such wastefulness and likened it to the barbaric extravagance of the old régime, and was told that its manufacture gave work to mechanics who otherwise would have nothing to do. Knowing, as I did, that Austria is obliged to import its coal, and has unsurpassed facilities for making electricity

MODEL TENEMENTS IN VIENNA

from water power, I suggested that hydroelectric plants
and the electrical equipment of their railways might have
given the needed relief to labor and at the same time have
enabled the state railways to operate more economically.
To this there was no adequate reply.

I know nothing as to welfare clinics for children, but here,
too, I saw what seemed to my untutored eye such elegance
of equipment for the health and amusement of the children
of the poor as I cannot believe exists elsewhere in the world.
If ten of the richest men in New York were to vie with one
another in providing a health kindergarten, if such a thing
might be, the result in beauty and in artistic and hygienic
arrangement might approach what has been provided for
the poor folk of Vienna.   I ask you to see to it, Mrs. Astor-
bilt, that your children's toothbrushes match in color and
material their tooth mugs — it is most important. How
many kindergartens are thus functioning in Vienna?   I
have no idea, but there are many.   The children arrive at
seven in the morning and remain under constant care and
supervision until six in the evening, for which the charge is
merely nominal, from two to four shillings — that is to say,
at most fifty-six cents a week, including meals.

Turning now to the economic side of this pleasant picture,
whence came the wealth which provided all this?   From
the rich, who under the guise of taxation have been im-
poverished, if not to a man, certainly to a family.   What
contribution do the poor themselves make?   Well, in the
first place the poor have little or nothing, and as the Socialists themselves say, in some literature which was provided
me (in English), "The Municipality of Vienna does not
put any interest on the capital invested [in these under-
takings].   When the building is completed *the capital outlay
is reckoned at zero.* [Italics mine.]   Accordingly the Municipality can confine itself strictly to levying from its tenants

the mere cost of upkeep and repair.   The rents vary from
15 to 20 groschen per month per square metre." That
works out to something almost infinitesimal.   I hate figures;
the reader may do it for himself.   A square metre is 10¾
square feet, and 100 groschen are equal to one Austrian
shilling, or fourteen cents.   This is "the housing *rent*," and
I go on to read that "the housing *tax*" on a worker's dwelling
amounts to a little more than one shilling per month, and
on a modest middle-class home a few shillings per month.
Large apartments and business premises are more severely
taxed.   *Natürlich!*   Is it any wonder that for this accommodation, which may fairly be described as luxurious, there
is an unlimited demand?

Austria is a Catholic country — next to Spain, perhaps
the most Catholic country in Europe.   The population has
declined, but marriage has risen from an average of 19,000
annually for the years 1910–1913 to 25,000 annually for
1919–1924, and the Church sees to it that the marriages are
fruitful.   Birth control, one certain way out of the world's
economic distress, is taught to be a crime.   Let me add that
68,000 dwellings of all kinds have been erected since the fall
of the Hapsburgs.   One more question, and a most important one: Are the people thus mothered and fathered by
the benevolent despotism of the Socialist happy?   Distinctly not.   They are as unhappy as it is within the power
of a pleasure-loving Viennese to be.

Once again it seems best to let my comment upon the
model tenements of Vienna stand as it was originally
printed.   What has happened since is history, fresh in the
minds of all of us.   There has been a second revolution, this
time accompanied by much bloodshed;   for a while civil
war seemed imminent, but fortunately the disturbance
quieted down almost as quickly as it arose.   It is claimed by

Dollfuss and his adherents that the great buildings which I have described were designed to serve as forts, and that they were full of the munitions of war. I do not believe they were so designed, although they might serve that purpose for a time, and I can well believe that men with guns and ammunition housed in them could give a very fine imitation of war. But it was soon over. The number of deaths was no doubt exaggerated on one side and minimized on the other, but they were enough; the truth will never be known. Dollfuss at present, to all intents and purposes a dictator, may wish to remain one, or he may be playing John the Baptist to a Hapsburg king. History is in the making. We shall see what we shall see.

The world is greatly interested in the Russian experiment in government, but the country is so vast and the people are so ignorant that no one knows what will happen or when. In Austria Socialism may be studied; one can go there easily in safety and in comfort, and one can talk to the people freely — my wife did so in her mother's tongue. The people she interviewed — and she talked to men and women — were not contented; they did not like the old order of things especially, but it gave them work. They said their fine surroundings were a mockery; they wanted work and food, which the Socialists were unable to provide. Having once completely robbed the rich, Socialism could go no further. Our fool legislators in Washington, with their slogan "Soak the rich," may well take warning.

I think I am right in saying that wherever Socialism has been tried it has blown up. And to quote my friend, Dr. Johnson, finally and perhaps for the last time: "Depend upon it, Sir, it is very difficult to change the existing order of things."

But there is another picture and a pleasanter one. "He studied medicine in Vienna," says someone, wishing to pay tribute to the skill of some excellent physician, and when that physician comes and is through prescribing for his patient he will tell you how happy he was to work under the watchful eye of this great man or that, and of the joys of his student days, and how he longs to go back. I visited the great infirmaries and hospitals, famous all over the world, and thought for a time that I would take advantage of the opportunity of having something cut out of me or something useful inserted in my anatomy; but, after feeling myself carefully all over, I determined to carry on as is for a while longer. I shall soon be coffin-ripe anyhow, and at my age capital repairs are expensive and may be dangerous.

The centre of Alt Wein is no doubt the Hofburg. The centre of Vienna is the Opera House. Paris for art, Vienna for music! The people live upon it; it seems more necessary to them than bread; it is not so with me. I went to the opera several times, — a good husband is obliged to make concessions to his musical wife, — but I was more interested in Sacher's, immediately behind the Opera House. It was once the most exclusive, most expensive, and, they say, the naughtiest hotel in Europe. (Reader, if you did not see the Lunts in that naughty, delightful play, *Reunion in Vienna*, you missed something!) Old Man Sacher has been dead for some time; Frau Sacher died quite recently. Their hotel faded, however, like everything else in Vienna during the War, and with the extinction of certain Archdukes and their ladies, who seldom appeared in the rather dingy public dining room, its glory departed, and will never return. If the mirrors in its *chambres séparées* could portray what they once reflected! If walls had ears and mouths too! But it is better as it is. Vienna will live down her scandals — all but one, which I must refer to, however shocking it may be. *The famous Danube is Brown, not Blue.*

XIV

I AND BUDAPEST

WHEN you tell a man or a woman in Vienna that you are going to Budapest, the eyebrows are raised, as who should say, "I wonder why?" If the subject is continued, a concession may be made and you may be told that "the old city, Buda, is interesting, but . . ." Or you may be told that the "new city, Pest, is beautiful, but . . ." Now the fact is that Budapest is both interesting and beautiful; it is one of the finest cities in Europe. The entrance to it is, speaking generally, Vienna, and the Austrians and the Hungarians hate each other cordially; they always have, and seemingly they always will. My time permitted me to go either to Budapest or to Prague. I chose the former. I should have gone to both; I shall have to go back.

The first, I might say the only, bit of modern, up-to-date enterprise I saw in Vienna was not Viennese but Hungarian. In the office of the American Express Company I observed a sign calling attention to a certain all-inclusive ticket from Vienna to Budapest and return — a ticket which gave one the choice of half a dozen of the best hotels; meals (except breakfast, which naturally one takes in his room, or where he will), and other things, and all for a ridiculously small sum. The ticket was issued by the Hungarian government. In other words, an effort was being made to sell to tourists the idea of going to Budapest, the Hungarians relying, quite naturally, upon the charm of the city to keep the tourist there once it gets him.

I have, no doubt, been fortunate in the Hungarians I have known. Where is the book-collector who does not know Gabriel Wells? I knew him first, twenty-five years ago, as Gabriel Wiess. Disliking the Germans, when the War broke out he changed his name to Gabriel Wells, and he said that when the United States entered the War, as he prophesied we should, he would change it again to George Washington. But we told him that he had gone far enough, and that everyone knew what his initials G. W. stood for anyway. So, although he is a Hungarian and honored in his native city, for which he has done much, Gabriel Wells he remains, and he divides his time between New York and London. Effendi (the late F. N. Doubleday) once told me that Gabriel Wells's word was as good as a certified check.

I once knew another Hungarian whose check sometimes came back to me with that horrid little notation thereon, "No funds," but my friend was so cultivated, so altogether charming, that our cordial relations continued until his death.   This man — bless his memory — told the truth with the utmost reluctance, and I once said to him, "Alois, why do you not tell the truth more frequently?" "Eduard," he replied, "let me make it clear to you. We Magyars are a very old race; we have a civilization of a thousand years. A thousand years ago, at a time when your ancestors were savages hunting in the swamps of what is now London, my ancestors had discovered that a man who tells the truth is very likely to be disagreeable." *Veritas odium parit.*

My friend had an excellent education; he had never gone to school, but had had tutors in everything. He spoke Hungarian, a most difficult language, faultlessly, no doubt; German like a native, English acceptably, and French sufficiently. His profession — so far as he had a profession — was architecture. He was very handsome, and he was an accomplished horseman. Forty years ago he used to

drive tandem up Fifth Avenue, — a great art, — and
through Central Park, the observed of all observers. He
wrote verses and I could talk English literature to him as I
would to my college-professor friends. He drank little,
never smoked, and he had one accomplishment of which he
was really proud: he played the piano magnificently. His
great joy was to get two Steinway pianos in a large empty
room, seat Joseffy at one of them, place himself at the other
— and spend the day. Except when he was angry, he concealed the fact that he thought Americans barbarians.

I knew another — but enough: the Hungarian, man or
woman, is a delightful companion. Shall I be understood
if I say that every man should go to Budapest before he is
married, taking with him a robust constitution and a lot of
money, and be careful how he spends them?

The country to the west and south of Vienna is beautiful;
indeed, some of the finest scenery in Europe is not far off,
and were it possible for the Austrian to live on landscape
and music, he would be the most fortunate of mortals. Unluckily, however, he requires food. From Vienna we made
only one excursion — to Melk, that noble old monastery
built on a great mountainous rock which projects into the
Danube, an unsurpassed location. Those old monks had
an eye for the picturesque — and for many other things.
The road to Melk — we went by motor — is the road the
crusaders took in their journeys overland to and from
Jerusalem. I have always been interested in the crusades,
those enormous surges of people who, prompted by piety,
avarice, love of adventure, or what not, trudged wearily
thousands of miles, it may be, in the hope of at last reaching
the Holy Sepulchre. And of all who started, how many
arrived, and in what condition! And what a welcome
awaited them in the City of Peace!

Seven hundred years ago this now almost deserted road was occasionally a busy thoroughfare — and once the scene of one of the romances of history. For along this road Richard I of England, Richard Cœur de Lion, on his return from Palestine was caught, in the dress of a serving man, it is said, while attempting to make his way home, and thrown into Dürrenstein Castle, there to be discovered by the troubadour Blondel, according to the story, singing, for the purpose, under his window. There is the castle; it is a ruin now, as so many old castles are, but the legend remains. And at the foot of the castle is a small town with a fine church and the Richard Cœur de Lion Inn, where we had a glass of the wine of the country. There has been a place of refreshment there always, it is said.

We had received an invitation from the Abbot of Melk to have lunch with him, which we accepted gladly. "The meal is not much," the Abbot said, passing me the menu, "but all from the heart." The wine was excellent, but I was careful, as I always am in drinking strange vintages. I knew that the Abbey cellars were famous; indeed, the immense monastery was the outgrowth of several centuries of profitable traffic in wine.

The Abbot, who was a delightful old man, became much interested when I told him — my wife acting as interpreter — that I had seen his famous Gutenberg Bible sold at auction in New York. This is the Bible that Dr. Rosenbach bought for $106,000 and sold to Mrs. Harkness, who gave it to the Library at Yale. "Has it a good home?" the Abbot inquired. I assured him that it had, that it was in the keeping of an especial friend of mine, Professor Chauncey B. Tinker, who would see that no harm came to it. "I was sorry to part with it," the old man went on to say, "but we have many noble books in our library, which you shall see after lunch, and we had to have money for

some very necessary repairs. We are very poor now."
But he seemed happy, as why should he not be? Content
with this world, sure of the next, no wife to order him about
— an Abbot has much to be thankful for. I have never
before thought of turning Abbot. It is a matter deserving
consideration.

The country east of Vienna shortly becomes as flat and
uninteresting as Kansas or Nebraska, and for the same
reason — it is one huge wheat field, mile after mile of
slightly undulating plains, with hardly a house or a barn in
sight, without a tree or a fence to indicate where one property ends and another begins. But presently one notices
markers, just such stones as we employ to indicate a ceme-
tery lot. And I thought of individualistic England with
the limits of every man's farm indicated by hedges or ditches
or fences of stone or wood or wire, sometimes by all of them,
lest by some mischance a man or an animal should stray
beyond bounds.

After a journey of about five hours the train rolls into an
indifferent railway station and you are at the end of your
journey. Driving to the hotel, you instantly realize that the
city is very beautiful but very foreign. To see signs all over,
and not one which by any possibility you can make out, is
an unusual experience. The Hungarian language is very
difficult, resembling Finnish, one is told, which helps very
little. The words are immensely long, with accents, which
are equivalent to danger signals, over the vowels, violently
changing any sound which in one's ignorance one might
presume to give to them. I made out a list of perfectly
preposterous words one afternoon, but the only two that I
am sure of I scribbled in my guidebook — *Póggysdszkiád-
szás*, which to the best of my knowledge and belief means
luggage office, and when you seek a drug store you ask for a

Gyógyszébár. One of the daughters of the House of Vander-
bilt married a Count Széchényi — scion of one of the oldest
families in Hungary — and she has, I am told, learned to
speak the language perfectly, a great accomplishment.

Up to a century or two ago Latin was the language of the
court and of the courts. People who were interested in
reading had to learn the languages and the literatures of the
world, but a hundred years or so ago it was discovered that a
national literature was in the making, and the Hungarians
are now excessively proud of what they have accomplished
in poetry, in the drama, and in fiction. You never hear a
word upon the street that can be understood, but at your
hotel you are addressed very courteously in excellent English, and upon being shown to your room the windows are
thrown open and you look out upon a magnificent panorama: below is the terrace, and beyond the Danube, and
across the river rises the fine old city of Buda.

Pest, the "modern" city where the great hotels are, is built
upon the left bank of the Danube, which is flat, whereas on
the right, Buda, the "old" city, climbs, terrace upon terrace,
up the hills, and upon the topmost ridge is an old fortress
which has long ceased to serve any purpose, but it bulks
large in the history of the country, having been several times
besieged and at least once taken by the Turks. Below is a
magnificent palace built by Maria Theresa, and a noble old
church, with a glorious spire, which is known as the Coronation Church, a part of which dates back to the time of
Stephen, the first Christian King of Hungary. His Apostolic Majesty — a title conferred upon him by one of the
Popes a thousand years ago — became a Saint after his
death. And centuries later the title was renewed in favor
of Queen Maria Theresa, by virtue of which it was one of
the many titles assumed by the late Kaiser Franz Josef. It

is also known as the Church of St. Matthias, Matthias also being a Saint as well as a King. It is really not surprising that the Kings of Hungary were made Saints by the Roman Church when it is remembered how valiantly, for centuries, they fought the Turks, whose aim was to make all the world Mohammedan. Had the Turks been successful in keeping Buda, and had they captured and retained Vienna, we — you and I, reader — might to-day be Mohammedans and not Christians.

The last coronation to take place in this church was that of the unlucky King Charles, the successor of Franz Josef, and his Queen Zita. Their reign was brief, for in 1919 they were obliged to flee for their lives to Switzerland, where they remained for three years, during which Hungary had become some sort of socialistic republic — but, beyond painting the domes of some old churches red and temporarily disfiguring some historic monuments, the republicans did little. The government was seen to be weak and vacillating; at any rate Charles, who was an amiable man but a heavy drinker, probably inspired by his wife Zita, an ambitious woman, thought the time had come to regain his Kingdom if not his Empire. So from Switzerland he came with Zita by aëroplane to the estate of one of his followers, whence he took train, as he hoped, for Budapest. All went well for a time, but as the special train neared the city it was discovered that the tracks were torn up, and what was intended to be a triumphal entry was no entry at all but another flight, this time to the Island of Madeira, and in six months he was dead.

It is said that Charles was a coward; this may or may not be true, but it is certainly not true of his wife. She is a woman to be reckoned with, and she has a son, the Crown Prince Otto, who is now a handsome young god of twenty-two — biding his time, with his mother, in poverty in

Brussels. The claim is now made that Charles never gave up the throne of Hungary, that he declined to rob his children of their inheritance. "There must remain Hapsburgers in the world," he cried, when urged to yield his crown voluntarily and take a pension which was offered him. "Never, never! Otto will come after me." And no doubt he will; the stage is being set for him.

Hungary is at present a kingdom, governed by a Regent, not merely lacking but wanting a king. We saw the Regent, Admiral Horthy, who has been at the head of the government since Charles fled, more than twelve years ago, take the salute from the palace one Sunday morning while a great crowd stood with uncovered heads and a military band played the national anthem. His title is Regent, but he was dressed in the uniform of an Admiral of the Navy, although the Hungarian navy now ranks with that of Switzerland. Chaos will play with the hands of the Hapsburgs; there are plenty of them. They are a prolific race and will not die. Otto has seven brothers and sisters. Should the male line fail, the "pragmatic sanction" may again be invoked to put a queen upon the throne which was once Maria Theresa's.

Do you remember what the "pragmatic sanction" was? When Maria Theresa's father came to the throne he, by a famous edict (so called), settled the succession upon his daughter, but immediately upon his death Frederick the Great sought to overthrow her. A twenty-five-year war ensued, and, the lady winning not only on the battlefield but also in diplomacy, she became the greatest ruler in Europe. The encyclopædias say that the "pragmatic sanction" — both the term and the thing — is now obsolete, owing to the spread of constitutional government. But what is the constitution among friends — and enemies? Order, and Hungary seems orderly at present, will make for the status quo. How long will it last? This is one, and only one, of the many problems of the future.

The Italians have a saying, "See Naples and die," but I have no desire to die in Naples, or, at present, elsewhere. More properly one should say, "See Budapest and live." The two cities, separated by the Danube, which here varies in width from one to two thousand feet, are connected one with the other by six fine bridges, and luckily the river traffic, which is considerable, goes on well below the street level so that the noble Franz Josef Quai, on which the principal hotels of Pest are situated, is in reality a broad promenade, closed to vehicles. It is a mile long and is usually referred to as the Corso. It was on a fine Sunday afternoon that we first saw it, thronged with handsome men and women, well dressed and irreproachable in conduct. The hotels formed a long line, and in front of each was an open-air café crowded with people drinking coffee and eating *brioches*, those exquisite sweet rolls for which both Austria and Hungary are famous. And that reminds me of a story.

We have all eaten and enjoyed at good restaurants and cafés in Europe, and occasionally in New York, a crescent-shaped roll which has several names, according to the country one is in. In Austria it is called a *Kipfl*, which is a man's name. My story is how it came to be so called. For centuries Vienna stood foursquare against the Turk. The old wall which encircled Alt Wien was erected centuries ago and stood firm against almost continuous attack for nearly a hundred and fifty years. In 1683 the Turk came and sat down outside the wall with the fixed determination of starving out the city. The siege was a long one, and among other efforts made was that of mining the wall with the intention of making a breach in it. One night a baker working at his trade heard a noise — something unusual was going on under his cellar. An alarm was given and it was discovered that the Turks were engaged in making a passage to and under the wall which was to be filled with powder and exploded. The entrance to the mine was discovered and stopped, the mining Turks lost their lives, and Vienna was saved. The baker's name was Kipfl, and he was given the sole right to make rolls in the shape of a crescent, the emblem of Turkey. Patriotic people insisted upon eating *Kipfl*, as the crescents came to be called, and nothing else — the baker soon becoming prosperous and rich. And the story goes that when the Turks finally raised the siege they left behind them some bags of coffee which the Viennese soon learned to use. And now Vienna bread and rolls are famous the world over — and so is its coffee.

There is but one great international sport to-day. It is the game which Pip played with Estella to the delight of Miss Havisham, in *Great Expectations*. It is called " Beggar Your Neighbor," and it is being played the world over. By a series of tariff walls every nation tries to beggar every other, with such brilliant success that perhaps a quarter of the world's productive energy is now unemployed. This game is played with unexampled skill in southeastern Europe, where no one will trade or have anything to do with a member of any nation except his own. This "self-determination" of small nations is amusing and annoying to the traveler when he comes upon a new nation every few hours, though I am bound to confess that customs officers gave us little trouble. They asked the customary questions about cigars and cigarettes, and received the customary answers. They asked how much money we had and in what form, looked at our passports and our letter of credit, made curious little notations thereon with an indelible pencil, and disappeared. But it is a horrid blunder to offer a Hungarian a piece of Austrian silver, or vice versa. Except in the hotels, the people shrink back from it as from an adder. A German word is never heard in Hungary, and a German play or opera is a thing taboo.

I soon discovered why my Viennese friends spoke so slightingly of the charms of Budapest. Dislike of its people and envy of its relative prosperity are the cause. I once heard a German college professor say, at my own dinner table, — he came to the table wearing black kid gloves, a long frock coat, russet shoes, a celluloid collar, and a blue tie upon which an adoring wife had embroidered pink forget-me-nots, — I heard this Herr-Professor-Doctor say that, one hour east of Vienna, one was in the Orient. I did not know enough at the time to contradict him. If the statement still calls for denial, I now deny it. Vienna has an architecture which has influenced all of Austria: it is baroque — and magnificent. Budapest is, however, if anything, Gothic, with scarcely a suggestion of the East. The Parliament Building is magnificent and as Gothic as the House of Parliament in London. We were conducted all over it with great ceremony, and regretted that it was too early in the season for us to spend an evening in the long portico café where the townspeople dine and sip their coffee and drink wine from the famous Rathskeller.

I have said that Budapest is in the centre of the greatest wheat-raising countries in Europe, hence it is that the city ranks next to Minneapolis in milling. Its streets are immaculately clean; one almost hesitates to knock the ashes from his cigar, and as for throwing a piece of paper away carelessly, it is not done: a receptacle is always at hand — and used. And I suspect that the people are clean too, beyond those of any other nation, for there are baths, medicinal and other, everywhere.

To a stranger the history of Hungary is especially complex. Her union with Austria was forced upon her, and but for the regard of the Magyars for their Queen Elizabeth, the Austrian Empress, Franz Josef's wife, separation of the two countries would probably have come sooner than it did. The death of the old Emperor and the flight of his successor afforded the occasion.

History comes rolling in as one takes his place on a bench with his back to the river, facing the splendid hotels and watching the crowd. Suddenly my wife, who has eyes like a hawk and who always, for reasons which I never could understand, keeps one of them on her husband, said to me: "Do you see that man over there, in a gray suit, without a hat, looking at us? I have seen him somewhere; I think I recognize him. He has been at Oak Knoll — I am sure of it. Go over and speak to him."

"In Hungarian, I suppose," was my obvious answer.

"No; he speaks English, I am sure."

While we were debating the matter, the man, who seemed to me a perfect stranger, separated himself from the crowd, came over, and, bringing his heels together, made a stiff little bow, saying: "I think I cannot be mistaken; I had the honor of visiting you in Philadelphia. I never hoped that I should have the pleasure of seeing you in Budapest." Then it dawned upon me that years ago, in the early days of the War, I had picked up at my club a man, a handsome young officer in the Austrian army who was pleasantly occupied in doing "missionary work" in the United States while his compatriots were fighting. It was indeed he. We called him Captain — his name I had forgotten, if I ever knew it. This chance meeting made our brief stay in Budapest delightful. He appropriated us, went everywhere with us, lunched and dined with us, never offering to pay a penny for anything — I am quite sure he did n't have a penny.

Ewing Galloway

THE FINANCE MINISTRY BUILDING, BUDAPEST

Now for a story which, among many, he told us in the library at Oak Knoll! He did not like the army, he said, but what was he to do? The army was a tradition in his family — "it was either the army or raise pigs." He chose the army; he was a petty officer and he wanted a captain's commission. An examination was necessary; he must be able to do this and that — nothing very difficult, as it seemed to me. Finally he had to pass an oral examination. This was not so easy. So he went to Budapest to do what we should call "intensive study." But no sooner had he arrived than he met a girl, — a very beautiful, compliant girl, — the most beautiful girl he had ever seen. With her he spent many delightful hours; examinations were forgotten, study could not be thought of when that beautiful young woman occupied his every hour, day and night.

But put off is not done with — the day of examination approached. My friend, after bidding a fond adieu to the lady, packed up a lot of books and went into the country to study at a little inn, far from the seductions of a great city. But unluckily at this inn was a maid, — servant, that is, — also the most beautiful young girl he had ever seen. With her he spent many delightful hours, etc. But he must pass that examination or go to pig-raising. He was in a terrible predicament; what was to be done? In the army was an old man, a friend of his family, famous for his gallantries. To him he went and frankly recounted his difficulties.

"General," he said, "I fell in love. You, I know, are not too old to sympathize with me." (The General, who was well over seventy, sighed.) "But I must pass that oral. What is to be done? Can you not discover what questions I shall be asked? In confidence, General, in perfect confidence. My honor, the honor of my family, is at stake. Perhaps you have at this moment a pretty woman waiting for you somewhere."

The General nodded his head.   "To whom do you report for your oral?" he said.

"To General ——."   He mentioned some name I have forgotten; it makes no difference.

"He knows nothing but one thing, and very little of that. He is afraid of showing his own ignorance.   He will ask you to tell him of the rifle of 1892 — of anything else he knows nothing.   Learn all there is to know about the rifle of 1892.   I think you will have no difficulty."

My friend made another fond adieu to the maid — servant — and locked himself in his room with his books and a pot of strong black coffee.   At the end of twenty-four hours there was nothing, no detail, of the rifle of 1892 which he did not know.   The day of the fateful examination came. My friend entered the room alone to find an old man covered with decorations in a profound slumber; to rouse him was to kick a sleeping dog.   Presently the General turned uneasily in his chair, opened his eyes, and growled, "What do you want?"

"My oral, General," said my friend, bringing his heels together and leaping into the air.   Nothing was said for a time; then the old man remarked brusquely: —

"What do you know of the rifle of 1905?"

The rifle of 1905! My God, nothing!

But my friend did not lose his presence of mind.   He began in a dull, monotonous voice, "In order that one may understand the rifle of 1905, it is first necessary that one should know thoroughly the rifle of 1892.   This excellent arm," and on and on, and on.   The General was seen to nod; as he went off into a doze, he was heard to murmur, "Come to the rifle of 1905."

"Immediately, General," and on and on he went, talking in a voice which would soothe a nervous child.   The General was sound asleep.   If the young cadet stopped talking he might wake, and so, with only a momentary pause, he continued to talk about the only rifle of which he knew anything, occasionally bringing in with a firm voice, "the year 1905." At last the General opened his eyes, looked around, and uttered the Hungarian equivalent of "Excellent!" My friend brought his heels together, leaped into the air, made a salute, and left the room a Captain. There is a pretty maid — servant — at the inn. And there is a lady waiting for a Captain in Budapest.

Do you remember? — Of course you don't; you are too young. During our own Spanish-American War, the American Commander in Chief in Cuba, who was a man weighing two hundred and fifty pounds, was seen in a hammock, sound asleep, one afternoon after an excellent lunch, with two young orderlies gently fanning him and keeping the flies from annoying him. Seeing which, a young soldier remarked, sententiously, "This is what Sherman meant when he said, 'War is hell.' "

I one day asked my friend the Captain — we called him Captain and he may have been one — to take us to a good characteristic Hungarian restaurant. This he took to be an invitation to lunch at all the expensive restaurants in the city, and I saw that it was his intention to include the suburbs, also. I hinted, plainly, that I should like to visit the National Casino, which is the rendezvous of the Hungarian nobility, but this he told me was very bad, whereas I knew, from report, that it was famous for its cuisine. It was to the Casino that Edward VII, as Prince of Wales, once wished to take his friend, the Vienna Rothschild. The manager, however, protested, so the story goes, saying, "Naturally you are welcome, Your Royal Highness, and we are proud to have you, but you 'll excuse — the by-laws of the Casino will not permit us to entertain your companion"; whereupon the Prince renounced the privilege of dining at the Casino. We did, however, visit the Márványménnyásszóny (Marble Bride) and had our lunch at the Apostles, a famous place in the centre of the city. How different is life in any of our great cities at home! Nature has showered her blessings upon us; we have in the greatest variety shellfish, fish, meats of all kinds, vegetables in profusion, but we do not take time to enjoy them. The fact is that we do not know either how to prepare and eat good food or how to drink a glass of wine, and that curse, prohibition, which the Mid-West fastened upon us for so many years, completed our disgrace. I was told, not long ago, of a man who, dining with a friend, was offered as an apéritif a large glass of Benedictine!

A midday meal, which in Europe is something to look forward to and back upon, takes with us the form of the "quick lunch" in order that we may hasten back to our jobs. We who are, as our politicians never tire of telling us, "a nation of inexhaustible resources," live indeed from hand to mouth. It is merely one of our bad habits: there is no necessity for it; nothing is gained by it. I wish that my old friend Kit Morley's "Two Hours for Lunch Club" might be established throughout the country, as so many other things have been, by the illegal but benign fiat of the President; that anyone taking less than two hours for lunch might be deprived of his "blue vulture." Ultimately we might be a wiser, happier, and healthfuler people. After all, this is only carrying a step further the saying of a Vice President, now dead: "What this country needs is a good five-cent cigar" — to which I would add, "and time to smoke it." All over Europe one is struck with the expression of content, if not of satisfaction, upon the faces of those about one, and I remember that the English economist and philosopher, Herbert Spencer, when he was

MILLENNIUM MONUMENT, BUDAPEST

Which commemorates the thousand years of Hungary's existence

asked in New York, fifty years ago, what seemed to him to be especially characteristic of us, replied, "A sort of 'do or die' expression upon your faces." With the passing of years this expression has developed into one of apprehension. Most of us look as though we had lost our last cent — and many of us have, and this at the end of fifty years of unexampled, if misdirected, effort. What have we to show for what Andrew Carnegie called our "triumphant democracy"? We have fooled ourselves, and, more important still, we have given a wrong lead to the world. Having no standard of success but that of wealth, we became money-mad, and honesty was thrown to the winds. Seemingly we have neither the ability nor the integrity to govern ourselves without the direction of a lot of crooks. It is not pleasant to write these words, but why should I not? I never expect to run for public office. They would not have me on a school board — they would prefer a bootlegger.

One thinks constantly when traveling abroad of how drab our life is at home. There is nothing interesting or picturesque to do, no respectable place to go to have a good time. We have in our employ, and have had for some years, a Viennese butler, a well-educated man; his history is a romance and not mine to tell, but he is a gentleman and a philosopher, occupying, on my small estate, a pretty little cottage which I built for him. Not long ago, on his day off, I asked him what he intended to do with his time, — where was he going? — for of course he has a Ford. "Oh, nothing much," he replied. "I have some odd jobs to do in my garden, and I shall listen in on my radio. Where should I go in my car? If I could go to a good beer garden and hear some music, I would do so, but to ride twenty miles to get an ice-cream cone is not good enough. I prefer to stay at home."

How entirely the art of living has decayed in this country!
We were taught to do nothing but work, and there is now
no work to be had.   What a commentary upon our scheme
of government!   That the richest nation in the world, with
all the coal and wheat and oil and every other mortal thing
except tea, coffee, and rubber, should be flat on its back,
pawing the air!   For this condition there is blame enough
to go round, even after the bankers and the lawyers have
taken theirs.

One blessing at least we have, but it is not of our making
— we are free from attack.   There is something, no doubt,
in the slogan, "United we stand, divided we fall"; we shall
not be divided by pressure from without.   I am not of
those who indulge themselves in eloquent folly in speaking
of our country.   I read the other day that "we are not so
much a nation as an aspiration."   This sounds like nonsense
to me.   Nor am I of those who indulge themselves in the
eloquent folly of speaking of this as "God's Country," meaning thereby that it is not yet what a distinguished German
novelist said Europe was: "A bankrupt museum."   We
made a noble start, but left the rails somewhere.   "We
were, however," as Gerald Chittenden says in his *Reflections
of a Resident Expatriate*, "the first people to conceive the idea
of furnishing opportunity to all citizens and then to do something to interpret the dream in action. . . .   This ini-
tiative is our great contribution to world civilization.   It
will remain whatever happens to us."

In the excellent company of our new-found companion we
saw much which under less fortunate conditions would have
escaped us.   I cannot say that he could tell us very much
about the museums of the city, and for this I thanked him,
but he named the churches as we passed them, — correctly,
I hope, — explained the monuments, and was really elo-

quent when he came to that of Louis Kossuth, the Hungarian patriot — my old friend Louis K. Comstock, of New York, who is known to everyone in the electrical trade, is named after him.

One has the feeling of being very far from home in Budapest. This is due, not to the people or one's surroundings, but to the language. One cannot get accustomed to hearing conversation all about and not by any chance hearing a familiar word. But the music that one hears is magnificent. At the hotel half a dozen men with fiddles, a piano, and a *czimbalom* play weird, melancholy rhapsodies until one feels that his heart is breaking, and then after a few chords they break into a waltz that makes the recollection of the cacophonous noise that passes for dance music at home and elsewhere seem like a nightmare. For the equivalent of a dollar any orchestra would play waltzes from *The Merry Widow*, and again and again the "Blue Danube," until I thought my wife would desert me in favor of that Captain whose morals I suspected to be reprehensible.

The shops are excellent, the people have style and taste. Men's and women's tailoring establishments abound, prices are low, and the "fit" admirable. One of the specialties of the city is "jewelry," and we bought a lot of trash, which we saw being made, similar to that which, a few years before, we had bought in Egypt, being told that the stones were semiprecious and came from India. I do not doubt that the "stones" were glass — most jewelry is.

All during my stay in Budapest and Vienna I had been ruminating upon the difference between the Royal House whose empty palaces we had been tramping over and the House of Windsor, which alone among the great nations of the world has kept its crown upon its head. The Hapsburgs are dead or in exile. William Hohenzollern, covered with whiskers and disgrace, is in Holland; the Romanoffs were murdered in cold blood; George V is respected as no other man has been in my time.

When I was last in London there was a story going around regarding the activities of the Royal Family in a certain week during which someone had kept tabs on it. Everyone had been busy with philanthropic or humanitarian duties, and no one is more so than the Prince of Wales. Here is a reported day which cannot be regarded as typical, for no man could stand such a strain. The Prince had breakfasted at the Palace with the King to meet someone. Then he had flown to the North of England to affect an interest in a cattle fair. Then he had visited some miners who are out of work, have been for years, and seemingly will continue to be. During his visit he inadvertently trod on the foot of a small boy, who began to whimper. Quick as a flash he said, "Don't cry; be a man; tread on mine!" (There may be no truth in this story, but it is much that such a story can go uncontradicted.) Then he flew back to London, handed out some tennis trophies, and at ten at night, in the uniform of a Colonel of the Welsh Guards, attended a city dinner. This spells WORK.

Compared to Austria, Hungary is prosperous; her lands are fertile and she cannot starve. The World War was not of her making, but she suffered severely by it. At the end she was torn asunder, losing two thirds of her territory. I bought one day a picture postcard which shows more plainly than words the partition of Hungary. Upon pulling a string, portions of the old kingdom separate themselves from the centre portion, in the midst of which is Budapest, and a part joins itself to what is now Czechoslovakia, Rumania, and what not. One afternoon we were driving along a magnificent boulevard to a park near which is the

Tomb of the Unknown Hungarian Soldier. Close by is a tall flagstaff upon which the national flag floated at half-staff. At its base two young cadets stood at attention with fixed muskets. They are relieved every hour, and the watchword is, "We 'll take it back."

When Prince Otto — whose full name is Otto Robert Maria Anton Karl Maximilian Heinrich Xavier Felix Fenatus Ludwig, and many more — thinks that the time is ripe, or his mother thinks so for him, he will make his way to whichever capital city, Vienna or Budapest, will rise to meet him, and we shall have another war, and so on, and so on. Southeastern Europe has always been in a turmoil and will remain so; it is full of age-old antipathies. Byron may have had it in mind when he said, "Man is an unlucky rascal." And Gibbon called history a "register of the crimes, follies, and misfortunes of mankind."

"Did you see this, that, or tother thing in Salzburg?" inquired my up-and-doing daughter, and, upon being answered in the negative, she demanded, "Why then did you go?" My reply, "To rest my feet," roused her to fury. We went to Salzburg with a fixed determination to see as little as possible, for the Belgian blocks of the footways in Vienna, and to a lesser extent in Budapest, are very fatiguing. But Salzburg is a delightful city, straddling a swiftly flowing river. It seems always to have been a favorite place of residence for a long line of rich and powerful bishops, who, looking for a locality preëminently suitable for palaces from which they could dispense hospitality and royally entertain their numerous lady friends, pitched, almost automatically, upon this little jewel box. There are many, far too many, fine churches and other evidences of former ecclesiastical magnificence, but its churchly glory has departed, and it now exists largely for its music. Mozart was born here, and in the summer it is crowded with musickers from all over the world. How happy I was to escape them!

When we were there the town was just beginning to awaken from its winter's sleep, the trees were just coming into leaf, and we spent some days very pleasantly in an excellent hotel — the Österreicherhof — doing little but looking at mountains. Soon I found myself getting tired of "noble wild prospects" and bethought me of Dr. Johnson's remark that "the noblest prospect a man ever sees is the highroad that leads him to England." I felt London pulling at my heartstrings, and, taking my wife gently but firmly by the hand, led her to the railway station.

And we had been in our little flat in Jermyn Street just long enough to unpack, settle ourselves, and remark, "This is the life," when the door opened and in walked Gabriel Wells and Professor Tinker. How delighted we were to see them! Both men speak English faultlessly, especially Gabriel, and after all the filthy languages which had been polluting our ears, what a relief!

"And so you are just come from Budapest! Is it not a beautiful city, and did you call on my brother?" said Gabriel. "But never mind, we 'll talk it over together at the Hungarian Restaurant while Mrs. Newton and the Professor are dancing a *czárdás*."

I think my wife will be the undoing of the Professor.

XV

THE BRONTË COUNTRY
MY FIRST VISIT

WHEN a small stone parsonage at the top of a narrow
miserable street which climbs out of a poor neglected little
hamlet in Yorkshire, well off the beaten track of travel,
attracts, annually, some seven or eight thousand pilgrims,
one may say without fear of contradiction that something is
to be seen there. Such, however, is hardly the case. There
are, indeed, some books, papers, oddments of furniture,
pictures, and clothing, but nothing very important. One
makes the effort to visit this dreary dwelling set in a graveyard, not for what one sees, but for what one feels there.
Because it was, a hundred years ago, the home of the greatest number of geniuses that ever lived in one small house at
the same time, anywhere. Father, son, and three daughters. What a family!

In the first place, it is important to remember that it was
not an English family. I doubt if an English family could
interest, increasingly, the whole world. The father, Patrick
Brunty, was Irish, as wild as they make 'em, and his lady
was Cornish. And when two young people, each of the
opposite sex, settle down to the business of life in a desolate
country, children are almost certainly bound to occur, and
they occurred in this family with the regularity of clockwork.
Six in seven years. Then the lady died, of exhaustion and
cancer. Whereupon a maiden aunt, the lady's sister, was

sent for and would possibly have become the second Mrs.
Brontë but for the fact that

> . . . that annual blister,
> Marriage with deceased wife's sister,

had not, at that time, been pricked.   The Reverend Brontë,
— to give him the title and the name that he finally decided
upon, — therefore, feeling the need of a helpmate, wrote a
long-winded letter to a maiden lady he had, seemingly,
behaved badly to years before and offered to let bygones be
bygones if she would come and share with him his bed and
board.   "I have, too," he said, "a *small* but *sweet* little
family."   Six children, the eldest seven years old, mark
you!   Is it any wonder the lady declined the honor?   He
repeated his offer, whereupon the lady said, "Not at any
price," or words to that effect; and the matter was dropped.
But only to be taken up in another quarter, with the same
result.   Few young women cared, even in those days, to
settle down on the moors of Yorkshire to care for six ready-
made children with the certainty — almost the certainty —
of as many more in as many years.   "Blessed is the man
that hath his quiver full of them," no doubt, but there is
reason in all things.   Therefore the aunt was invited to stay
on; she did not like it much, but she did; since her time the
professional aunt has become extinct.   One by one the
children died, and now the world — that is to say, men and
women from all over the world, in motor cars chiefly, climb
that miserable little street which runs up a hill at an angle
of almost forty-five degrees and makes a town, to see the
house where once they lived.

Many years ago, nearer fifty than forty, I had a friend —
he is dead now — who, like myself, was a member of a little
club which devoted itself to the study of English literature.

His name was Henry Houston Bonnell; unlike myself, he was not only pious, but good, really good. When I first knew him he was not rich, but he inherited wealth, and in between the various philanthropic activities to which he devoted his life he became a book-collector and a student of the English novel. He concealed from his friends — at least from me — the fact that he wrote hymns. I am glad of this. I knew that he was a churchman and interested in the Fathers, and I knew, too, that he was the author of a book on the Works of Charlotte Brontë, George Eliot, and Jane Austen, but I had no idea that he had an important collection of Brontë until, one day when we were lunching together, he asked what I would advise him to do with his collection. He explained to me fully his position. He had no son, and neither his wife nor his daughter was keenly interested in his first editions. He had been collecting (as I knew) for many years. It seemed a pity that his Brontë collection, which included everything that came his way, — books, letters, drawings, memoranda, writing desks, samplers, memorabilia of all sorts of the Sisters Brontë,— should be broken up. If once disseverated (the word is Gabriel Wells's) it could never be reassembled. What would I advise him to do with it?

It is a question that sooner or later every collector asks. If he be poor, the question is quickly answered: turn the lot into the salesroom. But if the man is possessed of ample means and does not wish to see his life's work (or recreation) shattered at a blow, then what? To whom, and when, and how? Books, or anything else, in the possession of the ardent collector are, or should be, as dear to him as his heart's blood. And museums are cold places.

Most men when they ask advice have already made up their minds what they will do; they merely want to be confirmed in a conclusion they have already reached. I saw at once that Bonnell wanted to leave his collection to the Brontë Society of Haworth, the society of worshipers at the shrine of that family of which the world now only asks, "Which was the greatest genius?" I could not dissuade him from doing so, nor did I try to.

After much consideration I have reached the conclusion that Americans who buy English literary material should not return it to the country of its origin. But at the time Bonnell consulted me I had no fixed decision on this subject. Were the question to be put to me now, — were my friend Ellis Ames Ballard to consult me as to the disposition of his wonderful Kipling collection, or Morris L. Parrish to discuss with me the ultimate destination of his collection of Lewis Carroll, — I should say: "The whole is greater than the sum of the parts; keep the collection intact, if you can, in some public institution in which you are or should be interested, as a permanent testimonial to your skill and intelligence. But, in any event, keep it in this country."

If this land of ours is ever to be as interesting to us as Europe is, we must take steps to make it so. We must keep what we have and acquire more. We do not find England returning her works of art to the countries of their origin. Not likely. When the English part with their treasures they exact gold in exchange, and we, having bought, should keep. And if, when your collecting day is done, you must sell, the auction room is the place. It is the battlefield on which, perchance, you have won your victories. Why should not some follower in your own steps have his chance? But at the time Bonnell talked with me my ideas had not fully crystallized.

Several years passed, when, quite unexpectedly, I read in the paper of Bonnell's death: a gentle and a generous soul had passed on. Then one day came a letter from his widow. She, too, wished to consult me as to certain

literary property which her husband had left to the Brontë
Society, but there were certain restrictions; would I advise
her? I would. The intent of Bonnell's will was clear.
But Mrs. Bonnell had certain authority as to when and
what; on these points my advice was, I believe, good. I
would, I said, give everything; I would make the gift as
distinguished as possible; I would keep nothing back, as
under the will she had a right to do. But I would give
nothing until the Brontë Society had, in addition to a name,
a fixed place of abode, in a fireproof room or building.
In due course Mrs. Bonnell communicated with the Secretary, saying that when the Society was prepared properly
to house and care for the gift she would send the entire
collection to Haworth.

Curiously enough, a few months later, in London, my
old friend Thomas J. Wise, whose library of modern English books — that is to say, books printed since 1640 —
is without equal in any private library, in an after-dinner
conversation asked if I had ever known a Philadelphian by
the name of Bonnell. I replied that I had, intimately;
why? "Well," said Wise, "he left, I understand, a valuable
collection of Brontë material to the Brontë Society which his
widow is holding back on one excuse or another; evidently
we are going to be wangled out of it." It is not often that
Tom Wise can be set right, but in this instance he was
wrong and I told him so. I said if Mrs. Bonnell had given
the impression that she did not intend to carry out the terms
of her husband's will fully and completely, I was at fault,
not she; that she was acting under my advice to send
nothing until a suitable fireproof building, or at least a
room, was provided. "Well," said Tom, "that is being
done, but we shall never see a stick of it." "Nonsense," I
replied, "I know whereof I speak. As soon as the Society

informs Mrs. Bonnell that her terms are complied with, you can rest assured that every item of the collection will come forward."

At that time the parsonage, the old home of the Brontë family, was still the residence of the incumbent at Haworth, and his life was being made miserable, by Americans chiefly, who wanted to see the house in which the Brontës had lived. To live in a historic house, in a shrine, where one is interrupted constantly, day after day, year after year, by inconsiderate visitors must be frightfully annoying. One gets fed up with the interest and frequently misdirected enthusiasm of strangers, and finally becomes, if not positively rude, at least disobliging. At that time the property of the Brontë Society was housed elsewhere. Then, most luckily, a gentleman of large means came forward and offered to purchase the old house and, after making it fireproof, present it to the Society. His generous offer was immediately accepted, and the old house, which had many years ago been enlarged by the addition of a gable wing, was turned into a museum. Except for the new wing, the house is exactly as it was when the Brontës lived in it, and, as it is of stone and well built, so it is likely to remain for centuries. No one was more pleased than was Mrs. Bonnell at what had been done, and immediately she took such steps as were necessary to make her late husband's gift effective. Again I was consulted, and at my suggestion Arthur Swann, the well-known auctioneer of the American Art Association, was employed to supervise the packing and transportation of the collection. I was flattered at Mrs. Bonnell's confidence in asking me to send the books to England, but I was afraid to trust myself with the job, fearing that a copy of a book I have long wanted to add to my collection of English novels, *Wuthering Heights*, might stick to my fingers.

While all this was taking place, I was wondering why I

THE PARSONAGE AT HAWORTH

had never visited Haworth. The Bonnell transaction supplied the necessary incentive and the next time I went to England I made my first visit. I have said that Haworth is off the beaten track of the tourist; this makes it all the more wonderful that it should have so many visitors. It is four miles from Keighley (pronounced Keethly) and ten from Bradford, a now flourishing city given over to the cloth trade. It is the introduction of power looms for the manufacture of cloth which gives interest to the first chapters of *Shirley*.

We went directly from London to Harrowgate, a popular resort in the North of England. I do not care for English resorts, much, but it is a good point from which to motor to the Brontë country. The car we hired to take us to Haworth was a ramshackle affair, driven by an inexperienced lad, and I felt my heart leap into my throat when we came to the last hill and observed that our progress up this hill was slowed down to a mere crawl by a great motor lorry ahead of us filled with coal. I felt certain that if anything caused either our car or the lorry to stop we should never be able to start again on such a steep hill, *except backwards*, and I then and there made a vow that if I ever had occasion to visit Haworth again I would enter the town from the top of the hill rather than from the bottom. Fortunately nothing happened, and I quoted to myself Dr. Johnson's remark, "Sir, most apprehension is needless pain."

At last we passed the Black Bull, where towards the last of his unlucky life Branwell used regularly to get drunk; then the church of which the old man, Patrick, was rector and in which all the members of the family, except Anne, are buried; and finally the parsonage in which they lived. I have used the word "rector." This is not quite exact: he performed the duties of a rector, but he was an "incumbent." An incumbent holds his job for life and can only with difficulty be detached from it. I mention the places of interest in the order of meeting them as one ascends the narrow and sordid street.

Strangers go to Haworth but for one purpose: to do honor to the Brontës; and in a moment we had paid our sixpences and stood in the little stone-floored passage, with doors opening to right and left and with cement steps in the rear leading to the rooms above. It was hardly necessary to read the inscriptions over the doors, we knew it all so well. To the right, the father's study, where, for the most part, he took his meals quite alone, for he was an irascible and self-centred dyspeptic who thought of himself and little else. To the left, the parlor, the dining room, the living room — all in one, where the lightning came down from heaven and touched the Brontë children, unequally certainly, but as certainly touched them all. It is in this room that the Bonnell collection is housed, and over the fireplace, under a large photograph of my old friend, is this inscription: —

THE MEMORIALS OF THE BRONTË FAMILY CONTAINED IN THIS ROOM
ARE THE GENEROUS GIFT OF THE LATE
MR. HENRY H. BONNELL OF PHILADELPHIA,
AN AMERICAN CITIZEN,
WHO BECAME A LIFE MEMBER OF THE BRONTË SOCIETY 25 YEARS AGO
AND WAS FOR MANY YEARS A DISCRIMINATING COLLECTOR OF
BRONTË TREASURES. IN BEQUEATHING HIS VALUABLE
COLLECTION TO THIS SOCIETY FOR EXHIBITION
IN THE BRONTË PARSONAGE MUSEUM,
MR. BONNELL WAS, WITHOUT DOUBT, ACTUATED IN LARGE MEASURE
BY THE UNANIMITY, IN HIGH APPRECIATION OF THIS GIFTED FAMILY
BY ENGLISH SPEAKING PEOPLES ON BOTH SIDES OF THE ATLANTIC.
THE YEAR OF OUR LORD 1929.

"Actuated in large measure by the unanimity, in high appreciation." What does this mean? I thought the inscription badly composed, and the exhibits — well, the fact is that exhibits in glass cases almost always leave me cold. Priceless treasures such as fill the great museums of the world must, of course, be so exhibited, but books, autograph letters, and other little memorabilia such as I am accustomed to handle in my own library and in the libraries of my friends can hardly be looked at with any pleasure in glass cases. And there is too frequently a hodgepodge of articles of questionable value and interest. In fact, the less there is to litter up the place where the lightning once came down, the better. A few prints and pictures, good ones, a few articles of furniture, — if possible, pieces which once belonged to the individual or the family whose home the house once was, — that is all that is necessary. It is what one does not see, or sees only with the mind's eye, that is important.

Later we ate sandwiches and drank ale at the Bull, stuck our heads into the church, — by this time it was too dark to see much, and the church is uninteresting, — and motored to Bradford and caught a train up to London.

A week later we were visiting our friends, the Britten Austins, at their home, Guestling Hall, not far from the delightful old town of Rye, and one afternoon Austin suggested that we make a call upon a great man who had recently bought a big house, Fairlight Hall, in the neighborhood. So a motor was ordered and soon we were in the presence of Sir James and Lady Roberts, whose names at first meant nothing to me.

"Have you been long in England? Where have you been?" said Sir James.

We told him; finally saying, "And only a week ago we were in the Brontë country and spent a day at Haworth."

"You don't say so!" exclaimed Sir James. "Tell me about the museum. I was born in that parish, and recently purchased the parsonage and did it over to meet the views of a Philadelphia lady who has since presented her husband's Brontë collection to our Society. I hope you were pleased with what you saw. Tell me about it."

"What a coincidence!" I replied. Then followed the story which I have tried to tell and which ended with (here I took a long chance, for Sir James might have been its author) my criticism of the wording on the tablet in the Bonnell room.

"You write a better one and send it to me, and I will have it cut and replace the one now there. I seem to remember that I have heard the inscription complained of before." This was most gracious of our host, and I should have done so, but the fact is that it is very much easier to criticize an inscription than to write one.

Here endeth the prolegomenon of my Brontë paper.

XVI

THE BRONTË COUNTRY
MY SECOND VISIT

ALL his life Robert Browning wanted to write a play, a
good acting play; he wrote several, — one for Macready,
— but on the stage all were impossible, and he certainly
would be surprised if he were told that out of *The Ring and
the Book* the genius of Walter Hampden had produced an
excellent acting drama, *Caponsacchi*. And he would be still
more amazed to learn that out of his courtship of an intro-
spective invalid a play had been made, *The Barretts of
Wimpole Street*, which ran a solid year in London and had
a reasonable success in New York. Its success was deserved; it was an excellent period and costume play, it was
brilliantly acted, and it had humor. This let loose several
Brontë plays, which were too gloomy to be popular; the
girls were not interesting, and the morose old father, reading
his Bible and getting what comfort he could out of the
"begat" chapter in Genesis, was neither dramatic nor convincing. *Wild Decembers*, by Clemence Dane, — the title
taken from a line in one of Emily Brontë's poems, — was
perhaps the best of the plays, but all had short runs; they
served, however, to revive an interest in the family which a
hundred years ago lived and moved upon the moors of the
West Riding of Yorkshire.

"West Riding of Yorkshire!" What does this mean?
If you ask a reasonably well-informed Englishman, he will
tell you that Yorkshire, being the largest of English counties,

is divided into three judicial districts — North, East, and West — called ridings, having reference to the several circuits which His Majesty's judges ride in the course of their judicial duties. But a scholar will tell you, as one once told me, that "riding" was once "triding," an Old English word meaning a third (as farthing means a fourth), and suggest reference to the Oxford English Dictionary. As I have several editions of this great work, before which every head should bow in reverence, I was able to look up the word "riding"; my scholarly friend was right.

I cannot explain how it is, but until my interest in the Brontës was aroused by the plays I had never read Mrs. Gaskell's famous *Life of Charlotte Brontë*, although I have had a copy of this book upon my shelves for years. And just here it is necessary to say a word. If one reads Mrs. Gaskell's *Life* it is most important to know what edition one is reading. If a first, or a reprint of a first, it contains a number of misstatements which led to much unpleasantness, and in one case to a threat of a lawsuit. These misstatements were withdrawn in subsequent editions. Mrs. Gaskell was a fine novelist; she wrote at least two admirable books, *Mary Barton* and *Cranford*, and her *Life of Charlotte Brontë* is one of the best biographies in the language. It is also a work of art — that is the trouble with it. She was asked by Charlotte's father to write the official biography, as it were, and she very conscientiously studied the subject. She traveled far, interviewed many people, and read letters by the hundred; then, having formed in her own mind the sort of woman Charlotte was, she, unluckily for her name and fame as a biographer, distorted or suppressed such facts as did not fit into the picture she was painting. This is the right of the novelist; it is not the right of the biographer. It would be difficult to write a book with a finer atmosphere than Mrs. Gaskell's *Life*, but Mr. E. F. Benson has written

CHARLOTTE BRONTË

After the crayon portrait by George Richmond

a much more accurate one. Moreover, an immense amount of new material has been discovered since Mrs. Gaskell's *Life* was published in 1857.

My aroused interest in the Brontës led me to look up several microscopic manuscripts which have been in my library for years. One of them, *A Leaf from an Unopened Volume*, from the pen of Charlotte, consists of nineteen pages, three and one-half by four and one-half inches, and can be read only by one with distorted vision or with the aid of a powerful reading glass. There are also, in the Oak Knoll Library, two similar manuscripts by Branwell Brontë, bought at the Buxton Forman sale. These reminded me that years ago, when Clement Shorter, the real creator of the Brontë Saga, was spending a week-end at Oak Knoll, we were talking of these manuscripts and he told me that he had once owned most of them; that he and Tom Wise had jointly purchased them from Mr. Nicholls, Charlotte's husband, back in 1895; that Wise had kept most of his, but that he (Shorter) had disposed of his from time to time as he became interested in other things. For some reason Shorter and Wise and I had never much discussed the Brontës; we were intimate for some years before Shorter died and for a time used to meet in London, once a week, at the Rendezvous, a restaurant in Soho, for lunch and to talk books. I remember one verse of a jingle which Colonel Ralph Isham wrote on the back of a menu card, one day when he joined us: —

> Between Newton and Shorter and Wise,
> Confusion is apt to arise,
> But Newton is Shorter, at least by a quarter,
> And certainly Shorter is Wise.

It now seems curious that Mrs. Gaskell and Shorter, and indeed all the early students of the Brontë cult, entirely missed the significance of these tiny manuscripts. They seemed to think that *Jane Eyre* sprang full fledged from Charlotte's brain, whereas the fact is that from her twelfth, certainly from her fourteenth year she had constantly been writing lurid tales of love and blood, yet only now are these novels, or novelettes, being published; they suggest a very different Charlotte from the one Mrs. Gaskell drew. The story of "Caroline Vernon," for example, covering sixty-seven octavo pages, now in the Widener Library at Harvard, was written eight years or more before *Jane Eyre*, yet it clearly foreshadows the violent scenes of that novel. We are indebted to Miss Fannie E. Ratchford, Librarian of the Wrenn Library, University of Texas, for decoding or transcribing this story, together with several others, and publishing them under the general title, *Legends of Angria* — Angria being a fanciful country, the scene of these tales. In "Caroline Vernon," the Duke of Zamorna (actually Lord Byron), as bold and bad as his prototype, has words about Caroline with Lord Northangerland which might well pass in a brothel or a barroom, at the end of which Northangerland snatches something from his breast. "It was a pistol. He did not draw the trigger, but dashed the butt end viciously at his son-in-law's mouth. In an instant his lips were crimson with gore. If his teeth had been fastened into their sockets like soldered iron, he would have been forced to spit them out with the blood with which his mouth was filled and ran over." This, mark you, from the pen of that seemingly demure young woman who, writing to her lifelong friend, Ellen Nussey, warned her to be careful of her reading, saying, in effect: You may read the tragedies but not the comedies of Shakespeare; avoid Byron, especially *Don Juan* (which I suspect that Charlotte herself knew well), and "in fiction read only Scott; all novels after his are worthless" — at the same time particularly recommending one of the dullest of them, *Kenilworth*. Now the fact is, and it is just beginning to be understood, that Charlotte was two distinct persons, as distinct from each other as Dr. Jekyll and Mr. Hyde. One was the plain, prim, industrious, and self-repressing governess; the other, the violently impassioned young woman who fell in love with her schoolmaster, a married man, and who occasionally so far forgot herself as to write the same Ellen Nussey that "her heart was a hot-bed for sinful thoughts." And again: "If you knew my thoughts, the dreams that absorb me, the fiery imagination that at times eats me up, you would pity and I dare say despise me." All this was discovered but suppressed by Mrs. Gaskell, who preferred to develop what may be called the governess side of her character.

It was the appearance of the *Legends of Angria* upon my reading table that thoroughly aroused my interest in the Brontës and led me to reread all the novels and, for the first time, most of the many biographies. Soon I wanted to go again to Haworth, and any excuse is a good one if it will take me to England. I was determined to go in "wild December," and, having read of the snow and wind and rain and sleet of the Yorkshire moors, I prepared to meet the elements halfway. Upon my arrival, there were none to meet. I will not say that the weather was altogether pleasant, but it was not tempestuous, and I was surprised and disappointed. I wanted to see the moors as Emily Brontë saw them, but to do this I shall have to go again.

Mrs. Gaskell suggests that the parsonage is small; it is not so much that the house is small as that the family was large: eight persons, not counting the servant, Tabby, who lived to be ninety. It may be worth while in the interest of the exact fact to say that the hall or passage which leads from the front door is five feet six inches wide; that it separates two rooms, each about thirteen feet square — the one

on the right-hand side being Mr. Brontë's study, the other,
the living room.   I visualize the Reverend Patrick Brontë
as a typical Victorian father — self-centred and selfish,
doing his duty as he saw it, but carefully shutting his eyes
that he might not see much.   He was the sort of man of
whom it is customary to say that a cold and severe bearing
concealed a warm heart; I hate such concealment.   There
were, of course, a kitchen and a sleeping closet for the
servant; and then, after ascending the stone stairs to the
second floor, there were four bedrooms and a tiny hall room
without a fireplace, the width of the passage below.   The
family adjusted itself to the house.   Mr. Brontë and his son
occupied the front bedroom over the study; his sister-in-law,
Miss Branwell, the room over the living room, from which
she governed the family as best she could.   Accustomed to
the benign climate of the South of England, she hated that
of Yorkshire, and doubtless said so.   This leaves the tiny
hall room and the back rooms for the five girls.

But we are interested chiefly in the children, of whom
there were six, five girls and a boy, all studious and very
precocious.   The first-born was Maria; at the age of ten
she used to read such newspapers as came her way and was
as keenly interested in politics as her father.   To develop
the interests of his children, Father used to stand them in a
row and make them answer such questions as these: —

Q.   Anne, what does a child like you most want?

A.   Age and experience.   (Anne was four at the time of
this ordeal.)

Q.   Emily, what had I best do with Branwell when he is
naughty?

A.   Reason with him, and if he won't listen to reason,
whip him.   (It is a pity this advice was not taken.)

Q.   Charlotte, what is the best book in the world?

A.   The Bible.

Q. Charlotte: And the next best?

A. The book of nature.

Q. Maria, how can one best spend one's time?

A. In preparation for eternity.

Presently the two eldest girls were packed off to a boarding school, one of them, Elizabeth, having just recovered from the measles and whooping cough. Shortly afterwards Charlotte, being then eight, and Emily, six years of age, joined them. This made the house quieter for Father. The school, which will live forever as Lowood in *Jane Eyre*, actually at Cowan Bridge, was intended for the daughters of indigent clergymen. It would seem almost murderous to send four small, delicate children to such an establishment as the one maintained by the Reverend Carus Wilson, but such was the custom of the time. Wilson was a poet as well as a schoolmaster (perhaps this recommended him to Mr. Brontë, who also wrote verse), and a verse from one of Wilson's poems may be indicative of his attitude to small children. This may have been written for the small girls to recite, or perchance to sing: —

> It 's dangerous to provoke a God
> Whose power and vengeance none can tell;
> One stroke of His almighty rod
> Can send young sinners quick to hell.

The two elder girls were not well when they arrived at the school, and the treatment they received was not calculated to prolong their lives. They soon became ill, were taken home; died of consumption and were buried in the vault in the church in which their mother already lay. Charlotte and Emily stayed on, desperately homesick and very unhappy. An account of their lives, overcolored somewhat, may be read in the early pages of *Jane Eyre*. Anne, the youngest and most amiable of the children, escaped this experience; she was too young to go, and the father, who

had originally been a school-teacher, attended to the education of the son, Branwell, himself, and was in no small
measure responsible for his shipwreck.

Presently Charlotte and Emily are brought home to teach
themselves and each other, with such oversight as Aunt
Branwell could give. This condition lasted for several
years, and it was in this period that their writing began.
Children forbidden to play must find an outlet for their
activities, and writing stories in microscopic hand became
the amusement of the four children.

Later on, another boarding school looms for Charlotte,
and presently for Anne, one kept by a Miss Wooler at Roe
Head.   Here Charlotte met Ellen Nussey, who became her
lifelong friend, to whom she wrote many letters; over five
hundred have been preserved, although Mr. Nicholls, after
his marriage to Charlotte, told his wife to tell her friend to
destroy them.   Mercifully, for us, she did not do so.   After
a year or so at Roe Head, Charlotte again came home and
remained until her governessing days began.   We may be
sure that she was not idle.

The family income, all in all, was not too bad.   Mr.
Brontë had the house and two hundred pounds per annum,
and Miss Branwell had her own annuity of fifty pounds,
but the question was: In the event of Father's death, what
was to become of the children?   The girls' interests were
sacrificed that their brother might become a portrait
painter; for the girls themselves there was but one trade —
teaching.   They all hated it and they all adopted it.
Girls are more fortunate to-day.

There is, in the National Portrait Gallery, a curious canvas from the brush of Branwell.   The canvas has been
folded twice in the middle, once along its length and once
along its width; it is from this portrait that we get our

THE BRONTË SISTERS

After the painting by Patrick Branwell Brontë

impressions of the appearance of the girls. Of Charlotte
we have besides the drawing of George Richmond, made in
1850, also in the National Portrait Gallery, which does all
that an excellent portrait painter can do for a very plain,
not to say homely woman with a crooked mouth. We
know that she was very small; she describes herself as
"stunted." Harriet Martineau thought her "the smallest
creature she had ever seen, except at a fair." I take her to
have been from her earliest childhood intelligent and studious, always reading or writing; very nearsighted, suffering
from headaches, nervous, irritable, neurotic, secretive,
domineering, and quick to take offense — in a word, the
finest possible specimen for the laboratory of Herr Freud,
but in those days psychoanalysis was unheard of.

Charlotte was singularly ill fitted to be a governess, and
generally went around with a chip on her shoulder, rather
disliking children and they disliking her. If she was asked
to take them out for a walk, she was being imposed upon;
if she was not asked, she was being neglected. In the
family boat she pulled stroke oar; she it was who decided
that it would be best for them to open a school in the parsonage. But before doing so she and Emily must complete
their own education, and to this end, borrowing some
money from Aunt Branwell, they were taken by their father
to a school in Brussels. It is not difficult for us to recon-
struct the lives of the two girls on the Continent. They took
no part whatever in the life which went on around them;
they were lonely and unhappy, severely critical of everything, but conscientiously industrious. The word "Protestant" might have been coined to describe them. The news
that reached them from home was not satisfactory; Branwell was behaving badly, drinking himself, and not too
slowly, to death at the Black Bull, only a stone's throw from
their home, and of which he had become a distinguished

ornament.   Presently Aunt dies and the girls return home.
After the funeral the will is read and it is discovered that a
small legacy, some four hundred pounds, has been left to
each of the girls, Branwell, on account of his bad conduct,
receiving a few trinkets only.   After a family conference it
is decided that Emily shall stay at home to look after her
father and Branwell; Anne shall resume her position as
governess, in which she is fairly happy; and Charlotte will
return to Brussels, ostensibly to perfect her French, in
which she is becoming very proficient. Of her real reason,
her desire to be near Héger, her teacher, with whom she
was desperately in love, she of course said nothing.   I shall
return to this subject presently.

After an unhappy year in Brussels, Charlotte goes home,
Branwell dies of drink and opium, and then one fine day,
almost by chance, Charlotte opens Emily's private desk and
discovers notebooks full of poetry.   Emily's sensitive nature
is outraged and there is a violent scene.   Charlotte confesses
that she, too, has written poetry, and Anne, not be to
outdone, brings forth her little hoard of verse.   And thereby
hangs a tale, for without this chance discovery the world
might never have known that the sisters could write such
terrific and passionate novels as *Wuthering Heights* and *Jane
Eyre*.   Anne's stories, like her verses, amount to nothing;
they would never be mentioned but for the genius of her
sisters; she was the most normal of the children.   She made
the best governess and, having less imagination than her
brother and her sisters, soonest tired of the world of fancy
in which they lived — the world where the "Angrians" and
the "Gondals" lived.

After Emily's anger had cooled, the three girls decided to
publish a volume of *Poems*, anonymously — that is to say,
not under their own names, but under names which were
not indicative of the sex of the writers: Currer, Ellis, and

Acton Bell (C for Charlotte as well as Currer, E for Emily as well as Ellis, A for Anne as well as Acton). Charlotte undertook to find a publisher, and after some correspondence Messrs. Aylott and Jones of Paternoster Row agreed to do the job upon the payment of thirty-odd guineas, with a further sum for advertising. In due course the book, a slender volume of one hundred and sixty-five pages, appeared. Fourteen review copies were sent out, and at the end of a year, when an accounting was asked for, it was discovered that just *two* copies had actually been sold! To finish the history of this waif: several years later, when the sisters had become famous, Smith, Elder and Company took over the sheets and brought the book out under their imprint; it had a reasonable success, but before this was done a few copies of the original edition were presented to men of note. Wordsworth, Tennyson, Lockhart, De Quincey, and Ebenezer Elliott, the Corn-Law Rhymer, an author popular in 1846, received copies; the last-named is in the Bonnell collection with an inscription in Charlotte's hand: "Presented to Ebenezer Elliott by the Misses Brontë." At the Kern sale, Charlotte's own copy, with her autograph on the flyleaf, dated "Manchester Sept. 21st 1846," and a further note, "Given to me by Mrs. Nicholls, the second wife of the husband of Charlotte Brontë, Reginald J. Smith, March 1915," brought thirty-six hundred dollars!

I have referred to Anne as soonest tiring of the world of fancy in which her sisters and her brother lived. It is necessary to enlarge upon this imaginary world. From their early youth they had accustomed themselves to the habit of writing short stories in a microscopic hand; Charlotte persisted to her twenty-fourth year, the other children perhaps for a longer, perhaps for a shorter time. These self-revealing manuscripts are to-day scattered far and

wide, in libraries and museums, public and private. Miss
Ratchford, in her *Legends of Angria*, recently published by
the Yale University Press, tells of how, on June 5, 1826,
Father Brontë "returned from Leeds with a box of wooden
soldiers for Branwell. . . . The children were asleep for
the night and the soldiers were placed where Branwell's
eyes lighted upon them when he awoke in the morning.
Catching them up, he ran to his sisters' room, calling them
to come to see his treasures. Out of bed they sprang,
Charlotte in the lead." (Naturally, she would be; she
always led.) "Snatching up the best of the lot, she claimed
it for her own, calling it the Duke of Wellington. Emily
likewise took up one and said that it should be hers; and
Anne, following her example, made her choice. Branwell
called his soldier Napoleon."

They were not English children, it will be remembered,
but Celts, with every Celtish characteristic. They believed
in fairies, sprites, gnomes, goblins, and all the rest, and it
was not difficult for them to endow their little wooden toys
with life and make them function as would their favorite
characters in history. They could not then suspect that
they were embarking upon a voyage which would carry
them to an unknown and far-away island off the coast of
Africa, at the mouth of the River Niger, where a magic city
would spring up, first known as Glass Town and then by the
more magnificent name of Verdopolis. Henceforth, and
for years, all four children lived in a world of make-believe
— a world entirely unsuspected by those around them.
They never spoke of it to any but themselves, but among
themselves they spoke of little else; and when they were
separated they wrote each other of some event in the life
of one of their favorite characters, and this news was received with as much interest as if it had happened to one of
themselves. This is a very pretty game for children, but it

becomes serious when played by three grown women and a grown man — if Branwell can be said ever to have grown up; the only robust thing about him was his vices. The children separated over their stories; Charlotte and Branwell developed the Angria fictions, Emily and Anne the Gondal stories. Verdopolis became the capital of a large and flourishing nation, Angria, on an island of which Branwell made an elaborate map, now in Mr. Wise's library. The Duke of Wellington, with fifteen thousand troops, landed and took possession of part of it; Wellington's Land, it became. City life is depicted, and life in a great city is not always nice: men do violence and keep mistresses. Mr. Wise, of London, has printed privately a number of these Angria stories; Hodder and Stoughton, some ten years ago, published thirteen of them; Miss Ratchford has printed five; and one, "The Spell, an Extravaganza," — so far as we know, the longest of these stories, — was published several years ago for George Edwin MacLean, by the Oxford University Press. There may be more.

While Angria, under the patronage of Charlotte and Branwell, was growing great in the tropics, Emily and Anne were developing another country in a colder climate, where the Gondals lived; of this country we know little. Anne, lacking imagination, probably tired of it, and Emily may have been too busy revolving in her mind a story which became *Wuthering Heights* to bother much about what happened to the Gondals. In any event, of them we know little; Charlotte, after her sisters' death, may have destroyed what records there were; she may have thought them sacred — we shall never know. She wrote: —

> We wove a web in childhood,
> A web of sunny air;
> We dug a spring in infancy
> Of water pure and fair;

We sowed in youth a mustard seed;
We cut an almond rod.
We now are grown up to riper age:
Are they withered in the sod?

How many of these youthful romances are there? Who
wrote which, and how did they come upon the market?
To answer some of these questions we must go back to my
old friend, Clement Shorter. In 1895 he was a struggling
journalist, keen as a good journalist is for "a story," with
more than a superficial interest in literature. He was beginning to be a collector and his reading brought him to the
Brontës. He learned that Mr. Nicholls, Charlotte's husband, was still living, but very old; that after the death of
Patrick Brontë he had given up the ministry and had gone
back to farming in the North of Ireland, from whence he
came. He guessed that Nicholls was poor and that his
interest in his first wife was waning, for he had long since
married a second. In any event, Shorter wrote him a letter
asking if he had any Brontë material that he would be willing to sell, and received no reply. Then one day, discussing
the matter with his friend Tom Wise, Shorter remarked
that he had a good mind to run over to Ireland and discover
if Nicholls had anything he would like to dispose of; he felt
sure that he had. Wise approved of this idea and offered
to finance the expedition, the thought being that they would
share in any plunder which might be obtained.

Shorter went and was welcomed; the bank notes which
he flashed before Nicholls would ease his declining years —
there was a mortgage on his farm, of course. And one may
well believe that the second Mrs. Nicholls was not sorry to
see a trunkful of old books, papers, and mementos of the
first Mrs. Nicholls, of whom she had heard much and
for whom she cared little, turned into Bank of England
notes. A deal was made; how much was paid I do not

know; Mr. Wise did not tell me, nor did I ask. But old Nicholls had tasted blood; soon he collected another lot, everything he had. By this time Shorter was coy. It was bought eventually, however, and Wise and Shorter had a corner on practically all the Brontë material extant, including miniature manuscripts, diaries, letters, with the publication rights; mementos and souvenirs of all kinds; and the manuscript of Anne's *The Tenant of Wildfell Hall*, now in the Morgan Library. It was a great discovery. What was the value of such material in a cabin in the North of Ireland, forty years ago? Or in London, for that matter? The trade was not eager for Brontë material in 1895, and a letter which to-day would fetch twenty or even fifty pounds went begging at as many shillings.

Shorter was eager to publish a book, but before doing so he had to deal with Ellen Nussey, who had some five hundred letters. Knowing nothing of the law of copyright, she had, indeed, printed them, but, as we have seen, Mr. Nicholls had urged their destruction years before and he would not permit their publication; so the entire edition, with the exception of perhaps half a dozen copies, had been destroyed. The letters themselves were Ellen's; the copyright Shorter had now secured from Nicholls. Ellen was by this time an old maid living quite alone in the West of England, feeling that she was, in effect, Charlotte Brontë and quite as interesting as all the Brontës put together. At first she declined to part with the letters; Shorter was frugal but persistent; finally they were obtained, and Shorter's book, *Charlotte Brontë and Her Circle*, was published. It was well received, and in 1908, the copyright of material in Mrs. Gaskell's *Life* having expired, Shorter published another book, *The Brontës: Life and Letters*. Shorter's work changed the whole aspect of the Brontë Saga. Had he not gone to Ireland just when and as he did, much, perhaps all the material he secured might have been lost or destroyed. His name will ever be remembered by all who are or may become interested in the Brontës — that is to say, by all who are or may be interested in English fiction, and in two women whose lives are at least as interesting as their books.

To return to the miniature manuscripts: Shorter was a busy man; he was not a student, and he missed entirely the significance of them, as Mrs. Gaskell had before him — for whom there was less excuse. They are almost impossible to read; Mrs. Gaskell brushed them aside, Shorter regarded them as museum pieces. Both Wise and Shorter took and kept what they wanted; the rest were sold from time to time as the market would absorb them. Most of the Bonnell material now in the Brontë Museum at Haworth came from various London dealers who had it from Shorter and Wise. We now know that these manuscripts in bulk — that is to say, in the number of words — are perhaps greater than the sisters' published novels put together, and they afford the key to what has heretofore been regarded as a mystery. "What geniuses they were!" people exclaim. Think of that demure little governess, Charlotte Brontë, without knowledge or experience in the world or in writing, producing such a thriller as *Jane Eyre!* The mystery becomes less mysterious when one discovers that she had been writing for years — pretty rough stuff, some of it, yet she was deeply offended when the critics told her that *Jane Eyre* was coarse. Coarse! What did people mean? The fact is that she had unconsciously been steeping herself in the crudest melodrama, and one's nature, like the dyer's hand, becomes subdued by that it works in.

Villette, which many critics think her best novel, is largely autobiographical. *Shirley* is a pleasant story. *Jane Eyre* is a thriller, plus such passion as mid-Victorian England was not accustomed to. It has some kinship with that once

famous melodrama, *Nelly, the Beautiful Cloak Model*. Some
of my readers may remember Nell and how virtue triumphs
in spite of obstacles in that play, in which the heroine (in
appearance strongly resembling Mae West) is constantly
pursued by a villain in evening dress, whose pockets are a
perfect arsenal. I can see Nelly now, leaping from an ele-
vated railway train to the street below, landing in a providentially provided feather bed. I can hear her scream as
she throws herself from Brooklyn Bridge, only to land on the
deck of a passing ferryboat. I can hear the crash, off stage,
as the ferryboat impales itself on the rocks of Hell Gate, just
beyond. But we have no anxiety for Nell; we feel that she
will surmount her difficulties without injury, even to her
complexion — I was about to say, to her nervous system,
but we know that she has none.

The contriver of *Nelly* was a mere mechanic. The author
of *Jane Eyre* was a genius, yet its plot is quite as incredible:
Mr. Rochester, who has led a violent and erotic youth, now
keeps a lunatic wife in charge of a drunken maidservant on
the third floor of his country house, no one else in his house
knowing anything of this. Jane Eyre, governess to his
illegitimate daughter, falls passionately in love with him
and he with her, also passionately. Jane, thinking Rochester a single man, is about to be married to him, when the
wife, discovering what her husband is about to do, tries to
burn him in his bed, bites her brother, and tears Jane's
bridal veil to tatters. Jane leaves the house and wanders,
penniless, over the countryside for days, in the rain, finally
reaching a house in which live three of her cousins, of whose
existence she had known nothing, only to find that she is
heiress to twenty thousand pounds and that a missionary
wants to marry her. She declines marriage, but fits herself
for the duties of a missionary, and is drifting towards
marriage when she hears a voice out of the midnight calling,

"Jane! Jane!" It is Rochester's voice! Jane hurries back to his house, only to find it in flames, Mrs. Rochester having set it on fire. The husband tries to rescue the wife, but fails; a burning beam falls on his face — he is stone blind! Mrs. Rochester jumps from the roof and is killed. Jane is now free to marry, which she instantly does; she has a baby, and her husband recovers his sight. All this from the pen of a young lady who has warned a girl friend to avoid Shakespeare's comedies as not fit reading for a young woman.

Charlotte from infancy painted in vivid colors — no delicate shading for her. She saw no merit to Jane Austen and did not hesitate to say so. And of humor she has but one single trace. She was, too, a secretive little minx; even after the third edition of *Jane Eyre* had been published and when her authorship was more than suspected, by reason of the identification of Lowood with Cowan Bridge, she wrote to Ellen Nussey: "Whoever has said that [I am publishing] is no friend of mine. . . . I scout the idea utterly. . . . Whoever, after I have distinctly rejected the charge, urges it upon me, will do an unkind and ill-bred thing. . . . If any one should presume to bore you on the subject, you can just say, with the distinct firmness of which you are perfect mistress, that you are authorized by Miss Brontë to say that she repels and disowns every accusation of the kind." When, presently, it was no longer possible for her to deny authorship, we find her bitterly resentful of criticism. She fell out with editors over reviews that had appeared in their magazines, and with her friends — Harriet Martineau, George Henry Lewes, and others — for what were, after all, very temperate criticisms. There is in the British Museum — I have handled it recently — a sheet of paper addressed to Lewes on which are written two lines only: "I can be on my guard against my enemies, but

God deliver me from my friends." What called forth this bitterness? The suggestion that the author of *Jane Eyre* was a woman. "Is this a private fight, or can anybody come in?" said an Irishman as he saw a brawl developing on a street corner. Charlotte Brontë was an Irishwoman, curiously lacking the humor of her race, but rejoicing in an argument; a verbal battle, with her, was what a fight is to an Irishman. John Gibson Lockhart said that Charlotte was worth fifty Trollopes and Martineaus rolled into one, with fifty Dickenses and Bulwers to keep them company; this is high praise, but he called her "a brazen miss," and this spoiled everything.

We now return to Haworth and fancy ourselves in the living room of the parsonage when the post brings a letter saying that *two* copies of the *Poems by Currer, Ellis and Acton Bell* had been sold in a year; but, as Charlotte subsequently wrote, "Ill success failed to crush us," and already each of the three sisters was at work upon a novel. Charlotte finished hers first, *The Professor;* six publishers rejected it, including Smith, Elder and Company, who, however, said that a three-volume novel would receive consideration. In the middle of the nineteenth century there was a convention that a novel should be issued in monthly parts, with illustrations; or, if not in parts, in three volumes. The circulating libraries which supplied fiction to their subscribers were all-powerful; a novel must be in three volumes, well printed on good paper, and the price, they said, must be thirty-one shillings and sixpence the set. So Charlotte, who was never idle, completed her three volumes, which she called *Jane Eyre*, and Emily, who had her two-volume *Wuthering Heights*, took her sister Anne's one volume, *Agnes Grey*, and made a three-volume cluster. All appeared in the same year, Smith, Elder and Company taking *Jane Eyre* (ultimately Charlotte received five hundred pounds for it), an obscure publisher by the name of Thomas Cautley Newby agreeing to print 350 copies of *Wuthering Heights* and *Agnes Grey* upon the down payment to him of fifty pounds; these terms were accepted. Shorter tells us that he deceived the girls, printing only 250 copies, and was subsequently, with great difficulty, pried loose, by Smith, Elder and Company, from the copyright of what is now generally conceded to be one of the greatest novels in the English language, or in any language. Newby was a printer rather than a publisher, and a poor one at that. Through him Anthony Trollope first tasted the delights of authorship. In the same year, 1847, that saw the birth of *Wuthering Heights* there appeared *The Macdermots of Ballycloran.* Newby would certainly be amazed could he know that two novels for which he paid nothing are now prime bibliographical rarities, worth, in good condition — shall we say £1000 each?

Wuthering Heights! What a novel! As Charlotte, with all her knowledge of her sister and wild Decembers on the moors, did not "get" *Wuthering Heights,* how should the ordinary novel-reading public of 1850 do so? It is tragedy, and has been compared, not improperly, with *Lear.* Emily was the supreme genius of the family. What we really know of her is little — and noble. The introduction to an edition of *Wuthering Heights* recently published in the "World's Classics" by the Oxford University Press[1] says:

---

[1] In preparing the second edition of *Wuthering Heights,* Charlotte revised the only edition published in Emily's lifetime and did more than systematize the punctuation and arrange the paragraphing. She modified the Yorkshire dialect and softened or refined certain phrases and passages which she thought objectionable. This is indefensible, but Charlotte did not realize that she was tampering with a book which was to become a classic. In the *new* "World's Classics" edition, the first edition of 1847 is reprinted for the first time. It is a well-printed little volume, in large type, on good paper, and can be had for one dollar or less. All who are interested will wish to secure a copy. The introduction is by Professor H. W. Garrod.

"The first critics of *Wuthering Heights* supposed it to be an inferior work of Charlotte Brontë. That was just stupid. Later critics have seen in it a superior work of Branwell. That is just clever. A nearer approach to common sense is furnished by Mr. Chesterton, who conjectures that it was written by an eagle." I prefer the explanation which is given by Mr. Benson, who developed his theory without soaring. He suggests that the early chapters were written by Branwell. This idea was first advanced, so far as I can learn, many years ago by T. Wemyss Reid; but Mr. Benson elaborates, and I feel proves, both by reasoning and by internal evidence, that it is the work of two separate hands and minds.

The construction of the book is inconceivably clumsy. In its opening chapters a man named Lockwood — a lay figure, as it turns out — goes to call on his neighbor and landlord, one Heathcliff — he has no other name. He is received in the kitchen of an old farmhouse on the moors by his host, a man of middle age, a gypsy in aspect — coarse, brutal, and vulgar in his manners. Lockwood unwisely attempts to make friends with a bitch pointer, and, left alone for a moment, is attacked by the bitch and a pair of sheep dogs. He is rescued by an old woman who lays about her with a frying pan. "They won't meddle with persons who touch nothing," says the host upon his return. Lockwood is angry and departs; but, somehow fascinated, he repeats his call the next day, in a snowstorm. This time he meets a young man and a young and beautiful girl, whom he is told is the daughter-in-law of Heathcliff. He supposes that the young man is his son and is surprised when he discovers his name is Earnshaw. The manners of both young people make those of Heathcliff cordial by comparison. Lockwood thinks it time to go home; all agree, but he finds that night has set in and the snow lies in drifts. He inquires his way of the young woman. "Take the road you came," she tells him. He becomes frightened and begs to be permitted to stay the night. "I hope it will be a lesson to you to make no more rash journeys on these hills. As to staying here, I don't keep accommodations for visitors," says Heathcliff.

Lockwood decides that the storm outside is more hospitable than the inmates of Wuthering Heights, and starts to go. "I 'll go with him as far as the park," says Earnshaw, anxious to get him out of the house. "You 'll go with him to hell!" exclaims Heathcliff, cordially. Lockwood goes outside, is attacked by dogs, is again rescued by the old woman and conducted to a spare room in which he goes to bed. He cannot sleep; he dreams, hears noises and makes them — has the nightmare and inadvertently arouses his host, who, entering his room, curses him and asks how he ever got into that bed. "Lie down and finish out the night, since you *are* here; but, for heaven's sake! don't repeat that horrid noise: nothing could excuse it, unless you were having your throat cut!" Lockwood looks at his watch; it is three o'clock. Daylight comes at last; Lockwood goes home, goes to bed with a severe cold; and his housekeeper, Nelly Dean, to beguile the time, tells him the history of the family who occupy the house which he recently entered, — an uninvited guest, — known as Wuthering Heights. She talks to him for twenty-seven long chapters, interrupted occasionally by such asides as, "But, Mr. Lockwood, I forget these tales cannot divert you," at which Lockwood exclaims, "Mrs. Dean, you 've done just right to tell the story leisurely." Whereupon Mrs. Dean goes a generation further back into history, at last reaching the time of the opening chapter. *Wuthering Heights*, therefore, begins at the end, and Lockwood, who was evidently intended to play an important part in the story as it was begun (by Branwell?), was put to bed by Emily, who took the story over and made of it what it is.

Essays, volumes of praise, criticism, and conjecture, have been and will continue to be written about it. An eminent English barrister, Mr. C. P. Sanger, has recently made a profound study of its legal structure, with reference to the laws of inheritance and entail, all of which he finds faultless. "How Emily acquired her knowledge I cannot guess," he says. The ways of genius are indeed beyond discovery. Think of a young spinster in a far-off country parsonage, who never had a lover or even, so far as we know, a male friend, setting down in black on white such words of passion as those of Catherine's for Heathcliff and Heathcliff for Catherine, each married to another. Passion! Yes, but pure as snow, without a trace of sex. The passion of *Jane Eyre* is of another kind. And recall Heathcliff's death! He was very ill and went to his room; they sent for the doctor (Mrs. Dean is still talking). He came, they tried the door and found it locked; Heathcliff bid them be damned and sent the doctor away. It rained all night; the next morning Mrs. Dean walked out and saw the window of his room swinging open and the rain beating in. She forced an entrance into his chamber; his eyes were open, the bedclothes were dripping, and his face and throat were washed by the rain. He was dead and stark!

We now have three novels by as many Brontës floating under pseudonymous names upon the sea of London. One was a great success; everyone was talking of *Jane Eyre*. Somebody guessed that *Wuthering Heights* was by the same author; then Newby did something foolish or wicked, and Charlotte, with a Puritan conscience, thought it necessary to go up to London to set matters right. Emily saw no necessity for setting right another's blunders, so Anne went with her.   The picture of these two country girls, one of them almost a dwarf, leaving home, walking four miles to Keighley in a thunderstorm, taking a night train up to London, going to the Chapter Coffee House in Paternoster Row, — the only hotel they knew, where Charlotte had once stayed with her father when on her way to Brussels, — presenting themselves next morning at the office of Smith, Elder and Company in Cornhill, prepared to prove by their presence that they were two persons, not one, and that there was another girl at home — can anything be more amusing and pathetic?   Yes — their reception by Mr. Smith, his amazement at seeing them, his taking them in their home-made, high-cut frocks to the opera at Covent Garden that evening, with his mother as chaperon.   Did people stare and make remarks?   I 'll say they did.   Is it any wonder that Charlotte was excited, nervous, ill, with a sick headache, having sat up in the train all the night before, ready to die from exhaustion?   This is what Charlotte says of herself when she got home: "A more jaded wretch than I looked it would be difficult to conceive.   I was thin when I went, but I was meagre indeed when I returned, my face looking grey and very old, with strange deep lines ploughed in it — my eyes stared unnaturally."   Poor dear!   But with a pen ever ready to write, write, write;   it was the only outlet she had for her intense energy.   Words flowed from her pen like water from a fully turned-on tap — and in an order which could hardly be bettered.

As I lift my eyes, I see before me the living room in the parsonage;   it is evening.   For years the children had used this room as their work and play room: Jane Eyre and Heathcliff and Catherine had been born here.   Never again will Branwell come stumbling home from the Bull.   He is dead and his faults forgiven, if not forgotten.   The girls are quite alone.   Father has gone to bed, sticking his head in

the door, on his way, telling them not to sit up late. Charlotte is sewing, Emily is thinking as Anne reads aloud a
criticism of *Wuthering Heights* from the *North American Review*,
in which Ellis Bell is spoken of as "a man of uncommon
talents, but dogged, brutal and morose"; Emily listens to
this description of herself, half amused and half scornful.
Acton (that is Anne) is amazed at this portrayal of her sister.
Emily is not well; she is, in fact, very ill and has not been
out of the house since she went to the church to attend her
brother's funeral. A few weeks later she, too, is dead, and
Charlotte finds in her desk (the same desk which Bonnell,
my old friend, bought and kept in his home in Philadelphia
and which, at his death, his wife returned to the room from
whence it came) the manuscript of her last poem, a noble
swan song, the poem beginning: —

> No coward soul is mine,
> No trembler in the world's storm-troubled sphere:
> I see heaven's glory shine,
> And faith shines equal, arming me from fear.

This was in December 1848. In the following spring,
Anne, always delicate, became ill; the doctor said "consumption" and recommended pills and a change of air.
But it was too late; she went to Scarborough and a few days
later she, too, was dead, and was buried in the parish
churchyard. Her verses are gentle like herself: —

> I hoped that with the brave and strong
> My portioned task might lie;
> To toil amid the busy throng,
> With purpose pure and high.
> But God has fixed another part.

Charlotte is now alone. Her father, always nearsighted,
has undergone successfully an operation for cataract; he is
old, seventy-two; his churchly work is done largely by

curates. He spends much time in his study in meditation
— upon what? Nobody knows; perhaps upon his remarkable neckpiece or choker or stock, — whatever he calls it, —
which, bound many times around his neck, now covers his
chin almost to his nether lip. He never discards it; when
it becomes soiled he merely adds to its length. He suffers
much from quinsy. Is his neckpiece cause or cure?
Cause, one would say. Charlotte is patient and considerate, the correct Victorian attitude of child to parent.
At the behest of her publisher and to earn another five hundred pounds, she is writing another novel, *Shirley*. It opens
with her only trace of humor: "Of late years an abundant
shower of curates has fallen on the North of England."
This is worse than speaking disrespectfully of the equator,
and when it was discovered that these offensive lines were
written by a clergyman's daughter, the charge of coarseness
was renewed.

It was the publication of *Shirley* which blew to bits the
anonymity of its author, and Charlotte became famous
in her own person and personality. Again she went to
London, this time as the honored guest of Mrs. Smith, the
mother of her publisher. She now met for the first time
Thackeray, to whom she had dedicated the second edition
of *Jane Eyre*. Both tried to be polite and on their best
behavior; neither was too successful. In her praise of
Vanity Fair Charlotte had, it is generally believed, given
that great book its needed fillip. Its author had been
likened to Fielding: "Yes," she said, "as an eagle resembles
a vulture." There never was any mistaking her point of
view, either in praise or in blame; she always wrote with
intensity — I had almost said with violence. Thackeray
was prepared to acknowledge the obligation, but Charlotte
was difficult; unused to the ways of London society, she
spoke her mind. "Twice she took me to task for what she

held to be errors in doctrine. . . . She jumped too rapidly
at conclusions. . . . I found an astute little Joan of Arc
marching in upon us, rebuking our easy lives, our easy
morals." So wrote the great man. She met earls too,
and marquises, and Monckton Milnes, and of course breakfasted with Samuel Rogers, who entertained everybody.
She visited the Crystal Palace at the Great Exhibition;
she saw Rachel act, heard Thackeray lecture, and, to his
great confusion, entirely misunderstood a little joke of his.
After the lecture he told her that he had seen the Lord
Chancellor in the audience and he hoped for political
preferment. Charlotte feared that her friend would be
disappointed and said so. Thackeray retreated in confusion; jesting with the author of *Jane Eyre* was a serious
matter. In a word, she did London and London did her.
"Did Miss Brontë like the town?" "Yes, and no," was her
sententious reply.

Then she went home and produced what many critics
call her masterpiece, *Villette*. It had a great reception;
her name now was known far and wide. She was comparatively happy, her health was better, and her father
was, in his way, proud of his daughter. Slowly and
by degrees, curates, especially a certain curate, began to
seem less contemptible to her. Her first impressions of
the male sex were generally unfavorable. "Men," she
wrote, "are selfish, conceited, coarse and generally inferior
to women; only after one has accustomed oneself to the
creature one has taken for one's worse half can one be happy
with him."

In spite of this attitude, proposals were not a new experience to her. She had had three, all from the younger
clergy, when one evening her father's curate, Mr. Nicholls,
came to her and offered her his hand; it was all he had.
She promised her reply next day and, like a dutiful daughter

of the old school, replied, "Ask Papa." She was approaching forty, be it remembered. Papa, who had never considered the wishes or happiness of anyone but himself, was violently outraged. "He called her lover names; the veins on his temples started up like whipcord, his eyes became bloodshot." Charlotte became alarmed and sat right down and wrote a long letter to Ellen Nussey about it. She had promised, she said, never to speak to Nicholls any more; finally he became so agitated at the mere sight of Charlotte that he could not perform his holy office. Mr. Brontë called him an unmanly driveler and Nicholls gave up his job. Then there was some clandestine love-making; the consent of Father was at last secured and it was agreed that the lovers should marry. But on the day of the wedding the old man changed his mind again and declined to get out of bed; even the sight of new silk on his old stock would not tempt him. So Miss Wooler, who had been Charlotte's teacher twenty years before, took upon herself the father's office and gave the bride away. She married on the twenty-ninth of June, 1854, and was increasingly happy as the months rolled by until her death just nine months later. Mr. Nicholls remained as son and assistant to old Brontë seven years longer, until, at the age of eighty-four, the old man died; whereupon Nicholls gave up the ministry, returned to Ireland, became a farmer, married again, and died fifty-two years after the death of his first wife, at the age of eighty-eight.

We must now return to the books. Charlotte's comment on Emily's great novel is more than a little stupid. It hurts her that she should be thought capable of "an attempt to palm off an inferior and immature production [*Wuthering Heights*] under cover of one successful effort [*Jane Eyre*]." But the "Biographical Notice of Ellis Bell" and the "Editor's

Preface" to the second edition of *Wuthering Heights* are, for
the most part, admirable. There are some lovely phrases;
everyone who has written on the Brontës has quoted them.
I shall deprive myself of the pleasure of doing so, if I can —
all but one. She was, Charlotte says, speaking of Emily,
"stronger than a man, simpler than a child, her nature
stood alone." This is magnificent!

Emily has revealed this aspect of herself in her poem,
"No coward soul is mine"; then there is "The Old Stoic,"
and "Remembrance," the manuscript of which I had out of
the display case in the British Museum and reverently held in
my own hands, only a few months ago. It is written in the
tiny script that all the children employed upon occasion,
which they wrote with the utmost rapidity, and in which,
perhaps, all the important novels were originally written,
then copied out in "long hand" and sent to the publisher.
The manuscripts of *Jane Eyre*, *Shirley*, and *Villette*, now in the
British Museum, are practically free from erasure and ob-
viously not original manuscripts; nor is the manuscript of
The Professor, in the Morgan Library. The manuscript
of *Wuthering Heights* never came back from Mr. Newby.

It is disconcerting to read, as I have somewhere, that the
verse with which "Remembrance" begins, —

Cold in the earth — and the deep snow piled above thee,
Far, far removed, cold in the dreary grave!
Have I forgot, my only Love, to love thee,
Sever'd at last by Time's all-severing wave,

was not written to some early and earthly love of Emily's,
but to some imaginary "Gondal," and I refuse to believe it.
But to whom? To Branwell, perhaps, but the snow never
piled above his grave; he was buried in the parish church.
She was a magnificent pagan, a freethinker in the finest
sense of the word, and it must have bored her unutterably
to listen, respectfully, to her father's narrow and contro-

versial sermons hammered out year after year from the top
of the old three-decker pulpit in Haworth Church.   The
genius, she was also the drudge of the family.   Away from
the Haworth moors, she perished with homesickness; for
the privilege of staying at home she kept clean the house and
baked the bread.   She shrank from nothing; no coward
soul, indeed, was hers.   And if Charlotte had not led and
dominated the entire family, who would have done so?
The gentle and shrinking Anne, or the poor, weak, misguided Branwell?   Hardly.

Emily, when she wrote, drew upon her own wild and
unfettered imagination; nothing like *Wuthering Heights* had
ever passed through the mind of a woman and from her pen
to paper.   Charlotte, on the other hand, used every scrap
of her personal experience.   And what experience had she?
She had been a pupil and a teacher and a governess; yes,
and something more — she had been in love, with her professor, a married man considerably older than herself, a man
who was devoted to his wife, a man who was, moreover, a
Catholic while she was a rabid Protestant.   But knowing
her, as by this time we do, we are not surprised to learn that
she had first described this man to Ellen Nussey as of
"choleric and irritable temperament . . . a little black,
ugly being . . . an insane tom-cat and a delirious hyena."
But her hatred for him slipped into reverse and she fell in
love; her love was not returned, she was desperately unhappy and had to tell someone; therefore she went to
church, and, under seal of the confessional, unburdened her
mind to a priest.   She, Charlotte Brontë!   This is pure
conjecture, but is it not likely?   To Emily she wrote, telling
her that one day, being low in spirits, she had entered a
church and, observing people making their confession, was
seized with the desire of herself confessing.   She did so,
first telling the priest that she was a Protestant; and she

closes her letter by saying, "I think you had better not tell Papa of this." At another time, writing to Ellen Nussey, she said: "I returned to Brussels after Aunt's death against my conscience, prompted by what then seemed to be an irresistible impulse. I was punished for my selfish folly by a total withdrawal for more than two years of happiness and peace of mind." Poor girl! We can but pity her. She wrote in a burst of confidence most unusual in her; generally she was secretive, if not intentionally misleading.

Now the most striking incident in *Villette* is this selfsame confessional scene retold with all the dramatic intensity of which she was master: the scene where Lucy Snowe, — that is to say, Charlotte herself, — after a lonely walk, enters a church and falls upon her knees as if in prayer. She watches the penitents enter the confessional box and, their confession made, return therefrom consoled. "A pale lady kneeling beside her says in a low, kind voice: 'Go you now, I am not quite prepared.' Lucy enters and, ignorant of the formula, whispers into the ear of the priest, '*Mon père, je suis protestant.*' The priest inquires kindly why, being a Protestant, I come to him. I said, 'I am perishing for a word of advice.' "

By the time *Villette* appeared, the public, pretty well acquainted with Miss Brontë's habit of turning personal experience into copy, jumped to the conclusion (it, of course, knew nothing about Charlotte's letter) that she might be — probably was — relating some personal experience. "Absurd," said one. "Obscene," said another. "But listen," said a third, "can you not see the strong probability? . . ." Mercifully, by this time Charlotte was dead, and her husband, married again, turned farmer in the North of Ireland, was off the beaten track of literary gossip.

But the Brontë Saga kept on developing. Matthew Arnold wrote a long and rather tiresome poem on "Haworth

Churchyard" — I don't think he ever visited it, for he talks gloomily of "the grass blowing from one sister's grave, to another," whereas, in fact, they lie in the vault under the chancel floor. He has, however, some fine lines to her

> . . . whose soul
> Knew no fellow for might,
> Passion, vehemence, grief,
> Daring, since Byron died.

Meaning Emily, for the poem is dated April 1855, and Charlotte did not die until the last day of March in that year.

Two years after Charlotte's death Mrs. Gaskell's famous *Life* was published, and almost immediately discussions and dissensions arose which are only now quieting down; not that they have lost their interest, but by now the facts are probably as well known as they ever will be. Patrick Brontë was a self-centred and eccentric father of the Victorian type. Branwell, a victim of gin and opium, may or may not have had a violent love affair with a married woman much older than himself, in whose house he was a tutor; it makes no difference now. What part, if any, did he have in *Wuthering Heights?* This is important. Mr. Benson, in his considered biography, credits Emily with the great book, but thinks that Branwell had a hand in it, and gives his reasons, which I accept. Emily was the great genius of the family, of whom we know little, and that little is from the pen of Charlotte and her own poems. Only one letter from her pen, and that an unimportant one, is known; Mr. Wise has it.

Presently came a monograph from the pen of T. Wemyss Reid, to be followed promptly by *A Note on Charlotte Brontë*, by Swinburne, full of his violent and impassioned praise; this was in 1877. Twenty years later Clement Shorter fanned the flame to a white heat. "Charlotte's experience in Brussels made her an author," he said. What experience? people asked, and everyone took a hand in the answer — not in England only, but on the Continent. Damaging things were said and implied; finally, in 1912, May Sinclair came to the rescue of her idol, and in many and ill-tempered words sought to scotch defamatory rumors forever. In her book, *The Three Brontës*, she poured out vials of wrath upon any and all who believed that Charlotte could have had for M. Héger any other feeling than that of pupil for teacher; the fault, if fault there was, was Madame Héger's. Unluckily for Miss Sinclair and her theories, coincident with the appearance of her book there arrived in London the son of the man with whom Charlotte was said to be in love, with four heartbreaking letters from Charlotte; what was he to do with them?

To tell the story of these letters briefly, it will be remembered that Charlotte left Brussels suddenly and returned to Haworth. Why? We know now because of her love for the man she had once so vehemently derided. From the far-off parsonage in Yorkshire she had written, not such letters as a pupil would send to a one-time master, but letters crying for a reply — and in the same key. But such replies never came. How many letters were there, originally? We do not know; a good many, probably, for Charlotte was as violent a letter-writer as ever lived, but four only have been preserved, as by a miracle. Upon their arrival in Brussels, M. Héger, the recipient (M. Paul Emanuel of *Villette*, as Madame Beck, a most unpleasant person, is his wife), coolly read them, dictated replies to Madame Héger, tore the letters up, threw the scraps in a waste-paper basket, and gave the matter no further thought. Not so Madame Héger. She never liked or trusted Charlotte, so when her husband left the room she retrieved the pieces from the scrap-basket, stitched them together, and put them carefully away.

Twenty years passed; there were no more Brontës on earth, but their works had survived them, and a Frenchman had come to Brussels to lecture upon them. In his audience was the daughter of the Hégers, Mlle. Louise, who, recollecting something of the Brontës, was surprised to hear her father's and mother's treatment of them reflected upon. Thereupon the mother opened her jewel case and handed her daughter some letters — the girl read them and understood. Madame Héger died in 1889; at her death the letters came to the surface again, only to disappear and to reappear in the summer of 1913, of all places in the world, in the British Museum. Once again the Brontë Saga had received a fillip, and only the early outbreak of the Great War prevented the amazing incident from becoming more generally known. The story reads like a scene from a drama by Sardou; in all literary history I know no incident more striking.

When the letters were deposited, they were translated and published, and it was then seen that Mrs. Gaskell had had access to the letters, for (according to Benson) she quotes from three of them; but to publish the letters in their entirety would have destroyed the portrait she was painting, so she suppressed those portions which would not fit into her picture. In other words, she took a chance that the letters would disappear; she lost; and, as Benson says, Charlotte Brontë is a vastly more interesting and human figure than she would have been if her first biographer had won. To quote from these letters is difficult; they must be read completely. I have had one, however, photographed, and a page appears here with the permission of the always obliging officials of the British Museum.

In Shorter's *The Brontës: Life and Letters*, published in

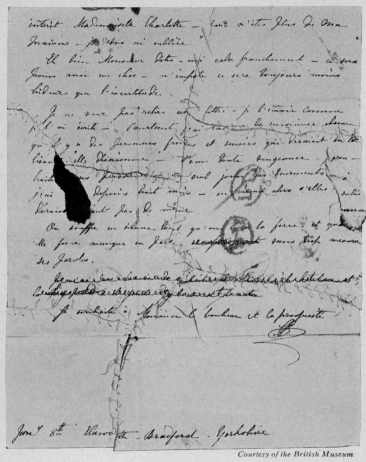

LAST PAGE OF ONE OF THE BRONTË-HÉGER LETTERS

1908, he says, "It is scarcely possible that time will reveal any more unpublished letters from the author of *Jane Eyre*," yet in the four big volumes, *The Brontës: Their Lives, Friendships and Correspondence*, edited by Wise and Symington and recently published, no less than three hundred new letters appear.   There never lived a more tireless correspondent than Charlotte; for her to see pen, ink, and paper was for her to use them; and what we write remains — sometimes forever.

The moors over which the Brontës walked a century ago are moors, in the old sense, no longer.   Good roads have been built and hundreds of cottages have sprung up in every direction.   There is now a sparse planting of trees and shrubbery in front of the parsonage, but the outlook from the windows remains gloomy beyond comparison: there is the church surrounded by graves and tombstones — flat, moss-covered slabs, for the most part, but some mounted on pedestals, looking like low tables.   The distance from the front door of the house to the churchyard is perhaps sixty feet.   The side of the house is not more than six feet from the nearest grave.   The Brontë girls, every time they looked out of the side window, could see the gravestone of Martha Pickle with this poetry thereon: —

> Grieve not, dear parents, shed no tears,
> I only sleep till Christ appears,
> Then at His coming I shall have
> A joyful rising from the grave.

A building bee took place in Haworth fifty years ago. The old church was razed and a new one erected, larger but somewhat along the lines of the old one, and the stone covering the vault in which the Brontës are buried can no longer be seen; the vault is in the chancel, and the tablets recording the births and deaths of the several members of the family are in the opposite end of the church — a stupid arrangement.

And at about the same time a gable end was added to the house, which is sometimes called "the rectory," sometimes "the parsonage." The rector was the incumbent; this suggests a matter of tithes. Patrick Brontë always signed himself "Minister." The family obtained water from a pump in the kitchen. In those days there was no such thing as hygiene, and the drinking water, filtered through a well-populated graveyard, seemed to have been excellent and people lived forever. Tabby, the servant, was over ninety when she died; Mr. Nicholls was eighty-eight, and Mr. Brontë was well over eighty. All the children died from their father's neglect, except Charlotte, who died in childbirth.

The museum is better cared for now than it was when I first visited it. The custodian, Mr. H. G. Mitchell, is an intelligent and obliging man. The photograph of my old friend Bonnell, which hangs over the fireplace in the living room, is fading and should be replaced by an oil portrait. But the inscription beneath it is still disturbing, and for this I can blame no one but myself.

INDEX

INDEX

348 INDEX

Hollywood, 200.
Holmes, Sherlock, 75.
Holy Roman Empire, 251.
Hoover, Herbert C., 247.
Horse racing, by moving pictures and by radio, 49. *See also* Ascot; Derby, the; Grand National.
Horthy, Admiral, Regent of Hungary, 282.
"Hundred Days," the, 253.
Hungarian language, 279, 280, 293.
Hungarians, 276, 277.
Hungary, history of, 286; its loss of territory, 294, 295.
Huntington, Henry E., 197, 203, 204, 210, 232.
Huntington Library and Art Gallery, 205.

INDIANS, 193–195, 195 *n.*
Irish Sweepstakes, 9, 10, 51, 59.
Irving, Henry, 78, 96.

JACOBS, W. W., 88.
James I, King, anecdote of, 73.
Jamestown, Va., 169.
Johnson, Samuel, 42; quoted on the shape of a dog, 65; remarks of, 67, 73, 77, 79, 87, 101, 119, 174, 201, 205, 243, 296, 303; quoted on Wapping, 70; quoted (*London*), 112; his house in Gough Square, 120–138; his Dictionary, 121–127; in need of money, 127, 128; affected by the death of his wife, 128; his reference to Americans, 129; his love of nicknames, 129; *Rasselas*, 129–131; celebration of anniversary of birth of, 139, 248; and Franklin, imaginary meeting of, 139–167; quoted (*Vanity of Human Wishes*), 252.
Johnson, Mrs. Samuel, death, 128; her grave, 128, 129.
Jones, Inigo, 76.
Jorrocks, Jack, quoted, 13, 28.

KATRINA, 186, 187.
Keller, Helen, 171–174.
King of Rome (L'Aiglon, Duke of Reichstadt), 253–256, 260.
Kipling, Rudyard, quoted, 98.
Kossuth, Louis, 293.

LAMB, CHARLES, 78.

Lehmann, Lilli, 194.
Leland Stanford University, 243, 245.
Lewes, George Henry, 324.
Lewis, Sinclair, 175, 210.
Libraries: Huntington, 205, 207–210; Boston, John Carter Brown, New York, Harvard, Yale, Morgan, of Congress, William L. Clements, Folger Shakespeare, 206, 207.
Liverpool, hotels, 40; cathedral, 42, 43.
Lockhart, John Gibson, on Charlotte Brontë, 325; receives copy of Brontë *Poems*, 317.
London, Elephant and Castle, 60, 61; Sunday morning in, 67–69; views of, 69; Marlborough House, 71; Carlton House Terrace, 71; The Mall, 71; Queen Victoria's Memorial, 71; Whitehall, 72; Cenotaph, 72; Abbey, 72; Westminster Hall, 72; bridges, 74, 75, 78–81; Embankment, 75, 78; Scotland Yard, 75; Water Gate of York House, 76; Savoy Theatre, 76; Hanway Street, 78; Temple, 78; Shakespeare's, 79; Monument, 79; Billingsgate, 81; Trinity Square, 82; Tower Hill, 82; Tower, 82, 83; Docks, 83, 84; Wapping, 84–88; Isle of Dogs, 88; Greenwich, 88, 89; Royal Military Hospital (Chelsea), 90, 91; Birdcage Walk, 91; Guards' Chapel, 91–94; Epstein statuary, 95; Leicester Square, 96; Piccadilly Circus, 97; Criterion, 97; "Lyons' Pop," 97, 98; transportation, system of, 100, 101; Dickens's, 101; the Albany, 101; Egyptian Hall, 102; Mayfair, 102; Devonshire House, 102, 103; Burdett-Coutts House, 103–106; Piccadilly, 107, 108; Cambridge House, 107, 108; Apsley House, 109; Hyde Park Corner, 109; St. George's Hospital, 109; Park Lane, 110, 111; Tyburn, 110–112; Marble Arch, 112; Sterne's (possible) grave, 113–116; the Gate, 117, 118; Arts Theatre Club, 118; Gough Square, 120–138.